EASY AND QUICK AIR FRYER COOKBOOK FOR BEGINNERS 2024

Lots of Healthy and Hot Air Fryer Meals for Your Whole Family and Busy People on a Budget

"Delicious Delights: Air Fryer Recipes for 2023

Crispy Air Fryer Broccoli

Air Fryer Cauliflower

ULTRA Crispy Air Fryer Chickpeas

Crispy Air Fryer Sweet Potato Tots

Honey Garlic Air Fryer Cauliflower Wings

Air Fryer Roasted Garlic

Crispy Air Fryer Brussels Sprouts

Air Fryer Corn (SO GOOD)

Air Fryer Carrots (tender + sweet!)

Crispy Baked Zucchini Fries

Air Fryer Bacon

Seriously Crispy Air Fryer Gnocchi

Air Fryer French Fries

Crispy Air Fryer Potato Wedges

Air Fryer Mushrooms

Crispy Air Fryer Eggplant Rounds

Lemon Parmesan Air Fryer Asparagus

Air Fryer Green Beans

Air Fryer Hard Boiled Eggs

Air Fryer Roasted Potatoes

Air Fryer Croutons (BEST texture!)

Air Fryer Pizza

Crispy Air Fryer Chicken Parmesan

Air Fryer Chicken Fajitas

Air Fryer Whole Chicken (so juicy!)

Perfect Air Fryer Salmon

Crispy Air Fryer Fish (lemon parmesan breading!)

Air Fryer Chicken Nuggets

Air Fryer Chicken Thighs

Air Fryer Meatballs (fresh, frozen)

Air Fryer Salmon Patties (Golden + Crispy)

Air Fryer Shrimp (Honey Lime)

Crispy Air Fryer Chicken Tenders

20 Minute Air Fryer Chicken Breast

Air Fryer Chicken Wings

Lemon Pepper Air Fryer Chicken and Broccoli

Air Fryer Burgers (Turkey or Beef)

Crispy Air Fryer Chicken Taquitos

Herb Crusted Air Fryer Pork Tenderloin

Air Fryer Grilled Cheese (SO crispy!)

Crispy Air Fryer Falafels

Air Fryer Cauliflower Chickpea Tacos

Crispy Seasoned Air Fryer Tofu

Air Fryer Baked Potatoes

Crispy Spicy Air Fryer Okra

Air Fryer Radishes

Air Fryer Sweet Potato Fries

Air Fryer Zucchini

Air Fryer Baby Potatoes

Air Fryer Broccoli Cheese Bites

Healthy Air Fryer Eggplant

Air Fryer Tortilla Chips

Air Fryer Asparagus

Air Fryer Pumpkin Fries

Lemon Garlic Air Fryer Roasted Potatoes

Air Fryer Cauliflower

Crispy Air Fryer Tater Tots

Air Fryer Roasted Beets

Air Fryer Shrimp

Easy Air Fryer Baby Back Ribs

Air Fryer Sponge Cake

Air Fryer Grilled Cheese

Air Fryer Onion Potatoes (Lipton Onion Soup)

Crispy Air Fryer Pork Belly

Best Air Fryer Salmon Recipe

Air Fryer Bacon Wrapped Scallops Recipe

Succulent Garlic Butter Shrimp

Golden Onion Rings with Tangy Dipping Sauce

Air Fryer Parmesan Roasted Potatoes

Air Fryer Hard Boiled Eggs

Scrumptious Air-Fried Donuts

Crispy Fried Pickles

Perfectly Crispy Air Fryer Carrots and Parsnips

Air Fryer Omelette

Air Fryer Sausages

Book Introduction:

Welcome to "Delicious Delights: 15 Air Fryer Recipes for 2023"! In this book, you'll embark on a culinary journey filled with delectable dishes prepared using the latest air fryer techniques. Discover the art of achieving perfectly crispy and delicious results without excessive oil or hassle.

Air fryers have revolutionized the way we cook, providing a healthier alternative to traditional deep-frying methods. Whether you're a seasoned chef or a beginner in the kitchen, this book is designed to cater to all skill levels. Each recipe has been carefully crafted to bring out the best flavors and textures using your air fryer.

Throughout the following chapters, you'll find an array of mouthwatering recipes that showcase the versatility of this remarkable kitchen appliance. From classic favorites like fried chicken tenders and crispy bacon-wrapped jalapeño poppers to unique creations like coconut shrimp and apple fritters, there's something to satisfy every craving.

Forget the greasy takeout or the long hours spent in the kitchen. With these air fryer recipes, you'll be able to whip up restaurant-quality dishes in no time. Enjoy the convenience of quick and easy meals without compromising on taste or healthiness.

So, dust off your air fryer, gather your ingredients, and get ready to embark on a culinary adventure. Let's dive into the first chapter and explore the wonders of air fryer cooking!

Chapter 1: Introduction to Air Fryer Cooking

In this introductory chapter, we will delve into the fascinating world of air fryer cooking. We'll start by understanding the basic principles behind this innovative kitchen appliance and its advantages over traditional frying methods.

The air fryer utilizes hot air circulation and a minimal amount of oil to create a crispy exterior while maintaining the juiciness and tenderness of the food. This means you can enjoy your favorite fried dishes with significantly less oil and fewer calories.

We will also discuss the various types of air fryers available in the market, their features, and how to choose the right one for your needs. Whether you prefer a compact model for individual servings or a larger capacity for family meals, we'll guide you through the selection process.

Furthermore, we'll provide essential tips and tricks for achieving the perfect air-fried results. From preheating techniques to optimal cooking times, you'll learn the secrets to consistently delicious dishes. We'll also address common troubleshooting issues and offer solutions to ensure your air fryer experience is smooth and enjoyable.

To whet your appetite, we'll conclude this chapter with a tantalizing recipe: Crispy Fried Chicken Tenders. This beloved classic will showcase the capabilities of your air fryer, delivering a golden, crunchy exterior with moist and tender chicken on the inside.

Stay tuned as we embark on a culinary journey filled with crispy goodness. Let's get started with the first recipe in Chapter 1:

Crispy Air Fryer Broccoli

Crispy Air Fryer Broccoli Recipe:
Ingredients:
- 1 pound (450g) fresh broccoli florets
- 2 tablespoons olive oil
- 1/2 teaspoon salt
- 1/4 teaspoon black pepper
- 1/4 teaspoon garlic powder (optional)
- 1/4 teaspoon onion powder (optional)
- 1/4 teaspoon paprika (optional)

Instructions:
1. Start by washing and drying the broccoli florets thoroughly. Cut them into bite-sized pieces.

2. In a large mixing bowl, combine the broccoli florets with olive oil, salt, pepper, and any optional seasonings you like, such as garlic powder, onion powder, or paprika. Toss the broccoli to evenly coat it with the oil and seasonings.
3. Preheat your air fryer to 375°F (190°C).
4. Place the seasoned broccoli in the air fryer basket in a single layer. Do not overcrowd the basket; you may need to cook the broccoli in batches if you have a small air fryer.
5. Air fry the broccoli at 375°F (190°C) for 12-15 minutes, shaking the basket or tossing the broccoli with tongs halfway through the cooking time. The cooking time may vary depending on the size of your florets and your air fryer, so check for doneness.
6. The broccoli is ready when it's tender on the inside and crispy on the outside, with slightly charred edges.
7. Once done, remove the broccoli from the air fryer and serve immediately. You can sprinkle some additional salt or seasonings if desired.

Notes:
1. Make sure the broccoli is well dried before seasoning and air frying it. Excess moisture can make the broccoli less crispy.
2. The optional seasonings are entirely customizable. You can experiment with different herbs and spices to suit your taste.
3. Don't overcrowd the air fryer basket. Cooking the broccoli in a single layer ensures even cooking and crispiness. If you have a small air fryer, cook the broccoli in batches.
4. Cooking times may vary based on your air fryer model, so keep an eye on the broccoli to prevent overcooking or undercooking. The key is achieving that perfect balance between tenderness and crispiness.
5. Serve the crispy air fryer broccoli as a side dish, with a dipping sauce, or use it as a topping for salads or bowls.
6. This recipe is quite versatile, and you can adjust the seasonings to your liking. It's a healthy and delicious way to enjoy broccoli with a satisfying crunch!

Certainly! Here are some additional tips and ideas for making the most of your crispy air fryer broccoli:

1. **Dipping Sauces:** Serve your air-fried broccoli with a variety of dipping sauces for extra flavor. Some popular options include ranch dressing, honey mustard, sriracha mayo, or a simple garlic aioli.
2. **Cheese:** For an extra indulgent twist, sprinkle grated Parmesan or cheddar cheese over the broccoli during the last few minutes of cooking. The cheese will melt and create a delightful crispy topping.
3. **Lemon Zest:** Add a zesty, fresh flavor to your broccoli by grating some lemon zest over it right before serving. The citrusy brightness pairs wonderfully with the crispy texture.
4. **Nuts and Seeds:** To add crunch and nutrition, sprinkle some toasted nuts (such as almonds or pine nuts) or seeds (like sesame seeds) over the air-fried broccoli.
5. **Spicy Kick:** If you like a bit of heat, try adding red pepper flakes or a pinch of cayenne pepper to the seasonings for a spicy kick.
6. **Balsamic Glaze:** Drizzle some balsamic glaze over the air-fried broccoli to give it a sweet and tangy flavor. This can elevate the dish and make it more gourmet.

7. **Bacon:** If you're not concerned about keeping it vegetarian, crumbled bacon is an excellent addition. Cook bacon separately, crumble it, and then sprinkle it over the broccoli before serving.
8. **Variety of Veggies:** Experiment with other vegetables alongside the broccoli, such as cauliflower, bell peppers, or asparagus. Just adjust the cooking times to accommodate the different vegetables' textures.
9. **Preheat the Air Fryer:** Preheating your air fryer for a few minutes can help ensure more even and consistent cooking.
10. **Cleanup Tip:** To make cleanup easier, you can line the air fryer basket with parchment paper, especially if you're using cheese or sticky sauces.
11. **Leftovers:** If you have any leftovers, you can use them in omelets, frittatas, or as a topping for a baked potato or pizza.
12. **Kids' Friendly:** Kids may enjoy these crispy broccoli florets, especially if you serve them with a favorite dipping sauce. It's a sneaky way to get them to eat their greens!

Remember that air fryers vary in terms of cooking times and temperatures, so be ready to adjust accordingly. With these tips and ideas, you can create a variety of delicious and crispy air-fried broccoli dishes that suit your taste and dietary preferences. Enjoy!

Air Fryer Cauliflower

Air frying cauliflower is a great way to make a delicious and healthy snack or side dish. Here's a basic recipe for air-fried cauliflower along with some helpful notes:

Ingredients:

- 1 head of cauliflower, cut into florets
- 2-3 tablespoons olive oil or cooking spray
- Seasonings of your choice (e.g., salt, pepper, garlic powder, paprika, cumin, Parmesan cheese, or your favorite seasoning blend)

Instructions:

1. **Prepare the Cauliflower:**
   ○ Wash the cauliflower and cut it into bite-sized florets. Make sure the florets are relatively uniform in size to ensure even cooking.
2. **Season the Cauliflower:**
   ○ In a large mixing bowl, drizzle the cauliflower florets with olive oil or use a cooking spray to coat them evenly. This helps the seasonings stick to the cauliflower.

- Add your choice of seasonings. You can be as creative as you like. Some people prefer a simple seasoning with just salt and pepper, while others like to add a variety of spices for extra flavor.

3. **Preheat the Air Fryer:**
   - Preheat your air fryer to 375°F (190°C). This step is essential to get a crispy and evenly cooked cauliflower.

4. **Air Fry the Cauliflower:**
   - Place the seasoned cauliflower florets in the air fryer basket in a single layer, making sure not to overcrowd the basket. You may need to cook in batches if you have a small air fryer.
   - Cook the cauliflower for about 15-20 minutes, shaking the basket or turning the florets halfway through the cooking time. The cooking time may vary depending on your air fryer's size and power. Check for doneness by poking a fork or toothpick into a floret; it should be tender and golden brown.

5. **Serve:**
   - Once the cauliflower is done, remove it from the air fryer and let it cool for a minute before serving. You can serve it as a snack, side dish, or even as a topping for salads.

Notes:

- **Don't overcrowd the basket:** It's essential not to overcrowd the air fryer basket to ensure proper air circulation. Cook in batches if necessary.
- **Check and shake:** Shake the basket or turn the cauliflower halfway through the cooking time to ensure even browning.
- **Experiment with seasonings:** Cauliflower is a versatile vegetable, so feel free to experiment with different seasonings and spices to suit your taste.
- **Adjust cooking time:** Cooking times can vary depending on the size of your cauliflower florets and the air fryer's power. Keep an eye on the cauliflower and adjust the cooking time as needed.
- **Serve with dipping sauce:** Consider serving your air-fried cauliflower with a dipping sauce like ranch dressing, tahini, or a yogurt-based dip for extra flavor.

Air-fried cauliflower is a healthier alternative to deep-frying, and it retains a nice crispy texture with a tender interior. Enjoy your air-fried cauliflower as a guilt-free snack or side dish!

Certainly! Here are some additional tips and ideas for air-frying cauliflower:

1. Breadcrumb Coating: For an extra crispy texture, you can coat the cauliflower florets in breadcrumbs or panko crumbs before air-frying. Dip the florets in beaten egg or a mixture of egg and milk before rolling them in breadcrumbs. This will give your cauliflower a crunchy crust.

2. Parmesan Cheese: Grated Parmesan cheese can add a wonderful flavor and crispiness to your air-fried cauliflower. After seasoning the cauliflower with your preferred spices, sprinkle some Parmesan cheese on top before air-frying.

3. Temperature and Time: Experiment with the temperature and cooking time to achieve the texture you desire. Higher temperatures (around 400°F or 200°C) will result in a crispier exterior, but you may need to reduce the cooking time to avoid overcooking.

4. Parchment Paper or Basket Liner: To make cleanup easier and prevent sticking, you can line the air fryer basket with parchment paper or a basket liner specifically designed for air frying. This can also help maintain the crispy texture of the cauliflower.

5. Sauce or Glaze: Once your cauliflower is air-fried, you can toss it in your favorite sauce or glaze for added flavor. For example, a buffalo sauce or honey garlic glaze can make your cauliflower wings or bites even more delicious.

6. Roasted Garlic: Roasting whole garlic cloves alongside the cauliflower is a fantastic idea. The roasted garlic becomes sweet and mellow, making it a delicious addition to your dish.

7. Dipping Sauces: Consider serving your air-fried cauliflower with various dipping sauces, such as tzatziki, sriracha mayo, barbecue sauce, or a homemade aioli. Dipping sauces can complement the flavors and add extra zest to your dish.

8. Frozen Cauliflower: You can also air-fry frozen cauliflower florets. Just follow the instructions on the package but typically, you'll need to preheat the air fryer and cook the frozen cauliflower for a few minutes longer than fresh cauliflower.

9. Mix and Match: Combine air-fried cauliflower with other vegetables like broccoli, carrots, or bell peppers for a colorful and flavorful mix. Adjust cooking times as needed for different vegetables.

10. Leftovers: If you have any leftover air-fried cauliflower, you can reheat it in the air fryer for a few minutes to restore its crispiness. It's a great way to enjoy the leftovers without losing their texture.

Remember that air fryers vary in size and power, so some trial and error may be needed to find the perfect settings for your specific model. Enjoy your air-fried cauliflower and have fun experimenting with different seasonings and variations!

ULTRA Crispy Air Fryer Chickpeas

Making ultra-crispy air fryer chickpeas is a delicious and healthy snack option. Here's a recipe along with some important notes to help you achieve that perfect crunch:

Ingredients:

- 1 can (15 ounces) of chickpeas (garbanzo beans)

- 1-2 tablespoons of olive oil or cooking spray
- Seasonings of your choice (see notes below)
- Salt, to taste

Instructions:

1. **Preparation:**
   - Preheat your air fryer to 375°F (190°C) for about 3-5 minutes while you prepare the chickpeas.
2. **Rinse and Drain:**
   - Open the can of chickpeas, drain them in a colander, and rinse them thoroughly under cold water. Pat them dry with a paper towel. Removing excess moisture is essential for achieving crispiness.
3. **Seasoning:**
   - Place the dried chickpeas in a bowl and drizzle with 1-2 tablespoons of olive oil, or you can use cooking spray for a lighter option. Toss to coat them evenly.
   - Add your preferred seasonings. Some popular options include:
     - Paprika
     - Cumin
     - Chili powder
     - Garlic powder
     - Onion powder
     - Smoked paprika
     - Cayenne pepper (for heat)
     - Salt (adjust to your taste)
   - Toss the chickpeas again to make sure they are evenly coated with oil and seasonings.
4. **Air Frying:**
   - Place the seasoned chickpeas in the preheated air fryer basket in a single layer. Do not overcrowd the basket; you may need to cook in batches.
   - Cook at 375°F (190°C) for about 15-20 minutes, shaking the basket or tossing the chickpeas every 5 minutes to ensure even cooking.
5. **Checking for Doneness:**
   - The chickpeas are done when they are golden brown and have a crispy texture. Keep an eye on them, as cooking times can vary depending on your air fryer model.
6. **Cool and Enjoy:**
   - Once done, remove the chickpeas from the air fryer and let them cool for a few minutes. They will continue to crisp up as they cool.

Notes:

1. **Seasonings:** Be creative with your seasonings. You can customize the flavor to your liking. Just be mindful of the salt content, as chickpeas tend to absorb salt quickly.

2. **Rinsing and Drying:** Properly rinsing and drying the chickpeas is crucial for achieving a crispy texture. Extra moisture can lead to steaming rather than crisping.
3. **Batch Size:** Don't overcrowd the air fryer basket. Cook the chickpeas in batches if necessary to ensure they have enough room to crisp up.
4. **Cooking Time:** Keep an eye on the chickpeas, as cooking times can vary depending on the air fryer's model and chickpea moisture content. They can go from perfectly crispy to burnt quickly.
5. **Storage:** Store any leftovers in an airtight container. Reheat in the air fryer for a few minutes to restore their crispiness.

These ultra-crispy air fryer chickpeas make for a great snack, salad topper, or even a crunchy addition to your favorite dishes. Enjoy experimenting with different seasonings to find your favorite flavor combination.

Certainly, here are some additional tips and variations to enhance your air fryer chickpeas experience:

Tips:

1. **Dry Chickpeas Thoroughly:** After rinsing the chickpeas, pat them dry with a kitchen towel or paper towels. The drier they are, the crispier they'll become.
2. **Preheat the Air Fryer:** Preheating your air fryer is crucial for even cooking and achieving that crispy texture. Let it reach the desired temperature before adding the chickpeas.
3. **Experiment with Spice Blends:** Get creative with your spice blends. You can use pre-made seasoning blends, such as curry powder, taco seasoning, or ranch seasoning, for a unique flavor.
4. **Smoked Chickpeas:** Add a smoky flavor by using smoked paprika and a touch of liquid smoke in your seasoning mix.
5. **Sweet and Savory:** For a sweet and savory twist, try adding a pinch of brown sugar or honey to your seasoning mix. This is a great option if you like a hint of sweetness in your snacks.
6. **Citrus Zest:** Add a burst of fresh flavor by grating citrus zest (lemon, lime, or orange) over the chickpeas before air frying. It will infuse them with a bright, tangy taste.
7. **A Touch of Parmesan:** After air frying, sprinkle some grated Parmesan cheese over the chickpeas while they are still warm. The residual heat will melt the cheese and create a savory coating.
8. **Herbs:** Fresh or dried herbs like rosemary, thyme, or basil can add an aromatic touch to your chickpeas.

Variations:

1. **Spicy Chickpeas:** If you enjoy a kick, add a generous pinch of cayenne pepper or crushed red pepper flakes to your seasoning mix.

2. **Buffalo Chickpeas:** Toss the chickpeas in a mixture of buffalo sauce and a bit of melted butter or olive oil before air frying for a spicy, tangy flavor.
3. **Everything Bagel Chickpeas:** Season your chickpeas with a blend of sesame seeds, poppy seeds, garlic flakes, onion flakes, and coarse salt for an "everything bagel" flavor.
4. **Taco Chickpeas:** Use taco seasoning mix, or make your own blend with cumin, chili powder, paprika, and a touch of lime zest for a Tex-Mex twist.
5. **BBQ Chickpeas:** Create a barbecue flavor with a mixture of paprika, brown sugar, garlic powder, and a bit of tomato paste or barbecue sauce.
6. **Sesame Ginger Chickpeas:** Combine sesame oil, grated ginger, and soy sauce for an Asian-inspired twist.
7. **Ranch Chickpeas:** Season with a homemade ranch seasoning blend made from dried herbs, garlic powder, onion powder, and buttermilk powder.
8. **Curry Chickpeas:** Create a flavorful curry blend with curry powder, turmeric, cumin, and coriander for an Indian-inspired snack.

Feel free to mix and match seasonings and variations to suit your preferences. Air fryer chickpeas are incredibly versatile and make for a healthy and satisfying snack with a satisfying crunch.

Crispy Air Fryer Sweet Potato Tots

Crispy Air Fryer Sweet Potato Tots are a delicious and healthier alternative to traditional deep-fried tots. They make for a great snack or side dish, and they're simple to prepare. Here's a recipe along with some notes to help you make the best sweet potato tots in your air fryer:

Ingredients:

- 2 large sweet potatoes
- 2 tablespoons olive oil
- 1/2 teaspoon salt
- 1/2 teaspoon black pepper
- 1/2 teaspoon paprika (optional)
- Cooking spray (for the air fryer basket)

Instructions:

1. **Prep the Sweet Potatoes:**
   - Wash and peel the sweet potatoes.
   - Cut the sweet potatoes into small cubes or pieces. You can also use a food processor with a grating attachment to shred them.
2. **Preheat the Air Fryer:**
   - Preheat your air fryer to 375°F (190°C) while you prepare the sweet potato mixture.
3. **Season the Sweet Potatoes:**

- In a large bowl, toss the sweet potato pieces with olive oil, salt, pepper, and paprika (if using). Ensure the sweet potatoes are evenly coated with the seasonings.
4. **Shape the Tots:**
   - Take a small amount of the sweet potato mixture and shape it into small tots or cylinders. You can use your hands or a small scoop to form them. Ensure they are compact and hold their shape.
5. **Air Fry the Tots:**
   - Lightly grease the air fryer basket with cooking spray to prevent sticking.
   - Place the tots in the air fryer basket in a single layer, ensuring they are not crowded. You may need to work in batches.
   - Air fry the tots at 375°F for about 10-15 minutes, flipping them halfway through the cooking time. Cook until they are golden brown and crispy.
6. **Serve:**
   - Remove the sweet potato tots from the air fryer and let them cool for a minute or two.
   - Serve them hot with your favorite dipping sauce.

Notes:

- Sweet Potato Varieties: You can use different types of sweet potatoes, but orange-fleshed varieties like the Beauregard or Garnet are commonly used for sweet potato tots due to their sweet flavor and vibrant color.
- Seasoning: Feel free to adjust the seasonings to your taste. You can add garlic powder, onion powder, or any other herbs and spices you prefer.
- Shape and Size: You can shape the tots into small cylinders, but you can also make them into traditional tater tot shapes or any other shape you like.
- Cooking Time: Cooking time may vary depending on the size and thickness of your tots and the specific air fryer model you use. Keep a close eye on them, and adjust the cooking time as needed.
- Dipping Sauces: These sweet potato tots pair well with various dipping sauces like ketchup, aioli, or a honey mustard sauce.

Enjoy your crispy air fryer sweet potato tots as a delicious and healthier snack or side dish!

Of course, here are some additional tips and variations to help you make the most of your air fryer sweet potato tots:

1. Baking Powder Trick: Some people find that adding a small amount of baking powder to the sweet potato mixture can make the tots even crispier. A pinch (about 1/4 teaspoon) of baking powder can help create a lighter, crunchier texture.

2. Panko Crust: For an extra crispy coating, you can roll the tots in panko breadcrumbs before air frying. This will give them a fantastic crunch.

3. Cheese: If you want to make your sweet potato tots extra indulgent, consider mixing in some shredded cheddar or Parmesan cheese into the sweet potato mixture. The cheese will add flavor and a cheesy texture to the tots.

4. Spices and Seasonings: Experiment with various spices and seasonings to change the flavor profile of your sweet potato tots. Smoked paprika, cumin, cinnamon, or even a dash of cayenne pepper can add an exciting twist to the recipe.

5. Gluten-Free Version: If you need a gluten-free option, use gluten-free breadcrumbs or almond flour instead of regular flour in the mixture or for coating the tots.

6. Freezing for Later: You can make a large batch of sweet potato tots, freeze them on a baking sheet, and transfer them to an airtight container or a freezer bag once they're solid. This way, you can have a supply of homemade tots that you can air fry whenever you want.

7. Preheat the Air Fryer: Always preheat your air fryer before cooking to ensure even cooking and a crispy exterior.

8. Avoid Overcrowding: It's essential to arrange the tots in a single layer without overcrowding the air fryer basket. Overcrowding can lead to uneven cooking and less crispy results.

9. Serve with Dipping Sauces: Sweet potato tots are delicious on their own, but they're even better when served with various dipping sauces. Consider options like sriracha mayo, barbecue sauce, or ranch dressing for a flavorful experience.

10. Healthier Option: If you want a lower-calorie option, you can reduce the amount of olive oil used or use a cooking spray to lightly coat the tots.

Experiment with these tips and variations to create sweet potato tots that suit your taste preferences and dietary needs. Whether you serve them as a snack, side dish, or party appetizer, crispy air fryer sweet potato tots are sure to be a hit.

Honey Garlic Air Fryer Cauliflower Wings

Honey Garlic Air Fryer Cauliflower Wings are a delicious and healthier alternative to traditional chicken wings. They are crispy, sticky, and full of flavor. Here's a simple recipe along with some notes to make the perfect batch:

Ingredients:

- 1 head of cauliflower, cut into bite-sized florets
- 1 cup all-purpose flour (or a gluten-free alternative)
- 1 cup milk (or a plant-based milk for a vegan version)

- 1 cup panko breadcrumbs (or regular breadcrumbs)
- 1 teaspoon paprika
- 1/2 teaspoon garlic powder
- 1/2 teaspoon onion powder
- Salt and black pepper to taste

For the Honey Garlic Sauce:

- 1/2 cup honey (or maple syrup for a vegan version)
- 1/4 cup soy sauce (or tamari for a gluten-free version)
- 2-3 cloves garlic, minced
- 1 teaspoon ginger, minced
- 1 tablespoon cornstarch
- 2 tablespoons water
- Optional: Red pepper flakes for heat

Instructions:

1. **Preheat your Air Fryer:** Set your air fryer to 400°F (200°C) and let it preheat for a few minutes.
2. **Prepare Cauliflower:** Wash and cut the cauliflower into bite-sized florets.
3. **Coating the Cauliflower:** In separate bowls, place the flour in one, the milk in another, and combine the breadcrumbs, paprika, garlic powder, onion powder, salt, and pepper in a third. Dip each cauliflower floret in the flour, then the milk, and finally coat it in the breadcrumb mixture. Ensure they are evenly coated, and shake off any excess.
4. **Air Fry the Cauliflower:** Place the coated cauliflower in a single layer in your air fryer basket. You may need to do this in batches depending on the size of your air fryer. Spray or brush the cauliflower with a light layer of oil to help them crisp up. Cook for about 15-20 minutes, flipping them halfway through, until they are golden and crispy.
5. **Make the Sauce:** While the cauliflower is cooking, prepare the honey garlic sauce. In a small saucepan, combine honey, soy sauce, minced garlic, and ginger. Heat over medium heat, bringing the mixture to a simmer. In a separate small bowl, mix the cornstarch and water to create a slurry. Add the slurry to the sauce and stir continuously until it thickens. If you want a bit of heat, add some red pepper flakes to taste.
6. **Toss the Cauliflower:** Once the cauliflower is done, place it in a large bowl, drizzle the honey garlic sauce over it, and toss the cauliflower until it's evenly coated with the sauce.
7. **Serve:** Serve your honey garlic cauliflower wings hot, garnished with sesame seeds, green onions, or even a sprinkle of parsley for some color.

Recipe Notes:

- Experiment with the spice level of the sauce by adjusting the amount of garlic, ginger, and red pepper flakes.

- Make sure your cauliflower is well-coated with the breadcrumb mixture to ensure a crispy texture.
- Don't overcrowd the air fryer basket. Cook in batches if necessary to maintain crispiness.
- You can use store-bought honey garlic sauce if you're looking to save time.

These honey garlic air fryer cauliflower wings are a crowd-pleaser, and they make for a great appetizer or snack. Enjoy!

Air Fryer Roasted Garlic

Air fryer roasted garlic is a simple and delicious way to enjoy the sweet, caramelized flavors of garlic without the need for a traditional oven. Here's a recipe and some notes to help you make this flavorful dish:

Ingredients:

- Whole garlic bulbs
- Olive oil
- Salt (optional)

Instructions:

1. **Prepare the Garlic:**
   - Choose whole garlic bulbs that are fresh and firm. Try to get bulbs with plump cloves.
   - Use a sharp knife to cut off the top 1/4 inch of the garlic bulbs to expose the tops of the cloves. This will make it easier to squeeze out the roasted garlic later.
2. **Drizzle with Olive Oil:**
   - Place the garlic bulbs in a small bowl or on a piece of aluminum foil.
   - Drizzle the exposed cloves with olive oil. Use enough to coat the cloves thoroughly but not drown them. About 1-2 teaspoons per bulb is usually sufficient.
   - You can add a pinch of salt if you like, which will enhance the flavors as the garlic roasts.
3. **Wrap or Place in the Air Fryer:**
   - If using aluminum foil, wrap each garlic bulb in a small, tight package.
   - Preheat your air fryer to around 350°F (175°C). If your air fryer doesn't have a preheat function, let it run for a few minutes at this temperature before adding the garlic.
   - Place the wrapped or unwrapped garlic bulbs in the air fryer basket.
4. **Roast in the Air Fryer:**

- Roast the garlic at 350°F (175°C) for 20-30 minutes, depending on the size of the bulbs and the desired level of caramelization. Smaller bulbs may be done in as little as 20 minutes, while larger ones may take closer to 30 minutes.
- Check the garlic cloves after 20 minutes. They should be soft, caramelized, and slightly browned. If they're not done to your liking, continue roasting in 5-minute increments.

5. **Cool and Serve:**
   - Carefully remove the roasted garlic from the air fryer and let it cool for a few minutes. Be cautious as it will be hot.
   - To extract the roasted garlic, simply squeeze the base of the bulb, and the soft, sweet cloves will pop out easily.
   - Use the roasted garlic in various dishes like mashed potatoes, spread it on bread, mix it into sauces, or add it to soups and stews.

Notes:

- The roasted garlic is incredibly versatile and can add a rich, sweet, and savory depth of flavor to your recipes.
- You can adjust the roasting time based on your preference. If you like a more pronounced caramelized flavor, roast for a longer time.
- Keep an eye on the garlic to prevent it from burning. It should be soft and caramelized but not charred.
- Roasted garlic can be stored in the refrigerator for a few days. To store for a longer time, you can freeze individual cloves in an airtight container or wrap them in plastic wrap and place them in a freezer bag.
- Experiment with different seasonings like herbs or spices to add extra flavors to your roasted garlic.

Tips:

1. **Use Fresh Garlic:** Start with fresh, plump garlic bulbs. Older, shriveled garlic may not produce the same rich, sweet flavor.
2. **Adjust Temperature and Time:** Air fryers can vary in temperature and airflow. You may need to adjust the temperature and cooking time based on your specific appliance. Keep an eye on the garlic as it roasts to avoid overcooking.
3. **Minimize Oil:** While olive oil is commonly used, you can experiment with other oils like avocado oil or grapeseed oil. Just be cautious not to use too much, as it can make the garlic greasy.
4. **Flavor Variations:** Try adding herbs such as rosemary, thyme, or oregano to the garlic before roasting for additional flavor. You can also sprinkle a bit of parmesan cheese for a cheesy twist.
5. **Easy Cleanup:** If you're using aluminum foil, it can help with cleanup. However, you can also use air fryer parchment paper or a silicone baking mat to prevent the garlic from sticking to the air fryer basket.

Recipe Ideas:

1. **Garlic Butter:** Mix the roasted garlic with softened butter to create a delicious garlic butter spread. Use it on bread, steaks, or roasted vegetables.
2. **Creamy Garlic Mashed Potatoes:** Mash the roasted garlic cloves into your mashed potatoes for a creamy, garlicky twist.
3. **Roasted Garlic Hummus:** Blend roasted garlic into your homemade hummus for a flavorful dip.
4. **Pasta Sauces:** Add roasted garlic to tomato sauces or cream-based pasta sauces to enhance their flavor.
5. **Roasted Garlic Soup:** Puree roasted garlic with vegetable or chicken broth to make a flavorful roasted garlic soup. Garnish with a drizzle of olive oil and fresh herbs.
6. **Pizza Topping:** Spread roasted garlic on pizza dough before adding your other toppings for a gourmet touch.
7. **Salad Dressing:** Combine roasted garlic, olive oil, vinegar, and your choice of herbs to make a flavorful salad dressing.
8. **Sandwiches:** Spread roasted garlic on sandwiches or wraps for an extra burst of flavor.
9. **Stir-Fries:** Add roasted garlic to stir-fries for a mellow, sweet garlic flavor.
10. **Savory Roasted Vegetables:** Toss roasted garlic with roasted vegetables like carrots, Brussels sprouts, or potatoes for a tasty side dish.

Feel free to get creative and experiment with different recipes and flavor combinations. Air fryer roasted garlic is a versatile ingredient that can elevate a wide range of dishes.

Crispy Air Fryer Brussels Sprouts

Crispy Air Fryer Brussels Sprouts are a delicious and healthier alternative to traditional fried Brussels sprouts. They make for a fantastic side dish or snack. Here's a recipe along with some notes to help you achieve that crispy and flavorful result:

Ingredients:

- 1 pound of fresh Brussels sprouts
- 2 tablespoons of olive oil
- 1/2 teaspoon of salt
- 1/4 teaspoon of black pepper
- 1/4 teaspoon of garlic powder (optional)
- 1/4 cup of grated Parmesan cheese (optional, for added flavor)

Instructions:

1. **Prepare Brussels Sprouts:**
   - Wash the Brussels sprouts and trim the stems.

- Cut them in half lengthwise for even cooking.
2. **Seasoning:**
   - In a large bowl, toss the halved Brussels sprouts with olive oil, salt, pepper, and garlic powder if you're using it. Make sure they're evenly coated.
3. **Preheat Air Fryer:**
   - Preheat your air fryer to 375°F (190°C) for a few minutes.
4. **Air Frying:**
   - Place the seasoned Brussels sprouts in the air fryer basket in a single layer. Avoid overcrowding to allow for even cooking and crispiness.
   - Cook for 12-15 minutes, shaking the basket every 5 minutes to ensure all sides get crispy.
5. **Optional Parmesan Cheese:**
   - If you'd like to add some extra flavor, sprinkle grated Parmesan cheese over the Brussels sprouts during the last 2-3 minutes of cooking. This will allow the cheese to melt and become slightly crispy.
6. **Serve:**
   - Once the Brussels sprouts are crispy and browned to your liking, remove them from the air fryer.
7. **Garnish and Enjoy:**
   - You can garnish with more Parmesan cheese or a squeeze of fresh lemon juice for added flavor.

Recipe Notes:

- **Don't Overcrowd:** Overcrowding the air fryer basket can lead to uneven cooking. If you have a large batch, it's better to cook in multiple batches.
- **Consistent Size:** Try to cut the Brussels sprouts to a similar size for even cooking. Smaller sprouts may cook faster, so keep an eye on them.
- **Oil Usage:** You can adjust the amount of olive oil based on your preference. More oil may result in slightly crispier Brussels sprouts, but they can still be quite crispy with just a light coating of oil.
- **Customize Seasonings:** Feel free to experiment with your favorite seasonings. You can try different herbs, spices, or even a drizzle of balsamic glaze for added flavor.
- **Check for Doneness:** Keep an eye on the Brussels sprouts as cooking times can vary depending on the air fryer model. They should be tender on the inside and crispy on the outside when done.

Crispy Air Fryer Brussels Sprouts are a delicious and guilt-free snack or side dish that can be enjoyed by themselves or with your favorite dipping sauce.

Certainly, here are some additional tips and notes for making the perfect crispy air fryer Brussels sprouts:

- **Parchment Paper or Liner:** While not necessary, using parchment paper or a silicone liner can help prevent sticking and make cleanup easier. Just make sure it's air fryer-safe.
- **Preheating:** Preheating the air fryer is essential for consistent cooking. It helps achieve that initial crispiness.
- **Basket Placement:** For even cooking, place the Brussels sprouts in a single layer without stacking them. If your air fryer has multiple trays or layers, use them to maximize the cooking area.
- **Adjust the Temperature and Time:** Cooking times and temperatures can vary depending on the air fryer brand and model. Start with the recommended temperature and time, but feel free to adjust to your liking. If they're not crispy enough, you can cook them a bit longer.
- **Fresh vs. Frozen Brussels Sprouts:** Fresh Brussels sprouts are ideal for this recipe, but you can make frozen ones work as well. Just make sure to thaw and pat them dry before seasoning and air frying.
- **Variations:** Get creative with your seasonings. You can try adding a pinch of smoked paprika, red pepper flakes for some heat, or even a little honey for a touch of sweetness.
- **Serve with Dipping Sauces:** Crispy Brussels sprouts go well with various dipping sauces, such as aioli, ranch, balsamic glaze, or a simple lemon and garlic yogurt sauce.
- **Leftovers:** If you have leftover Brussels sprouts, you can reheat them in the air fryer for a few minutes to restore their crispiness. They may not be as crispy as freshly cooked, but they'll still be delicious.
- **Nutritional Benefits:** Brussels sprouts are high in fiber, vitamins, and antioxidants. Air frying them with minimal oil preserves more of their nutritional value compared to deep frying.
- **Experiment and Enjoy:** The beauty of air frying is its versatility. Don't be afraid to experiment with different ingredients and seasonings to create your unique twist on crispy Brussels sprouts.

Remember that practice makes perfect, and you can adjust the cooking time and seasonings to suit your personal taste. Enjoy your crispy air fryer Brussels sprouts!

Air Fryer Corn (SO GOOD)

Air frying corn is a quick and delicious way to enjoy this classic side dish with a crispy twist. Here's a simple recipe for making air fryer corn, along with some helpful notes:

Ingredients:

- 4 ears of corn, husked and cleaned
- 2 tablespoons of olive oil
- Salt and pepper to taste

- Optional seasonings: garlic powder, paprika, cayenne pepper, or grated Parmesan cheese

Instructions:

1. **Preheat the Air Fryer:** Preheat your air fryer to 375°F (190°C) for a few minutes.
2. **Prepare the Corn:** While the air fryer is preheating, brush each ear of corn with a thin layer of olive oil. This will help the corn become crispy and golden brown.
3. **Season:** Sprinkle salt, pepper, and any optional seasonings (garlic powder, paprika, cayenne pepper, or Parmesan cheese) over the corn. You can customize the seasonings to your taste.
4. **Air Fry:** Place the seasoned corn ears into the air fryer basket, making sure they are not overcrowded. You may need to cook them in batches if your air fryer is small.
5. **Cook:** Cook the corn at 375°F (190°C) for 12-15 minutes, turning the ears halfway through the cooking time. Cooking time may vary depending on your air fryer, so keep an eye on them. The corn should be tender and slightly charred.
6. **Serve:** Once the corn is done, remove it from the air fryer and let it cool for a minute or two. Serve it hot with a drizzle of additional olive oil or a sprinkle of Parmesan cheese if desired.

Notes:

1. **Husk and Clean the Corn:** Make sure to remove the husks and silk from the corn before cooking. You want the corn to be clean and ready for seasoning.
2. **Preheat the Air Fryer:** Preheating is essential for even cooking and ensuring that the corn gets crispy. It also reduces the cooking time.
3. **Customize the Seasonings:** Feel free to get creative with your seasonings. Smoked paprika, cumin, chili powder, or even a squeeze of fresh lime juice can add unique flavors to your air-fried corn.
4. **Watch the Cooking Time:** Cooking times can vary between different air fryer models, so it's essential to keep an eye on the corn as it cooks to prevent burning. You may need to adjust the cooking time based on your specific air fryer.
5. **Serve Immediately:** Air-fried corn is best enjoyed immediately while it's still hot and crispy. It's a fantastic side dish for BBQs, picnics, or as a simple weeknight meal.

Air-fried corn is a delightful twist on a classic favorite, and it's perfect for when you want a quick and tasty side dish. Enjoy!

Certainly! Here are some additional tips and variations to enhance your air fryer corn experience:

1. Butter and Herb Variation:

- After brushing the corn with olive oil, spread a thin layer of softened butter over each ear.
- Sprinkle with a mixture of fresh or dried herbs like thyme, rosemary, and parsley.
- This adds a rich, savory flavor to the corn.

2. Mexican Street Corn (Elote) Style:

- After air frying the corn, spread a layer of mayonnaise or Mexican crema on each ear.
- Sprinkle with crumbled queso fresco or grated Cotija cheese.
- Add a dash of chili powder, cayenne, or Tajin seasoning.
- Squeeze fresh lime juice on top for that classic Elote taste.

3. Parmesan and Herb Crust:

- In addition to olive oil, brush the corn with Dijon mustard for extra flavor.
- Mix grated Parmesan cheese with breadcrumbs and your choice of herbs (such as basil, oregano, or thyme).
- Coat the corn with the Parmesan and herb mixture for a crunchy, cheesy crust.

4. Grilled Corn Effect:

- If you want that grilled corn effect, you can also place the seasoned corn directly on the air fryer grill rack or grate instead of using the basket.
- Make sure to turn the corn halfway through to get those grill marks.

5. Spicy Corn:

- Add some heat by mixing a little cayenne pepper or chili powder into the seasoning.
- You can also drizzle the corn with hot sauce after cooking for an extra kick.

6. Leftover Corn Ideas:

- If you happen to have leftover air-fried corn, you can cut the kernels off the cob and use them in various dishes. They're great in salads, salsas, or mixed into pasta.

7. Cleaning Your Air Fryer:

- Corn kernels can leave residue in your air fryer. Make sure to clean it promptly after use to prevent any burnt-on debris. Refer to your air fryer's manual for proper cleaning instructions.

Remember that the cooking time might vary based on the size and freshness of the corn, as well as the specific model of your air fryer. It's always a good idea to test a few ears of corn first to get the timing just right for your particular setup.

Enjoy experimenting with these variations, and air-fry your corn to suit your taste preferences. It's a versatile side dish that can complement various meals and cuisines.

Air Fryer Carrots (tender + sweet!)

Air-fried carrots are a delicious and healthy side dish that's easy to make. They come out tender on the inside and slightly crispy on the outside. Here's a simple recipe and some tips to ensure your air-fried carrots turn out sweet and delightful.

Ingredients:

- 1 pound of fresh carrots, peeled and cut into even-sized sticks or coins
- 1-2 tablespoons of olive oil or cooking spray
- Salt and pepper to taste
- Optional seasonings (such as garlic powder, paprika, rosemary, or honey)

Instructions:

1. **Prepare the Carrots:** Wash, peel, and cut the carrots into uniform-sized pieces. This helps ensure even cooking.
2. **Season the Carrots:** In a bowl, toss the carrot pieces with olive oil or use a cooking spray to coat them evenly. Season with salt and pepper, and any additional seasonings you prefer. Be creative with your seasoning choices, but remember that simple salt and pepper can also work wonders.
3. **Preheat the Air Fryer:** Preheat your air fryer to 380°F (190°C) for a few minutes.
4. **Air Fry the Carrots:** Place the seasoned carrot pieces in the air fryer basket in a single layer, ensuring they are not crowded. You may need to do this in batches depending on the size of your air fryer. Crowding the basket can result in uneven cooking.
5. **Cook the Carrots:** Air fry the carrots at 380°F (190°C) for 12-15 minutes, shaking the basket or tossing the carrots halfway through the cooking time to ensure even browning. The exact cooking time may vary depending on your air fryer's model and the size of the carrot pieces. Aim for a tender interior and slightly crispy exterior.
6. **Check for Doneness:** At the end of the cooking time, check the carrots for doneness. They should be tender when pierced with a fork and have a nice caramelized exterior. If they need more time, you can air fry them for an additional 2-5 minutes, checking every minute to prevent overcooking.
7. **Serve:** Remove the air-fried carrots from the air fryer, season with a bit more salt and pepper if necessary, and serve immediately.

Notes:

1. **Carrot Size:** Cut the carrots into evenly sized pieces to ensure they cook uniformly. Thicker pieces may need a bit more time, so adjust accordingly.
2. **Oil Usage:** Use just enough oil to lightly coat the carrots. You can use olive oil or cooking spray to keep them from sticking and help with browning.
3. **Seasoning:** Experiment with different seasonings to find your favorite flavor combinations. Herbs, spices, or even a drizzle of honey can add a unique twist to your air-fried carrots.
4. **Batch Size:** Avoid overcrowding the air fryer basket to ensure the carrots cook evenly and get crispy.

5. **Checking Doneness:** Keep an eye on the carrots as they cook to prevent overcooking. The total cooking time may vary based on your air fryer's performance.

Air-fried carrots make a fantastic side dish for various meals and are a great way to enjoy the natural sweetness of this nutritious vegetable.

Certainly! Here are some additional tips and ideas to enhance your air-fried carrots:

1. Pre-Soak the Carrots: If you have the time, you can soak the carrot pieces in cold water for about 30 minutes before air frying. This can help them become even more tender on the inside.

2. Honey Glaze: For a touch of sweetness, consider drizzling honey or maple syrup over the carrots before air frying. This will create a caramelized glaze.

3. Balsamic Vinegar: Add depth of flavor by drizzling balsamic vinegar over the carrots after they've cooked. The acidity pairs well with the sweetness of the carrots.

4. Parmesan Cheese: Sprinkle grated Parmesan cheese over the carrots during the last few minutes of cooking for a cheesy, savory twist.

5. Dipping Sauces: Serve your air-fried carrots with a variety of dipping sauces. Classic choices include ranch dressing, hummus, or tzatziki.

6. Spice It Up: Experiment with different spice blends like cumin, coriander, or red pepper flakes for a unique flavor profile.

7. Citrus Zest: Grate some fresh lemon or orange zest over the carrots before serving to brighten the flavor.

8. Panko Crust: For an extra crispy exterior, dip the seasoned carrot pieces in beaten egg, then coat them with a mixture of panko breadcrumbs and your favorite seasonings before air frying.

9. Don't Overcrowd the Basket: Overcrowding the basket can lead to uneven cooking. It's better to cook the carrots in batches or use a larger air fryer if you have a substantial amount to cook.

10. Reheating: Air-fried carrots are best enjoyed fresh, but if you have leftovers, you can reheat them in the air fryer for a few minutes to restore their crispiness.

11. Customize the Cut: Experiment with different cuts, such as carrot ribbons or carrot fries, for a change in texture and presentation.

12. Serve with Protein: Air-fried carrots pair well with various proteins like roasted chicken, grilled fish, or even a vegetarian burger.

13. Keep It Healthy: Air frying is a healthier alternative to traditional frying, but remember not to overdo the oil or use excessive amounts of high-calorie seasonings if you're aiming for a healthier dish.

Air-fried carrots are versatile and can be customized to suit your taste. Whether you prefer them savory, sweet, or spicy, these notes and ideas should help you create a delicious and nutritious side dish for your meals.

Crispy Baked Zucchini Fries

Crispy baked zucchini fries are a healthier alternative to traditional deep-fried french fries. They're delicious, easy to make, and a great way to use up excess zucchini. Here's a recipe along with some helpful notes:

Ingredients:

- 2 medium zucchinis
- 1 cup panko breadcrumbs
- 1/2 cup grated Parmesan cheese
- 1 teaspoon Italian seasoning
- 1/2 teaspoon garlic powder
- 1/2 teaspoon salt
- 1/4 teaspoon black pepper
- 2 large eggs
- Cooking spray or olive oil

Notes:

1. **Prepare the Zucchini:**
   - Wash and dry the zucchinis. Trim the ends and cut them into strips resembling the shape of fries. You can choose to peel them or leave the skin on for added texture and nutrition.
2. **Preheat the Oven:**
   - Preheat your oven to 425°F (220°C) and place a wire rack on a baking sheet. This helps air circulate around the zucchini fries for even crisping.
3. **Breading Station:**
   - Set up a breading station with three shallow dishes. In the first dish, place the panko breadcrumbs mixed with the grated Parmesan cheese, Italian seasoning, garlic powder, salt, and pepper. In the second dish, beat the eggs.
4. **Coating the Zucchini:**
   - Take each zucchini strip and dip it into the egg, ensuring it's fully coated. Let any excess egg drip off.

- Next, roll the zucchini strip in the breadcrumb mixture, pressing the breadcrumbs onto the surface to create an even coating. Place the coated strip on the wire rack on the baking sheet.
5. **Baking:**
   - Once all the zucchini strips are coated and arranged on the wire rack, lightly spray them with cooking spray or drizzle a bit of olive oil over them. This helps them crisp up in the oven.
   - Bake in the preheated oven for about 20-25 minutes or until they are golden brown and crispy. You may want to flip them halfway through the baking time for even browning.
6. **Serving:**
   - Once the zucchini fries are done, remove them from the oven and let them cool slightly. Serve them hot with your favorite dipping sauces like marinara, ranch, or tzatziki.

Notes and Tips:

- Make sure the zucchini strips are evenly coated with the breadcrumb mixture to ensure they turn out crispy.
- If you don't have panko breadcrumbs, you can use regular breadcrumbs, but panko tends to make the fries extra crispy.
- Experiment with different seasonings and spices to customize the flavor of your zucchini fries.
- Keep an eye on the baking time, as the thickness of the zucchini strips and your specific oven may affect how long they need to bake. You want them to be golden and crispy, but not overcooked.
- These zucchini fries are best enjoyed fresh out of the oven for maximum crispiness.

Certainly! Here are a few more tips and variations to enhance your crispy baked zucchini fries:

Tips:

1. **Use a Baking Rack:** Placing the zucchini fries on a wire rack on top of a baking sheet helps them cook evenly and prevents them from getting soggy on the bottom.
2. **Even Slicing:** Try to slice the zucchinis into uniform strips so that they cook evenly. This ensures some won't be overcooked while others are undercooked.
3. **Don't Overcrowd:** Avoid overcrowding the baking sheet, as this can cause the zucchini fries to steam rather than crisp up. If needed, bake them in batches.
4. **Dipping Sauces:** Get creative with your dipping sauces. In addition to the classic choices like ketchup, mayonnaise, or mustard, consider healthier options like Greek yogurt-based dips with herbs and spices.
5. **Seasoning:** You can customize the seasoning to your liking. Add a pinch of cayenne pepper for some heat or smoked paprika for a smoky flavor.

Variations:

1. **Gluten-Free:** If you're on a gluten-free diet, use gluten-free breadcrumbs and ensure that all your ingredients, including the Italian seasoning, are gluten-free.
2. **Vegan:** To make these fries vegan, replace the egg wash with a mixture of plant-based milk (e.g., almond or soy milk) and a bit of cornstarch. Use vegan Parmesan cheese or nutritional yeast for the cheesy flavor.
3. **Herb-Crusted:** Add fresh herbs like chopped parsley, thyme, or rosemary to the breadcrumb mixture for an extra burst of flavor.
4. **Cheese Variation:** Experiment with different types of cheese. Instead of Parmesan, try cheddar, mozzarella, or a mix of your favorite cheeses.
5. **Sweet Potato Fries:** You can apply a similar coating and baking method to sweet potato fries for a different twist.
6. **Dill Pickle Zucchini Fries:** Create a tangy twist by using dill pickle-flavored breadcrumbs or adding some pickle juice to the egg wash for zesty zucchini fries.
7. **Baking Temperature and Time:** You can adjust the baking temperature and time slightly to achieve your desired level of crispiness. Higher temperatures may result in a quicker, crisper fry, but be cautious not to burn them.
8. **Experiment with Dips:** In addition to the classic dipping sauces, try creamy avocado ranch, honey mustard, or even tzatziki for a Mediterranean twist.

Feel free to get creative with the recipe and tailor it to your preferences. Crispy baked zucchini fries are a versatile and healthy snack or side dish that you can adapt to suit your taste and dietary requirements.

Air Fryer Bacon

Air fryer bacon is a quick and easy way to cook crispy bacon with minimal mess and fuss. Here's a simple recipe and some important notes to keep in mind when cooking bacon in an air fryer:

Ingredients:

- Bacon strips
- Optional: Pepper, maple syrup, or brown sugar for flavor variation

Instructions:

1. **Preheat the Air Fryer:** Preheat your air fryer to 350-400°F (175-200°C). The exact temperature may vary depending on your air fryer model, so consult the user manual for guidance.
2. **Prepare the Bacon:** Lay out the bacon strips on a clean cutting board or plate. You can season them with some ground black pepper, drizzle a little maple syrup, or sprinkle brown sugar for added flavor, but this step is optional.

3. **Arrange in the Basket:** Place the bacon strips in a single layer in the air fryer basket. Make sure they aren't overlapping to ensure even cooking. You might need to cook in batches if you have a lot of bacon to prepare.
4. **Cook the Bacon:** Cook the bacon at the preheated temperature for about 8-12 minutes. Cooking time will depend on the thickness of the bacon and the temperature you've chosen. Keep a close eye on it to avoid overcooking or burning. You can check it at the 8-minute mark and decide if you want it crispier.
5. **Drain Excess Fat:** As the bacon cooks, the fat will drip into the bottom of the air fryer basket. You may want to carefully drain the excess fat during the cooking process to prevent any smoke or splattering. Make sure to use oven mitts or tongs to avoid burning yourself.
6. **Remove and Serve:** Once the bacon reaches your desired level of crispiness, carefully remove it from the air fryer basket using tongs and place it on a plate lined with paper towels to absorb any remaining grease.
7. **Serve:** Serve your air fryer bacon hot and enjoy!

Notes:

1. **Bacon Thickness:** The cooking time will vary based on the thickness of the bacon. Thicker bacon may require more time, while thinner bacon may cook faster. Adjust the cooking time accordingly.
2. **Bacon Quantity:** Avoid overcrowding the air fryer basket, as it can lead to uneven cooking. It's better to cook bacon in batches if necessary.
3. **Watch Carefully:** Keep a close eye on the bacon, especially during the last few minutes of cooking, as it can quickly go from crispy to burnt.
4. **Draining Fat:** If the bacon is releasing a lot of fat during cooking, it's a good idea to drain the excess fat to prevent smoke and maintain a cleaner cooking environment.
5. **Experiment with Flavors:** Don't be afraid to experiment with different seasonings and flavors to make your air fryer bacon unique and delicious.

Air fryer bacon is a fantastic alternative to traditional stovetop or oven methods, as it cooks quickly and produces crispy results with less mess. Just be sure to follow these instructions and adjust based on your specific air fryer's settings and your personal preferences.

Certainly! Here are some additional tips and information about cooking bacon in an air fryer:

1. **Bacon Variations:**
   ○ You can use various types of bacon, including regular, thick-cut, and even turkey bacon, in the air fryer. The cooking times may vary, so adjust accordingly.
2. **Cooking Temperature:**
   ○ The recommended temperature range for air frying bacon is 350-400°F (175-200°C). Experiment with different temperatures to find the one that suits your taste and your specific air fryer.
3. **Air Fryer Accessories:**

- Consider using perforated parchment paper or an air fryer silicone mat to make cleanup easier. Just be sure that any paper or mat you use is rated for air frying.

4. **Bacon Prep:**
   - If you prefer a more hands-off approach, you can cut your bacon strips in half and lay them side by side in the air fryer basket. This reduces the need to flip the bacon during cooking.

5. **Flavor Enhancements:**
   - Get creative with your bacon by adding seasonings like smoked paprika, cayenne pepper, or garlic powder before cooking. You can also sprinkle it with brown sugar for a sweet and savory combination.

6. **Bacon Weave:**
   - If you want to use bacon as an ingredient in sandwiches or burgers, you can create a bacon weave by overlapping strips before air frying. This creates a sturdy bacon sheet that's perfect for layering.

7. **Bacon Wrapped Treats:**
   - Use air fryer bacon to wrap around various foods like asparagus, chicken, shrimp, or jalapeño poppers. It's a fantastic way to add flavor and texture to your dishes.

8. **Health Considerations:**
   - While air frying reduces the overall fat content compared to frying in a pan, bacon is still a high-fat food. Be mindful of your dietary preferences and requirements.

9. **Storage and Reheating:**
   - If you have leftover bacon, store it in an airtight container in the refrigerator. To reheat, you can briefly warm it in the air fryer to restore its crispiness.

10. **Safety:**
    - Be cautious when removing the bacon from the air fryer, as the basket and bacon can be hot. Use appropriate tools, like tongs or spatulas, and wear oven mitts if necessary.

Air fryer bacon is a convenient and delicious way to prepare this beloved breakfast item, but don't limit yourself to just breakfast – you can enjoy it in a variety of dishes and as a flavor-packed ingredient in various recipes. Experiment with different variations and flavors to find the perfect air fryer bacon recipe that suits your taste preferences.

Seriously Crispy Air Fryer Gnocchi

Air frying gnocchi is a fantastic way to achieve a crispy texture without the need for excessive oil or deep frying. Here's a seriously crispy air fryer gnocchi recipe along with some important notes:

Ingredients:

- 1 pound (450g) of store-bought or homemade gnocchi
- 1-2 tablespoons of olive oil
- Salt and pepper to taste
- Optional seasonings: garlic powder, Italian seasoning, paprika, or grated Parmesan cheese for extra flavor

Instructions:

1. **Preheat Your Air Fryer:** Preheat your air fryer to 400°F (200°C) for about 5 minutes.
2. **Prepare Gnocchi:** If you're using store-bought gnocchi, you can usually cook them straight from the package. If you're using homemade gnocchi, boil them briefly until they float to the surface, then drain them.
3. **Toss in Oil:** Place the gnocchi in a large bowl and drizzle with 1-2 tablespoons of olive oil. You want to ensure they are lightly coated. Toss to coat evenly.
4. **Season:** Season your gnocchi with salt, pepper, and any additional seasonings you like. This is where you can get creative with flavors. A pinch of garlic powder, Italian seasoning, or paprika can add a nice kick. Grated Parmesan cheese can be added for a cheesy, crispy finish.
5. **Air Fry:** Place the seasoned gnocchi in the preheated air fryer basket in a single layer. Avoid overcrowding; you might need to do this in batches if you have a small air fryer. You want them to have space for proper crisping.
6. **Air Fry Time:** Cook the gnocchi in the air fryer at 400°F (200°C) for about 10-15 minutes. You'll want to shake the basket or toss the gnocchi every 5 minutes to ensure even cooking. Cook until they are golden brown and crispy.
7. **Serve:** Once your gnocchi reaches the desired crispiness, remove them from the air fryer and serve immediately. They're great as a snack or served with your favorite dipping sauce.

Notes:

- **Don't Overcrowd:** Overcrowding the air fryer basket can lead to uneven cooking. Make sure your gnocchi are in a single layer with space between each piece.
- **Watch Closely:** Cooking times can vary depending on the brand and model of your air fryer. Keep an eye on your gnocchi as they cook to prevent burning.
- **Use Homemade or Store-Bought Gnocchi:** You can use either homemade or store-bought gnocchi for this recipe. Homemade gnocchi can be a bit softer, so boiling them briefly before air frying is recommended.
- **Experiment with Seasonings:** Gnocchi is a blank canvas for flavors. Experiment with different seasonings to suit your taste.
- **Serve Promptly:** Crispy gnocchi is best when served immediately. They tend to lose their crispiness if left to sit for too long.

Enjoy your seriously crispy air fryer gnocchi as a delightful snack, side dish, or even as a base for your favorite sauces and toppings.

Certainly, here are some additional tips and suggestions for making the most of your crispy air fryer gnocchi:

Dipping Sauces:

- Pair your crispy gnocchi with a variety of dipping sauces like marinara sauce, pesto, aioli, or a simple garlic butter sauce for added flavor.

Herbs and Greens:

- After air frying, you can toss your gnocchi with fresh herbs like basil or parsley and some arugula or spinach for a burst of color and freshness.

Protein Additions:

- Consider adding protein to make it a complete meal. Cooked and sliced sausage, grilled chicken, or shrimp can be added to your gnocchi for a heartier dish.

Serve as Appetizers:

- Crispy gnocchi also make great appetizers for parties or gatherings. Arrange them on a platter with different dipping sauces for guests to enjoy.

Gnocchi Variations:

- Experiment with different types of gnocchi. You can use regular potato gnocchi, sweet potato gnocchi, or even spinach gnocchi. Each will bring a slightly different flavor and color to your dish.

Healthier Option:

- For a lighter version, you can spray the gnocchi with cooking spray instead of tossing them in olive oil. This will reduce the calorie content while still achieving a crispy texture.

Gluten-Free Options:

- If you're following a gluten-free diet, look for gluten-free gnocchi, which is widely available. Make sure the brand you choose is suitable for air frying.

Experiment with Cheese:

- Besides Parmesan, try other cheeses like grated Pecorino Romano or crumbled feta for different flavors.

Leftovers:

- If you have any leftovers, you can reheat them in the air fryer for a few minutes to bring back some of the crispiness.

Temperature and Time Adjustments:

- The suggested temperature and cooking time can vary depending on your specific air fryer model. Experiment with the settings to find the perfect balance of crispiness to suit your taste.

Enjoy your seriously crispy air fryer gnocchi, and don't be afraid to get creative with toppings and seasonings to make it your own. It's a versatile dish that can be customized to your preferences.

Air Fryer French Fries

Air fryer French fries are a delicious and healthier alternative to deep-fried fries. They come out crispy on the outside and tender on the inside. Here's a simple recipe and some important notes to ensure your success:

Ingredients:

- Potatoes (Russet or Yukon Gold are great choices)
- Olive oil or cooking spray
- Salt and pepper, to taste
- Optional seasonings: paprika, garlic powder, onion powder, or your favorite seasonings

Instructions:

1. **Preparation:**
   - Preheat your air fryer to 375-400°F (190-200°C). The exact temperature can vary depending on your specific air fryer model, so consult your user manual for guidance.
2. **Potato Prep:**
   - Wash and peel the potatoes if desired. You can also leave the skin on for a more rustic look.
   - Cut the potatoes into uniform, thin strips, about 1/4 inch (6mm) thick. Thicker fries might not get as crispy.
3. **Rinse and Soak:**
   - Rinse the potato strips in cold water to remove excess starch.
   - Soak the potato strips in cold water for 30 minutes to an hour. This helps remove more starch, which is key to achieving crispy fries.
4. **Dry Thoroughly:**

- After soaking, pat the potato strips dry with a clean kitchen towel or paper towels. The drier they are, the crispier they will turn out.

5. **Seasoning:**
   - Place the dried potato strips in a bowl and toss them with a drizzle of olive oil or use a cooking spray to evenly coat them.
   - Season the fries with salt, pepper, and any other seasonings you like. Mix well to ensure even seasoning.

6. **Air Frying:**
   - Arrange the seasoned potato strips in a single layer in the air fryer basket. Do not overcrowd; you may need to cook them in batches.
   - Cook the fries for about 15-20 minutes, shaking or flipping them halfway through, or as per your air fryer's instructions. Cook until they're golden brown and crispy.

7. **Serving:**
   - Remove the fries from the air fryer and let them cool for a minute. They will become even crispier as they cool.

8. **Enjoy:**
   - Serve your air fryer French fries hot with your favorite dipping sauces, such as ketchup, mayo, or a homemade aioli.

Notes:

- You may need to adjust the cooking time and temperature depending on your specific air fryer model. Keep an eye on the fries as they cook to prevent burning.
- Don't skip the soaking step. It's crucial for removing excess starch, which can lead to limp fries.
- Make sure to space the fries apart in the air fryer basket for even cooking. Overcrowding can result in unevenly cooked fries.
- Experiment with seasonings to create unique flavor profiles. Paprika, garlic powder, and onion powder are excellent additions.
- You can also try using sweet potatoes or other root vegetables for a different twist on air fryer fries.

Enjoy your homemade air fryer French fries as a healthier and tastier alternative to traditional deep-fried fries!

Certainly! Here are some additional tips and information to help you make the best air fryer French fries:

Choosing the Right Potatoes:

- Russet and Yukon Gold potatoes are excellent choices for French fries due to their starchy texture, which results in a crispier exterior. However, you can use other potato varieties as well.

Cutting Consistency:

- Try to cut the potato strips as uniformly as possible. This ensures that they cook evenly and have a consistent texture.

Oil Usage:

- You don't need to drench the fries in oil. A light coating is sufficient for crispy results. Using an oil spray can help distribute the oil more evenly.

Shaking or Flipping:

- Shaking or flipping the fries halfway through the cooking time is crucial to ensure that all sides cook evenly. This helps prevent one side from becoming too crispy while the other remains soft.

Batches:

- If you're making a large batch of fries, cook them in batches. Overcrowding the air fryer basket will prevent proper air circulation and can result in less crispy fries.

Preheating:

- Preheating the air fryer is recommended for better results. It ensures the fries start cooking immediately when you put them in.

Storage:

- While fresh fries are the best, you can store any leftover fries in an airtight container in the refrigerator. Reheat them in the air fryer for a few minutes to regain some crispiness.

Dipping Sauces:

- Get creative with dipping sauces. Besides ketchup and mayonnaise, you can make garlic aioli, Sriracha mayo, or cheese sauce for a unique twist.

Healthier Alternative:

- Air frying significantly reduces the amount of oil used compared to deep frying, making it a healthier option. The fries will still be crispy, but with fewer calories and less saturated fat.

Experiment with Seasonings:

- Beyond the basic seasonings, you can get adventurous with your flavorings. Try truffle salt, Cajun seasoning, Parmesan cheese, or even a dusting of your favorite hot sauce.

Cleanup:

- Clean your air fryer basket and tray promptly after each use to prevent residue buildup and maintain the appliance's performance.

Air fryer French fries are not only delicious but also versatile. Feel free to get creative and experiment with different ingredients and seasonings to create your perfect batch of crispy fries. Enjoy your homemade fries!

Crispy Air Fryer Potato Wedges

Crispy air fryer potato wedges are a delicious and healthier alternative to traditional deep-fried potato wedges. They are easy to make and can be seasoned to your liking. Here's a basic recipe along with some notes to help you get the best results:

Ingredients:

- 4 large russet potatoes
- 2 tablespoons olive oil
- 1 teaspoon salt
- 1/2 teaspoon black pepper
- 1/2 teaspoon paprika (optional)
- 1/2 teaspoon garlic powder (optional)
- 1/2 teaspoon onion powder (optional)

Instructions:

1. **Prep the Potatoes:**
   - Scrub and wash the potatoes thoroughly.
   - Cut them into wedges. You can leave the skin on for added texture and flavor.
   - Try to keep the wedges similar in size to ensure even cooking.
2. **Season the Wedges:**
   - In a large mixing bowl, toss the potato wedges with olive oil to coat them evenly.
   - Season with salt, pepper, and any optional seasonings you like, such as paprika, garlic powder, or onion powder.
   - Mix well to ensure the wedges are coated with the seasonings.
3. **Preheat the Air Fryer:**
   - Preheat your air fryer to 400°F (200°C) for a few minutes. Check your air fryer's instructions for preheating time.
4. **Air Fry the Potato Wedges:**
   - Arrange the seasoned potato wedges in a single layer in the air fryer basket. You may need to cook them in batches if your air fryer is small.
   - Cook for about 15-20 minutes, flipping them halfway through. Cooking times may vary depending on the thickness of the wedges and your air fryer model. You want the wedges to be golden brown and crispy.

5. **Serve:**
   - Once the potato wedges are crispy and cooked to your liking, remove them from the air fryer and serve immediately.
   - You can serve them with your favorite dipping sauce, such as ketchup, aioli, or ranch dressing.

Notes:

1. **Potato Type:** Russet potatoes are a good choice for making potato wedges because they have a starchy texture that crisps up nicely in the air fryer. You can use other varieties, but the texture may vary.
2. **Even Sizing:** Cutting the potato wedges into similar sizes ensures that they cook evenly. This helps prevent some wedges from being undercooked while others are overcooked.
3. **Oil:** You can adjust the amount of oil based on your preference. Using too much oil can make the wedges greasy, while too little oil may result in less crispy wedges.
4. **Seasonings:** Feel free to experiment with seasonings to suit your taste. Smoked paprika, cayenne pepper, or rosemary are great options to add flavor.
5. **Cooking Time:** The cooking time can vary, so keep a close eye on the wedges, especially during the last few minutes of cooking. You can test for doneness by piercing a wedge with a fork or tasting for crispiness.

Air fryer potato wedges are a fantastic and guilt-free snack or side dish that's sure to be a crowd-pleaser. Adjust the seasonings and cooking time to your liking and enjoy!

Certainly! Here are some additional tips and notes for making the best crispy air fryer potato wedges:

Additional Tips:

6. **Preheating:** Preheating your air fryer is important as it helps the wedges cook more evenly and get crispy. Follow the manufacturer's recommendations for preheating, which typically takes about 3-5 minutes.
7. **Don't Overcrowd:** It's essential to arrange the potato wedges in a single layer in the air fryer basket. Overcrowding can lead to uneven cooking and less crispy results. Cook in batches if needed.
8. **Shaking or Flipping:** To ensure even cooking, it's a good idea to shake the basket or flip the wedges halfway through the cooking time. This helps all sides of the wedges get crispy.
9. **Use Parchment Paper or a Liner:** Consider using parchment paper or a silicone liner in the air fryer basket to prevent sticking and make cleanup easier. Just make sure it's safe to use with your specific air fryer model.
10. **Prevent Sticking:** Before placing the potato wedges in the air fryer, you can lightly spray the basket with non-stick cooking spray to further prevent sticking.

11. **Batch Cooking:** If you're making a large batch of potato wedges, keep the cooked batches warm by placing them in a preheated oven at a low temperature (around 200°F or 93°C) while you finish cooking the remaining batches.
12. **Experiment with Dips:** Potato wedges go well with various dipping sauces like barbecue sauce, honey mustard, or even a homemade aioli. Get creative with your favorite dips.
13. **Reheating:** If you have leftover potato wedges, you can reheat them in the air fryer for a few minutes to restore their crispiness. Make sure not to overcook them.
14. **Customize Your Seasonings:** The seasoning options are endless. Try using different herbs, spices, or even grated cheese for a unique twist on your potato wedges.
15. **Serve with Garnishes:** Garnish your crispy potato wedges with fresh herbs like parsley or chives for a visually appealing and flavorful touch.

Remember that air fryer models can vary, so it may take a bit of trial and error to perfect your potato wedges. These tips should help you achieve a crispy and delicious result. Enjoy your homemade air fryer potato wedges!

Air Fryer Mushrooms

Air-fried mushrooms are a delicious and healthy snack or side dish. They become crispy on the outside while remaining tender on the inside. Here's a simple air fryer mushrooms recipe along with some notes:

Ingredients:

- 8 oz (225g) whole mushrooms, cleaned and sliced if large
- 1-2 tablespoons olive oil or cooking spray
- Salt and pepper to taste
- Optional seasonings: garlic powder, paprika, thyme, or your favorite herbs and spices

Instructions:

1. **Prep the mushrooms:** Clean the mushrooms using a damp paper towel or a mushroom brush. If they are large, you can slice them into smaller pieces. Smaller mushrooms can be left whole.
2. **Season the mushrooms:** In a bowl, toss the mushrooms with olive oil or use a cooking spray to coat them evenly. This will help the seasonings stick to the mushrooms.
3. **Season with salt and pepper:** Season the mushrooms with salt and pepper to taste. You can also add any other desired seasonings or herbs to enhance the flavor.
4. **Preheat your air fryer:** Preheat your air fryer to 375°F (190°C) for a few minutes. Preheating ensures even cooking.

5. **Air fry the mushrooms:** Place the seasoned mushrooms in the air fryer basket. Make sure they are in a single layer, without overcrowding, to allow for proper air circulation. You may need to cook them in batches if you have a small air fryer.
6. **Air frying time:** Cook the mushrooms for about 10-15 minutes, shaking the basket or tossing the mushrooms halfway through the cooking time. Cooking time may vary depending on the size and type of mushrooms you're using. Check for doneness; they should be golden brown and crispy on the outside and tender on the inside.
7. **Serve:** Once the mushrooms are done, remove them from the air fryer and serve hot. You can sprinkle with additional salt or seasonings if desired.

Notes:

1. **Type of mushrooms:** You can use various types of mushrooms for this recipe, such as button mushrooms, cremini, shiitake, or oyster mushrooms. Each will have its unique flavor and texture.
2. **Seasonings:** Be creative with your seasonings. Try garlic powder, paprika, thyme, rosemary, or any of your favorite herbs and spices to customize the flavor to your liking.
3. **Oil:** Olive oil is a good choice for a rich flavor, but you can use any cooking oil or cooking spray. Be mindful not to use too much oil, as it can make the mushrooms too greasy.
4. **Don't overcrowd the air fryer:** For the best results, make sure there's enough space between the mushrooms to allow hot air to circulate. Overcrowding can lead to uneven cooking.
5. **Preheating:** Preheating the air fryer helps ensure consistent cooking and crispy results.

Air-fried mushrooms are a great addition to salads, sandwiches, or as a snack on their own. Enjoy your crispy, savory, and guilt-free treat!

Certainly, here are some additional tips and variations for air fryer mushrooms:

Tips:

1. **Mist with cooking spray:** Instead of tossing the mushrooms in oil, you can use a cooking spray to lightly mist them. This will help reduce the amount of oil used and still provide a crispy texture.
2. **Uniform size:** Try to keep the mushroom pieces as uniform in size as possible. This will help ensure even cooking.
3. **Adjust cooking time:** The cooking time may vary depending on the model and brand of your air fryer, as well as the size and moisture content of the mushrooms. Keep an eye on them and adjust the cooking time accordingly.
4. **Serve with dipping sauce:** Air-fried mushrooms pair well with various dipping sauces. Consider serving them with a garlic aioli, ranch dressing, or balsamic glaze for added flavor.

Variations:

1. **Stuffed mushrooms:** For a more elaborate appetizer, you can make stuffed mushrooms. Remove the stems from larger mushrooms, stuff them with a mixture of cream cheese, garlic, herbs, and breadcrumbs, and then air fry them until they're golden and bubbling.
2. **Parmesan-crusted mushrooms:** After air frying the mushrooms, while they're still hot, sprinkle them with grated Parmesan cheese. The residual heat will help melt the cheese and create a delicious crust.
3. **Asian-inspired mushrooms:** Toss the mushrooms with soy sauce, sesame oil, and a dash of rice vinegar for an Asian twist. Top with sesame seeds and chopped green onions before serving.
4. **Crispy mushroom "bacon":** Slice portobello mushrooms thinly and marinate them in a mixture of soy sauce, liquid smoke, and maple syrup. Then, air fry them until they become crispy. These make a great vegetarian bacon substitute.
5. **Herb-infused mushrooms:** Season your mushrooms with a combination of fresh or dried herbs like rosemary, thyme, and oregano. The herbs will infuse a fragrant aroma and savory flavor into the mushrooms.
6. **Spicy mushrooms:** If you like some heat, add a pinch of cayenne pepper or chili powder to the seasoning mix for a spicy kick.
7. **Mushroom medley:** Mix different types of mushrooms in a variety of colors and flavors for a diverse and visually appealing side dish.

Air-fried mushrooms are versatile and can be customized to suit your taste and the occasion. Whether you're looking for a healthy snack or a flavorful side dish, these mushroom recipes in the air fryer are sure to satisfy your cravings.

Crispy Air Fryer Eggplant Rounds

Crispy Air Fryer Eggplant Rounds are a delicious and healthier alternative to traditional fried eggplant. They are a great appetizer, side dish, or even a main course when served with your favorite dipping sauce. Here's a recipe along with some important notes:

Ingredients:

- 1 medium-sized eggplant
- 1 cup panko breadcrumbs
- 1/2 cup grated Parmesan cheese
- 1 teaspoon Italian seasoning (or a mix of dried herbs like basil, oregano, and thyme)
- 1/2 teaspoon garlic powder
- 1/2 teaspoon onion powder
- 2 large eggs
- Cooking spray (for the air fryer basket)

Notes:

1. **Selecting the Eggplant:** Choose a fresh and firm eggplant. The skin should be smooth and free from blemishes. Smaller eggplants tend to have fewer seeds and a milder flavor.
2. **Preparation:** Wash the eggplant and trim off the ends. You can peel it if you prefer, but it's not necessary. Slice the eggplant into rounds, about 1/2-inch thick. If your eggplant has a lot of seeds, you can lightly salt the rounds and let them sit for about 30 minutes to release excess moisture, then pat them dry with paper towels. This step can help make the eggplant less bitter and more crispy.
3. **Breading Station:** In a shallow bowl, beat the eggs. In another shallow bowl, combine the panko breadcrumbs, Parmesan cheese, Italian seasoning, garlic powder, and onion powder. You can also add a pinch of salt and pepper to the breadcrumb mixture for extra flavor.
4. **Coating the Eggplant:** Dip each eggplant round into the beaten eggs, allowing any excess to drip off, and then coat it in the breadcrumb mixture, pressing the breadcrumbs onto the eggplant to adhere well. Place the coated rounds on a plate or tray.
5. **Preheating the Air Fryer:** Preheat your air fryer to 375°F (190°C) for a few minutes. This will help ensure even cooking and crispiness.
6. **Cooking in Batches:** Lightly grease the air fryer basket with cooking spray. Place the breaded eggplant rounds in a single layer in the air fryer basket, making sure they are not touching. You may need to cook them in batches to avoid overcrowding, which can result in uneven cooking.
7. **Air Frying:** Cook the eggplant rounds for 10-12 minutes, flipping them halfway through the cooking time. The exact time may vary depending on the thickness of your eggplant rounds and the air fryer model you're using. They should be golden brown and crispy when done.
8. **Serving:** Serve the crispy air fryer eggplant rounds hot with your favorite dipping sauce, such as marinara sauce, garlic aioli, or tzatziki.
9. **Customization:** You can customize the seasoning and breadcrumb mixture to your taste. Try adding some paprika, cayenne pepper, or lemon zest for extra flavor.

Enjoy your crispy air fryer eggplant rounds as a tasty and healthier alternative to traditional fried eggplant!

Certainly! Here are some additional tips and variations to make your crispy air fryer eggplant rounds even more delicious:

Tips:

1. **Even Slicing:** Try to slice the eggplant rounds as evenly as possible to ensure they cook uniformly. A mandoline slicer can be helpful for this.
2. **Baking Instead:** If you don't have an air fryer, you can also bake the eggplant rounds in a preheated oven at 375°F (190°C) on a wire rack set over a baking sheet. This method will take a bit longer than air frying, so keep an eye on them to prevent overcooking.

3. **Spraying with Oil:** You can lightly spray the breaded eggplant rounds with cooking oil before air frying to help them become even crispier.
4. **Experiment with Dipping Sauces:** Explore various dipping sauces like honey mustard, balsamic reduction, or a yogurt-based sauce for a unique twist.

Variations:

1. **Spicy Eggplant Rounds:** Add some cayenne pepper or chili flakes to the breadcrumb mixture for a spicy kick.
2. **Herb-Crusted Eggplant:** Replace the Italian seasoning with fresh herbs like basil, parsley, or rosemary for a more herbaceous flavor.
3. **Gluten-Free Option:** Use gluten-free breadcrumbs and make sure your Italian seasoning mix is gluten-free if you have dietary restrictions.
4. **Vegan Version:** Substitute the eggs with a flax or chia egg (1 tablespoon ground flaxseed or chia seeds mixed with 3 tablespoons of water for each egg). Use vegan Parmesan cheese or nutritional yeast in the breadcrumb mixture.
5. **Greek Eggplant Rounds:** Season the breadcrumbs with Greek seasoning and serve the eggplant rounds with tzatziki sauce for a Mediterranean twist.
6. **Asian Flavors:** For an Asian-inspired version, use panko breadcrumbs mixed with sesame seeds and a pinch of five-spice powder. Serve with a dipping sauce made from soy sauce, rice vinegar, and a touch of honey.

Remember to adjust the seasoning and ingredients to suit your personal taste and dietary preferences. Crispy air fryer eggplant rounds are versatile and can be tailored to match a wide range of flavor profiles. Enjoy experimenting with this delicious recipe!

Lemon Parmesan Air Fryer Asparagus

Lemon Parmesan Air Fryer Asparagus is a delicious and healthy side dish that's quick and easy to prepare in your air fryer. Here's a recipe and some notes to help you make this tasty dish:

Ingredients:

- 1 bunch of fresh asparagus spears
- 2 tablespoons olive oil
- 2 tablespoons grated Parmesan cheese
- 1/2 teaspoon lemon zest
- 1 teaspoon lemon juice
- 1/2 teaspoon garlic powder
- Salt and pepper to taste

Instructions:

1. **Prepare the Asparagus:**
   - Wash the asparagus spears and trim the tough ends by snapping them off or cutting about 1-2 inches from the bottom. You can also peel the tough ends if you prefer.
2. **Season the Asparagus:**
   - In a large bowl, drizzle the trimmed asparagus spears with olive oil and toss them to coat evenly. Season with salt, pepper, and garlic powder. Mix well to ensure the asparagus is evenly coated with the seasonings.
3. **Air Fry the Asparagus:**
   - Preheat your air fryer to 400°F (200°C) for a few minutes.
   - Place the seasoned asparagus in a single layer in the air fryer basket. Depending on the size of your air fryer, you may need to do this in batches.
   - Air fry the asparagus for 8-10 minutes, shaking the basket halfway through to ensure even cooking. The asparagus should be tender and slightly crispy on the outside.
4. **Prepare the Topping:**
   - While the asparagus is cooking, mix the grated Parmesan cheese, lemon zest, and lemon juice in a small bowl.
5. **Finish and Serve:**
   - Once the asparagus is done, remove it from the air fryer and transfer it to a serving plate.
   - Immediately sprinkle the lemon Parmesan mixture over the hot asparagus while it's still in the air fryer basket. The residual heat will help melt the cheese and infuse the asparagus with flavor.
   - Serve the Lemon Parmesan Air Fryer Asparagus hot, garnished with a little extra lemon zest and a sprinkle of grated Parmesan if desired.

Recipe Notes:

- Be mindful of the asparagus thickness and your specific air fryer model. Cooking times may vary, so check the doneness of the asparagus as it cooks. Thicker asparagus may need a bit more time, while thinner ones might cook faster.
- You can adjust the amount of Parmesan cheese, lemon zest, and lemon juice to suit your taste. If you love a stronger lemon flavor, add more zest and juice.
- This dish is best served fresh from the air fryer, as the asparagus will be at its crispiest. However, you can also prepare the lemon Parmesan mixture ahead of time and add it to the asparagus just before serving.
- Feel free to customize the seasonings with your favorite herbs and spices. Fresh herbs like thyme or rosemary can be a great addition.

Certainly! Here are some additional tips and ideas for making the best Lemon Parmesan Air Fryer Asparagus:

1. **Preheat the Air Fryer:** Preheating your air fryer for a few minutes before cooking helps ensure even cooking and better results. It's a good practice to follow.

2. **Variations:** Get creative with your seasonings. Besides garlic powder, you can use other seasonings like smoked paprika, onion powder, or even a pinch of red pepper flakes for some heat.
3. **Lemon Variations:** You can use fresh lemon juice or bottled lemon juice, but fresh lemon zest will provide the best flavor. Use a microplane or fine grater to zest the lemon.
4. **Balsamic Glaze:** Drizzle a balsamic reduction or glaze over the finished asparagus for an extra burst of flavor. The sweet and tangy balsamic pairs well with the savory asparagus and Parmesan.
5. **Toppings:** Consider adding extra toppings like toasted pine nuts, slivered almonds, or chopped fresh herbs like parsley or basil for added texture and flavor.
6. **Serving Suggestions:** Lemon Parmesan Air Fryer Asparagus makes a great side dish for various meals. It pairs well with grilled chicken, steak, fish, or pasta dishes.
7. **Crispiness:** For extra crispiness, you can give the asparagus a light spray of cooking spray before air frying. This can help achieve a nice crispy texture.
8. **Batch Cooking:** If you're cooking for a crowd, you can prepare the asparagus in batches and keep them warm in a low-temperature oven (around 200°F or 95°C) until you're ready to serve. This will help ensure that everything is hot when you serve it.
9. **Leftovers:** If you have any leftovers, they can be refrigerated and enjoyed cold in salads or reheated in the air fryer for a few minutes.
10. **Double-Check Cooking Times:** As air fryer models may vary, keep an eye on your asparagus, and adjust the cooking time if necessary. You're looking for tender asparagus with slightly crispy edges.

Lemon Parmesan Air Fryer Asparagus is a versatile and flavorful side dish that's perfect for any season. With a few tweaks and personal preferences, you can make it your own and enjoy it alongside a variety of main dishes.

Air Fryer Green Beans

Air fryer green beans are a healthy and delicious side dish that can be prepared quickly and easily. Here's a simple recipe along with some notes to help you make the best air fryer green beans:

Ingredients:

- 1 pound of fresh green beans, trimmed
- 1-2 tablespoons of olive oil or cooking spray
- Salt and pepper to taste
- Optional seasonings: garlic powder, onion powder, paprika, or grated Parmesan cheese

Instructions:

1. **Preheat your air fryer:** Preheat your air fryer to 375°F (190°C) for a few minutes. This will ensure that it's hot and ready to cook the green beans.
2. **Prepare the green beans:** Wash and trim the ends of the green beans. You can leave them whole or cut them into smaller pieces if you prefer.
3. **Season the green beans:** Place the green beans in a mixing bowl, drizzle them with olive oil or spray them with cooking spray, and then season with salt and pepper. You can also add optional seasonings like garlic powder, onion powder, paprika, or grated Parmesan cheese for extra flavor.
4. **Toss to coat:** Toss the green beans in the bowl to evenly coat them with the oil and seasonings.
5. **Air fry the green beans:** Place the seasoned green beans in the air fryer basket in a single layer. It's essential not to overcrowd the basket, so you may need to cook them in batches if you have a smaller air fryer.
6. **Cook:** Cook the green beans in the preheated air fryer for about 8-10 minutes. Be sure to shake or toss them around every 3-4 minutes to ensure even cooking. The total cooking time may vary depending on your air fryer's size and power, so keep an eye on them to prevent overcooking. The green beans should become tender and slightly crispy.
7. **Serve:** Once the green beans are cooked to your desired level of doneness, remove them from the air fryer and serve immediately. You can garnish them with a little extra seasoning or grated Parmesan cheese if desired.

Notes:

- Be mindful of the batch size: It's important not to overcrowd the air fryer basket. If you have a small air fryer, you may need to cook the green beans in multiple batches to ensure they cook evenly.
- Customize the seasonings: Feel free to experiment with different seasonings to suit your taste. Herbs like thyme or rosemary can also be a great addition.
- Watch the cooking time: Cooking times can vary based on the air fryer model and the thickness of the green beans. Check them periodically to avoid overcooking, which can make them overly soft.
- Be cautious with oil: Using too much oil can make the green beans greasy, so start with a conservative amount and adjust as needed.
- Serve immediately: Air-fried green beans are best when served immediately, as they tend to lose their crispiness as they cool.

Certainly! Here are some additional tips and variations to consider when making air fryer green beans:

Tips:

1. **Prep the green beans:** Make sure to thoroughly dry the green beans after washing them. Excess moisture can prevent them from getting crispy.

2. **Use the right oil:** While olive oil is a popular choice, you can also use other high-heat oils like avocado oil, grapeseed oil, or canola oil. Cooking spray is another convenient option to ensure even distribution.
3. **Spice it up:** Experiment with different seasonings and spices to create different flavor profiles. Try adding red pepper flakes for some heat or a squeeze of lemon juice for a refreshing citrus twist.
4. **Don't forget to shake:** Shaking or tossing the green beans during cooking is essential to ensure they cook evenly on all sides. It helps to achieve that crispy texture.
5. **Check for doneness:** Green beans should be tender with a slight bite but not overly soft. If they're not done to your liking after the initial cook time, you can always air fry them for an additional minute or two.

Variations:

1. **Breaded green beans:** For a breaded and even crispier texture, you can dip the green beans in beaten egg and coat them with breadcrumbs or panko before air frying. This will give them a crunchy exterior.
2. **Asian-inspired green beans:** Toss the green beans with soy sauce, minced garlic, and a sprinkle of sesame seeds for an Asian flair.
3. **Lemon parmesan green beans:** Season the green beans with lemon zest, grated Parmesan cheese, and a little garlic powder for a zesty, cheesy flavor.
4. **Balsamic glaze:** After air frying, drizzle the green beans with balsamic glaze for a sweet and tangy touch.
5. **Honey-mustard green beans:** Whisk together honey, Dijon mustard, and a bit of olive oil to create a flavorful glaze for your green beans.
6. **Almond-crusted green beans:** Add a layer of crushed almonds to the green beans before air frying for a nutty crunch.
7. **Sesame green beans:** Season with sesame oil and sprinkle with sesame seeds for an aromatic, nutty taste.

Remember, the air fryer is a versatile kitchen tool, and you can get creative with your green bean recipes. Feel free to combine different seasonings and ingredients to suit your personal taste. Enjoy your air fryer green beans as a healthy and satisfying side dish!

Air Fryer Hard Boiled Eggs

Air frying hard-boiled eggs is a simple and convenient way to prepare them without the need for boiling water. Here's a recipe and some notes to guide you through the process:

Ingredients:

- Eggs
- Cooking spray (optional)

Instructions:

1. **Preparation:**
   - Start with cold eggs directly from the refrigerator. You can cook as many eggs as your air fryer can accommodate, as long as they're in a single layer in the basket or on the air fryer tray.
   - Preheat your air fryer to 270-280°F (130-140°C) for about 2-3 minutes.
2. **Air Frying:**
   - If your air fryer has a wire rack or a trivet, place the eggs on it. This helps to prevent them from getting direct contact with the hot surface and ensures even cooking.
   - If your air fryer doesn't have a wire rack or trivet, you can place the eggs directly on the air fryer basket or tray.
   - Cook the eggs at 270-280°F (130-140°C) for about 15-17 minutes. The cooking time may vary depending on your air fryer, so you may need to experiment a bit to find the ideal time for your specific appliance.
   - You can also give the eggs a light spray with cooking oil, but this is optional. It can help make peeling the eggs easier.
3. **Cooling and Peeling:**
   - Once the eggs are done, transfer them immediately to a bowl of ice water to stop the cooking process. Let them sit in the ice water for about 5-7 minutes.
4. **Peeling the Eggs:**
   - Gently tap the egg on a hard surface to crack the shell.
   - Roll the egg between your hands to loosen the shell.
   - Start peeling from the wider end (where the air sac is) as it's usually easier to get the peel off cleanly.
   - Peeling under running water can help remove any stubborn bits of shell.

Notes:

1. **Experiment with Cooking Times:** Air fryers vary in temperature and power, so you may need to adjust the cooking time to achieve your preferred level of doneness. A few minutes can make a significant difference, so start with the suggested time and adjust as needed.
2. **Freshness Matters:** Using fresh eggs can make peeling easier. As eggs age, the pH of the whites increases, making the membrane inside the shell stick more to the egg white. Fresher eggs are often easier to peel.
3. **Use a Wire Rack or Trivet:** Placing the eggs on a wire rack or trivet in the air fryer basket can prevent the eggs from getting brown spots from direct contact with the hot surface.
4. **Oil for Easier Peeling:** A light spray of cooking oil before air frying can make the eggs easier to peel, but it's optional.
5. **Safety Precautions:** Be cautious when handling hot eggs and equipment. Always use oven mitts or a towel when removing the eggs from the air fryer, and take care not to burn yourself.

Air frying hard-boiled eggs is a convenient method, especially if you want to make a large batch without boiling water. It's a time-saving option that can yield consistent results once you find the right cooking time for your specific air fryer.

Certainly! Here are some additional tips and variations for air frying hard-boiled eggs:

Additional Tips:

1. **Egg Size:** The size of the eggs can also affect the cooking time. Large eggs are the standard, but if you're using extra-large or jumbo eggs, you may need to adjust the cooking time slightly.
2. **Cracking the Eggs:** You can make a small X-shaped slit at the bottom of each egg before air frying. This can help prevent the eggs from cracking during cooking.
3. **Seasoning:** You can season the eggs before air frying them. Sprinkle a little salt, pepper, or your favorite herbs and spices on the eggs for added flavor.
4. **Deviled Eggs:** Air-fried hard-boiled eggs can be used to make delicious deviled eggs. After peeling, cut them in half, remove the yolks, mix with mayonnaise, mustard, and seasonings, then fill the egg white halves.
5. **Egg Salad:** Use your air-fried hard-boiled eggs to make a tasty egg salad. Chop the peeled eggs and mix with mayonnaise, mustard, chopped celery, onions, and your choice of seasonings.

Variations:

1. **Soft-Boiled Eggs:** If you prefer soft-boiled eggs with a runny yolk, reduce the cooking time to about 10-12 minutes in the air fryer.
2. **Smoked Hard-Boiled Eggs:** Add a smoky flavor by placing a small piece of wood chip (e.g., hickory, applewood) in the air fryer with the eggs. This will infuse the eggs with a subtle smokiness during cooking.
3. **Herbed Eggs:** Roll the eggs in dried herbs or spices before air frying for an added layer of flavor. This is a great way to infuse your eggs with a unique taste.
4. **Stuffed Eggs:** After peeling, cut the eggs in half, remove the yolks, and mix them with ingredients like cream cheese, chives, and bacon bits to create stuffed eggs.
5. **Pickled Eggs:** Once the eggs are cooked and peeled, you can place them in a jar of pickling solution (vinegar, water, salt, sugar, and spices) to make pickled eggs. Allow them to pickle in the refrigerator for a few days for a tangy snack.
6. **Curried Eggs:** Add curry powder or paste to your egg salad or deviled egg filling for a spicy twist.

Remember that cooking times and temperatures may vary depending on your specific air fryer model, so it's essential to experiment and keep an eye on the eggs to achieve your desired level of doneness and flavor. Enjoy your air-fried hard-boiled eggs in various ways, and get creative with the seasonings and recipes you use them in.

Air Fryer Roasted Potatoes

Air fryer roasted potatoes are a delicious and healthier alternative to traditional roasted potatoes. They come out crispy on the outside and tender on the inside, and you can customize them with your favorite seasonings. Here's a basic recipe and some notes to get you started:

Ingredients:

- 1 pound (450g) of small to medium-sized potatoes (such as red or Yukon gold)
- 2 tablespoons of olive oil
- 1 teaspoon of salt (adjust to taste)
- 1/2 teaspoon of black pepper (adjust to taste)
- 1/2 teaspoon of garlic powder (optional)
- 1/2 teaspoon of paprika (optional)
- 1/2 teaspoon of dried rosemary or thyme (optional)

Instructions:

1. **Preheat your air fryer:** Set the air fryer to 400°F (200°C) and let it preheat for a few minutes.
2. **Prepare the potatoes:** Wash and scrub the potatoes if needed. Cut them into bite-sized pieces, keeping them roughly the same size to ensure even cooking.
3. **Season the potatoes:** In a large bowl, toss the potato pieces with olive oil, salt, pepper, and any optional seasonings you prefer, such as garlic powder, paprika, or dried herbs. Mix well to ensure the potatoes are evenly coated.
4. **Air frying:** Place the seasoned potato pieces in the air fryer basket in a single layer, making sure not to overcrowd them. You may need to cook them in batches depending on the size of your air fryer. This will help the potatoes cook evenly and get crispy.
5. **Cooking time:** Cook the potatoes in the air fryer for about 20-25 minutes, shaking or tossing them halfway through the cooking time to ensure even browning. Cooking time may vary slightly depending on your air fryer and the size of the potato pieces. Keep an eye on them to prevent overcooking.
6. **Serve:** Once the potatoes are golden brown and crispy, transfer them to a serving dish, and season with additional salt and pepper if needed. You can also garnish with fresh herbs like parsley.

Notes:

1. **Potato size:** Using small to medium-sized potatoes works best for air frying. If you use larger potatoes, cut them into smaller pieces to ensure even cooking.
2. **Even cooking:** It's essential to arrange the potato pieces in a single layer in the air fryer basket to ensure they cook evenly. If they're too crowded, they may not get as crispy.
3. **Oil and seasonings:** The amount of oil and seasonings can be adjusted to your taste. Some people prefer to use less oil for a lighter option, but a little oil helps with crispiness.

4. **Seasoning variations:** Get creative with your seasonings! You can add your favorite herbs and spices, like cayenne pepper for heat or grated Parmesan cheese for a cheesy twist.
5. **Doneness:** Keep an eye on the potatoes as they cook, and adjust the cooking time as needed to achieve your desired level of crispiness.

Air fryer roasted potatoes make a great side dish or snack, and they're a versatile addition to your recipe repertoire. Enjoy your crispy, flavorful potatoes!

Certainly! Here are some additional tips and ideas for making the most delicious air fryer roasted potatoes:

1. Potato Varieties: Experiment with different potato varieties. While red or Yukon gold potatoes are popular choices, you can also try fingerling, baby, or even sweet potatoes for a unique flavor.

2. Preheating: Preheating your air fryer is essential for achieving crispy results. It helps start the cooking process right away, ensuring even cooking.

3. Soak in Water: For extra crispiness, soak the potato pieces in cold water for 30 minutes before drying and seasoning them. This helps remove excess starch.

4. Cooking Time Adjustments: The cooking time can vary depending on the air fryer's brand and model. If your potatoes aren't done after the suggested time, continue cooking in 5-minute increments until they reach your desired level of crispiness.

5. Shake or Flip: To ensure even cooking, remember to shake or flip the potatoes halfway through the cooking time. This helps all sides of the potatoes get crispy.

6. Size Consistency: Try to keep the potato pieces a consistent size to ensure they cook uniformly.

7. Optional Ingredients: You can get creative with additional ingredients. Consider adding diced onions, bell peppers, or even minced garlic for added flavor.

8. Parchment Paper or Liner: Using a piece of parchment paper or an air fryer liner can make cleanup easier and prevent sticking, especially when using minimal oil.

9. Dipping Sauces: Serve your air fryer roasted potatoes with a variety of dipping sauces. Classics like ketchup or mayonnaise are always a hit, or try something unique like a garlic aioli or a spicy sriracha mayo.

10. Serving Ideas: Roasted potatoes can be a versatile side dish. They're great with grilled chicken, steak, burgers, or as a breakfast side with eggs. You can also serve them with sour cream and chives for a snack.

11. Reheating: If you have leftovers, you can reheat the roasted potatoes in the air fryer at a lower temperature (around 350°F/175°C) for a few minutes to maintain their crispiness.

12. Seasoning Combinations: Get creative with seasoning combinations. Here are a few ideas:

- Italian: Use olive oil, dried oregano, basil, and grated Parmesan cheese.
- Cajun: Add cayenne pepper, paprika, and thyme for a spicy twist.
- Ranch: Toss the potatoes with ranch seasoning mix before air frying.

Remember that air fryers are very versatile, and you can adapt this basic recipe to suit your taste preferences. With a little experimentation, you can create your own signature air fryer roasted potatoes that everyone will love.

Air Fryer Croutons (BEST texture!)

Air fryer croutons are a delicious and easy way to add a crunchy topping to your salads, soups, or just enjoy them as a snack. They have a wonderfully crispy texture and can be customized with your favorite seasonings. Here's a simple recipe and some helpful notes for making the best air fryer croutons:

Ingredients:

- 4 cups of bread cubes (stale bread works best)
- 2 tablespoons of olive oil
- 1/2 teaspoon of garlic powder
- 1/2 teaspoon of onion powder
- 1/2 teaspoon of dried Italian herbs (oregano, thyme, basil, etc.)
- Salt and pepper to taste

Instructions:

1. **Preheat the Air Fryer:** Preheat your air fryer to 350°F (180°C).
2. **Prepare the Bread:** Cut your bread into bite-sized cubes. Stale bread is ideal for croutons as it holds its shape and absorbs the flavors better.
3. **Season the Cubes:** In a large bowl, drizzle the olive oil over the bread cubes and toss to coat them evenly. Add the garlic powder, onion powder, dried Italian herbs, salt, and pepper. Toss the bread cubes again to make sure the seasonings are evenly distributed.
4. **Air Fry the Croutons:** Place the seasoned bread cubes in the air fryer basket in a single layer. Depending on the size of your air fryer, you may need to do this in batches. Do not overcrowd the basket, as this will hinder even cooking. Air fry the croutons at 350°F (180°C) for 5-7 minutes, shaking or stirring them halfway through to ensure even cooking. Keep an eye on them as they can quickly go from golden brown to burnt.

5. **Check for Crispiness:** After the initial cooking time, check the croutons for desired crispiness. If they are not crispy enough, you can air fry them for an additional 1-2 minutes.
6. **Cool and Store:** Once your croutons are crispy and golden brown, remove them from the air fryer and let them cool. They will continue to crisp up as they cool down. Store your croutons in an airtight container once they have completely cooled.

Notes:

1. **Bread Selection:** While any bread can be used, using slightly stale bread (a day or two old) is best because it holds its shape during the cooking process and absorbs flavors well. You can use white bread, whole wheat, sourdough, or any bread of your choice.
2. **Seasoning:** Feel free to customize the seasonings to your liking. You can add grated Parmesan cheese, paprika, cayenne pepper, or any other herbs and spices you enjoy.
3. **Storage:** Store your croutons in an airtight container at room temperature. They should stay crispy for several days, but they're so delicious, they might not last that long!
4. **Serve:** Enjoy your air fryer croutons on salads, soups, or as a crunchy snack. They also make a great addition to charcuterie boards or as a topping for dips.

Making your own air fryer croutons not only allows you to control the ingredients but also results in a much fresher and tastier product than store-bought alternatives. Plus, it's a great way to use up any leftover bread you have on hand.

Certainly, here are some additional tips and variations to make the best air fryer croutons:

Additional Tips:

1. **Even Cubes:** Try to make the bread cubes as uniform in size as possible. This ensures even cooking and uniform crispiness.
2. **Don't Overcrowd:** Overcrowding the air fryer basket can lead to uneven cooking. If you have a lot of bread cubes, it's better to cook them in batches.
3. **Oil Consistency:** Use a good quality olive oil for flavor, but you can also use other cooking oils if you prefer. Make sure the oil is evenly distributed to avoid any dry, unseasoned croutons.
4. **Seasoning Alternatives:** Experiment with different seasonings and spices to create unique flavors. Smoked paprika, rosemary, thyme, and cumin are just a few ideas to get you started.
5. **Sweet Croutons:** You can also make sweet croutons for desserts by coating the bread cubes with melted butter and tossing them in a mixture of sugar and cinnamon before air frying.
6. **Custom Shapes:** Croutons don't have to be cubes. You can cut the bread into various shapes, such as sticks or triangles, for a different presentation.

Variations:

1. **Cheesy Croutons:** Add a generous sprinkle of grated Parmesan, cheddar, or any cheese of your choice to the bread cubes before air frying. The cheese will melt and create a delightful crispy layer.
2. **Spicy Croutons:** If you like some heat, add a pinch of cayenne pepper or chili powder to your seasoning mix for a spicy kick.
3. **Herbed Croutons:** Use a blend of fresh herbs like rosemary, thyme, and parsley instead of dried herbs for a more intense herbal flavor.
4. **Garlic Lovers:** Crush a few cloves of garlic and mix them with the olive oil before tossing with the bread cubes for a robust garlic flavor.
5. **Everything Bagel Seasoning:** Instead of making your own seasoning blend, you can use "Everything Bagel" seasoning mix for a quick and tasty twist.
6. **Gluten-Free Option:** Use gluten-free bread to make croutons suitable for those with dietary restrictions.

Air fryer croutons are a versatile and easy-to-make snack or topping that can be customized to suit your taste. Experiment with different bread types, seasonings, and shapes to create your perfect crouton. Enjoy the satisfying crunch they add to your dishes!

Air Fryer Pizza

Air fryer pizza is a quick and easy way to make a crispy, delicious pizza at home without using a traditional oven. Here's a basic recipe and some tips to help you make the perfect air fryer pizza:

Ingredients:

1. Pizza dough (store-bought or homemade)
2. Pizza sauce
3. Shredded mozzarella cheese
4. Toppings of your choice (e.g., pepperoni, bell peppers, mushrooms, olives, onions)
5. Olive oil (for brushing the pizza crust)
6. Cornmeal or flour (for dusting the air fryer basket)

Instructions:

1. **Preheat the Air Fryer:** Start by preheating your air fryer to 375°F (190°C). Preheating helps ensure that the pizza crust cooks evenly.
2. **Prepare the Dough:** Roll out the pizza dough on a lightly floured surface into your desired shape and thickness. You can make one large pizza or smaller individual ones.
3. **Dust the Basket:** Lightly dust the air fryer basket with cornmeal or flour to prevent sticking. This step is essential to ensure your pizza slides easily in and out of the air fryer.

4. **Assemble the Pizza:** Place the rolled-out dough in the air fryer basket. Spread a thin layer of pizza sauce evenly over the dough, leaving a border for the crust. Add your desired amount of shredded mozzarella cheese and your favorite pizza toppings.
5. **Brush the Crust:** Brush the exposed crust with a little olive oil. This will help it turn golden brown and crispy.
6. **Air Fry:** Carefully place the pizza in the preheated air fryer and cook at 375°F (190°C) for 10-12 minutes. Keep an eye on it, as cooking times may vary depending on the thickness of the crust and your air fryer's performance.
7. **Check for Doneness:** The pizza is done when the crust is golden brown, the cheese is melted and bubbly, and the toppings are cooked to your liking. You can use a fork or spatula to carefully lift the edge of the pizza and check the bottom to ensure it's crispy.
8. **Serve:** Carefully remove the pizza from the air fryer using tongs or a spatula, and place it on a cutting board. Let it cool for a minute, then slice and serve.

Notes and Tips:

1. **Don't Overload:** Be mindful not to overload your pizza with too many toppings, as this can make it difficult to cook evenly in the air fryer.
2. **Customization:** Get creative with your pizza toppings! You can use a variety of vegetables, meats, and even fresh herbs to customize your pizza.
3. **Preheating:** Preheating the air fryer is crucial for even cooking. It's recommended to preheat for at least 5 minutes before placing the pizza inside.
4. **Crust Thickness:** The thickness of your pizza crust will affect cooking time. Thinner crusts will cook faster, while thicker ones may need a few extra minutes.
5. **Temperature and Time:** Cooking times and temperatures can vary between different air fryer models, so it's a good idea to start with the suggested temperature and time and adjust if needed.
6. **Air Flow:** Ensure that the pizza has some space around it in the air fryer basket to allow for proper air circulation and even cooking.

Air fryer pizza is a fun and convenient way to satisfy your pizza cravings quickly. Experiment with different ingredients and crust styles to create your perfect air fryer pizza.

Certainly! Here are some additional tips and variations to enhance your air fryer pizza-making experience:

Tips:

1. **Pizza Stone or Pan:** If you have a small pizza stone or air fryer-specific pizza pan, you can use it to achieve a crispier crust. Preheat the stone or pan in the air fryer before placing the pizza on it.
2. **Frozen Pizza:** You can also make air fryer frozen pizza. Simply follow the instructions on the frozen pizza packaging and cook it in the air fryer. This is a convenient option when you're short on time.

3. **Rotate and Monitor:** Check the pizza periodically while it's cooking. Depending on your air fryer's design, you might need to rotate the pizza for even cooking. Be cautious not to let the cheese burn.
4. **Reheat Leftovers:** If you have leftover pizza, you can reheat it in the air fryer to restore its crispiness. Preheat the air fryer to 350°F (175°C) and reheat the pizza slices for a few minutes.

Variations:

1. **Calzone:** Fold the pizza dough in half, stuff it with your favorite pizza fillings, and crimp the edges to create a calzone. Air fry the calzone until it's golden brown and cooked through.
2. **Veggie Delight:** For a healthier option, load up your pizza with a variety of fresh vegetables, such as bell peppers, onions, tomatoes, spinach, and mushrooms.
3. **Barbecue Chicken Pizza:** Use barbecue sauce instead of traditional pizza sauce, and top the pizza with shredded cooked chicken, red onions, and mozzarella cheese for a sweet and savory twist.
4. **Hawaiian Pizza:** Top your pizza with tomato sauce, ham, pineapple chunks, and mozzarella cheese for a tropical flavor.
5. **Buffalo Chicken Pizza:** Toss cooked chicken in buffalo sauce and use it as a topping, along with blue cheese or ranch dressing drizzle. This is a spicy and tangy option for those who enjoy heat.
6. **Margherita Pizza:** Keep it simple with fresh tomato slices, fresh basil leaves, mozzarella cheese, and a drizzle of olive oil for a classic Margherita pizza.
7. **Breakfast Pizza:** Get creative with breakfast pizza by adding scrambled eggs, bacon, sausage, and cheese. Cook until the eggs are set, and you have a delicious morning meal.
8. **Dessert Pizza:** Use a sweet dough or pre-made cinnamon roll dough to create a dessert pizza. Top it with Nutella, sliced fruit, chocolate chips, or marshmallows, and air fry until it's a delightful treat.

Air fryer pizza is versatile, so feel free to experiment with different ingredients and flavors to suit your preferences. It's a great way to enjoy homemade pizza with a crispy crust in a fraction of the time it takes to bake one in a conventional oven.

Crispy Air Fryer Chicken Parmesan

Crispy Air Fryer Chicken Parmesan is a delicious and healthier twist on the classic Italian dish. It features breaded chicken cutlets that are cooked to perfection in an air fryer, topped with marinara sauce, melted cheese, and served with your choice of pasta or on a sandwich. Here's a recipe along with some notes to make it:

Ingredients:

- 4 boneless, skinless chicken breasts
- 1 cup all-purpose flour
- 2 large eggs
- 1 cup breadcrumbs (you can use Panko for extra crispiness)
- 1/2 cup grated Parmesan cheese
- 1 teaspoon Italian seasoning
- 1 teaspoon garlic powder
- 1 teaspoon salt
- 1/2 teaspoon black pepper
- Cooking spray
- 1 cup marinara sauce
- 1 cup shredded mozzarella cheese
- Fresh basil leaves (for garnish)
- Cooked pasta or sandwich rolls (for serving)

Instructions:

1. **Prepare the Chicken:**
   - Pound the chicken breasts to an even thickness (about 1/2 inch thick) to ensure they cook evenly.
   - In a shallow dish, place the flour. In another dish, beat the eggs. In a third dish, combine the breadcrumbs, Parmesan cheese, Italian seasoning, garlic powder, salt, and pepper.
   - Dredge each chicken breast in the flour, then dip it in the beaten eggs, and finally, coat it with the breadcrumb mixture. Make sure the chicken is well-coated at each step.
2. **Preheat the Air Fryer:**
   - Preheat your air fryer to 375°F (190°C) for a few minutes.
3. **Cook the Chicken:**
   - Lightly spray the air fryer basket with cooking spray.
   - Place the breaded chicken breasts in the air fryer basket, making sure they don't overlap. You may need to cook them in batches if your air fryer is small.
   - Cook for about 10-15 minutes or until the chicken is golden brown and reaches an internal temperature of 165°F (74°C). The cooking time may vary depending on the thickness of the chicken breasts and the air fryer model, so keep an eye on them.
4. **Assemble and Finish:**
   - Once the chicken is cooked, remove it from the air fryer.
   - Preheat your broiler in the oven.
   - Place the cooked chicken on a baking sheet or in an oven-safe dish. Top each chicken breast with a spoonful of marinara sauce and a generous sprinkle of shredded mozzarella cheese.

- Place the baking sheet under the broiler for a couple of minutes, just until the cheese is bubbly and golden brown. Be careful not to overcook and burn the cheese.
5. **Serve:**
   - Serve your crispy air fryer chicken Parmesan over cooked pasta or in a sandwich roll, garnished with fresh basil leaves.

Notes:

- Be sure to preheat your air fryer to ensure even cooking and crispy results.
- Spray the chicken with cooking spray before placing it in the air fryer to help achieve a golden, crispy crust.
- Don't overcrowd the air fryer basket; this can result in uneven cooking. Cook in batches if necessary.
- Cooking times may vary depending on your specific air fryer model and the thickness of the chicken breasts, so use a meat thermometer to check for doneness.
- The broiling step is essential to melt the cheese and give your chicken Parmesan that classic look and taste.
- Customize your chicken Parmesan by adding your favorite toppings or spices to the breading mixture or using different types of cheese.

Enjoy your Crispy Air Fryer Chicken Parmesan with your favorite sides or as a delicious sandwich!

Certainly! Here are some additional tips and variations for making Crispy Air Fryer Chicken Parmesan:

Tips:

1. **Use a Meat Thermometer:** It's crucial to use a meat thermometer to check the internal temperature of the chicken. This ensures that the chicken is fully cooked and safe to eat without overcooking and drying it out.
2. **Adjust Cooking Time:** Depending on your air fryer's wattage and size, you may need to adjust the cooking time. Keep an eye on the chicken to prevent overcooking. The chicken is done when it reaches an internal temperature of 165°F (74°C).
3. **Customize the Breading:** Feel free to add your favorite herbs and spices to the breadcrumb mixture to enhance the flavor. Paprika, oregano, and basil are good options to consider.
4. **Serve with Different Sides:** While serving the chicken over pasta is traditional, you can also serve it with a side salad, steamed vegetables, or on a sandwich with fresh greens and mayonnaise.

Variations:

1. **Gluten-Free Chicken Parmesan:** If you need a gluten-free option, substitute gluten-free flour and breadcrumbs for the regular ones in the recipe.

2. **Low-Carb Chicken Parmesan:** Skip the breading and flour to make a low-carb version of this dish. Season the chicken breasts and cook them in the air fryer, then top with marinara sauce and cheese.
3. **Vegetarian/Vegan Option:** You can make a vegetarian or vegan version by using plant-based chicken substitutes like seitan or tofu and vegan cheese. Follow the same breading and cooking steps.
4. **Different Cheeses:** While mozzarella is the classic choice, you can experiment with different cheeses such as provolone, cheddar, or a blend of Italian cheeses for a unique twist.
5. **Spicy Kick:** Add some red pepper flakes or hot sauce to the marinara sauce for a spicier version.
6. **Mushroom or Spinach Topping:** Sautéed mushrooms or spinach can make a delicious and healthy topping for your chicken Parmesan.
7. **Homemade Marinara Sauce:** While store-bought marinara sauce is convenient, making your own from scratch with fresh tomatoes, garlic, and herbs can take this dish to the next level.

Remember that Crispy Air Fryer Chicken Parmesan is versatile and can be customized to suit your taste preferences and dietary restrictions. Enjoy experimenting with different variations and making this classic Italian dish your own!

Air Fryer Chicken Fajitas

Air fryer chicken fajitas are a delicious and healthier alternative to the traditional stovetop or oven-cooked version. Here's a simple recipe and some notes to make the perfect chicken fajitas in your air fryer:

Ingredients:

For the Chicken Marinade:

- 1 pound boneless, skinless chicken breasts, sliced into thin strips
- 2 tablespoons olive oil
- 1 teaspoon chili powder
- 1 teaspoon cumin
- 1 teaspoon paprika
- 1/2 teaspoon garlic powder
- 1/2 teaspoon onion powder
- Salt and pepper to taste
- Juice of 1 lime
- 1 red bell pepper, sliced
- 1 yellow bell pepper, sliced

- 1 onion, sliced
- Flour or corn tortillas
- Toppings: Salsa, sour cream, guacamole, shredded cheese, and chopped cilantro

Instructions:

1. **Marinate the Chicken:** In a bowl, combine the olive oil, chili powder, cumin, paprika, garlic powder, onion powder, salt, pepper, and lime juice. Add the sliced chicken and toss to coat. Allow it to marinate for at least 30 minutes in the refrigerator, but longer is better for flavor.
2. **Preheat the Air Fryer:** Preheat your air fryer to 370°F (185°C).
3. **Prepare the Vegetables:** While the chicken is marinating, slice the red and yellow bell peppers and the onion.
4. **Cook the Chicken:** Once the air fryer is preheated, place the marinated chicken strips in a single layer in the air fryer basket. Cook for about 8-10 minutes or until the chicken is cooked through and slightly browned. You may need to shake the basket or flip the chicken halfway through for even cooking.
5. **Cook the Vegetables:** After the chicken is done, remove it from the air fryer and set it aside. Add the sliced bell peppers and onions to the air fryer basket. Cook for 5-7 minutes or until they are tender and slightly charred, shaking or flipping as needed.
6. **Assemble the Fajitas:** Warm your tortillas in the air fryer for a minute or two, if desired. Then, fill each tortilla with the cooked chicken and vegetables. Add your favorite toppings like salsa, sour cream, guacamole, cheese, and cilantro.
7. **Serve:** Serve your air fryer chicken fajitas hot and enjoy!

Notes:

- You can customize the marinade by adding more or less of the spices to suit your taste. If you like it spicy, consider adding some cayenne pepper or red pepper flakes.
- If your air fryer is small, you may need to cook the chicken and vegetables in batches to ensure they cook evenly.
- Don't overcrowd the air fryer basket; make sure there's enough space for air to circulate for even cooking.
- Experiment with different tortilla types, like whole wheat, spinach, or corn tortillas, for variety.
- Feel free to add other toppings like sliced jalapeños, diced tomatoes, or black beans for additional flavor and texture.

Air fryer chicken fajitas are quick, easy, and delicious, making them a great choice for a weeknight dinner. Enjoy your homemade fajitas!

Certainly, here are some additional tips and variations for making air fryer chicken fajitas:

Tips:

1. **Preheat the Air Fryer:** Make sure to preheat your air fryer before cooking. This helps ensure even and consistent cooking.
2. **Slicing Uniformly:** Try to slice the chicken and vegetables as uniformly as possible. This ensures they cook at the same rate.
3. **Cooking Time:** The cooking time may vary depending on your specific air fryer model. Keep an eye on the food to prevent overcooking, especially the chicken, as overcooked chicken can become dry.
4. **Add Some Heat:** If you like your fajitas spicy, you can add some chopped jalapeños or a pinch of cayenne pepper to the marinade.
5. **Don't Overcrowd:** Avoid overcrowding the air fryer basket to ensure that the chicken and veggies get that nice char and cook evenly.
6. **Use a Squeeze of Fresh Lime:** Before serving, give your fajitas an extra burst of freshness by squeezing a bit more fresh lime juice over them.
7. **Warm the Tortillas:** As mentioned in the main recipe, you can warm your tortillas in the air fryer for a minute or two to make them soft and pliable.

Variations:

1. **Different Proteins:** While this recipe uses chicken, you can easily make beef or shrimp fajitas in the air fryer using similar principles. Adjust cooking times based on the type of protein you choose.
2. **Vegetarian Fajitas:** If you prefer a vegetarian option, skip the chicken and make veggie fajitas by air frying a variety of vegetables like bell peppers, onions, mushrooms, and zucchini.
3. **Low-Carb Option:** Serve your fajita filling in lettuce wraps or on a bed of lettuce for a low-carb alternative to tortillas.
4. **Gluten-Free:** Use gluten-free tortillas or skip the tortillas altogether for a gluten-free option.
5. **Fajita Seasoning Mix:** Instead of mixing individual spices for the marinade, you can use store-bought fajita seasoning mix for convenience.
6. **Salsa Varieties:** Experiment with different types of salsas to add extra flavor. Try mango salsa, pineapple salsa, or a spicy habanero salsa.
7. **Cheese:** Add shredded cheese directly to the air fryer for the last minute or two of cooking to melt it over the chicken and veggies.
8. **Fresh Herbs:** Enhance the flavor by adding fresh herbs like cilantro, parsley, or fresh oregano to your fajitas.

Feel free to get creative and customize your air fryer chicken fajitas to suit your preferences. With these tips and variations, you can enjoy a variety of delicious fajita options.

Air Fryer Whole Chicken (so juicy!)

Air frying a whole chicken can result in a juicy and delicious meal with crispy skin. Here's a recipe and some notes to help you achieve the best results:

Ingredients:

- 1 whole chicken (approximately 3-4 pounds)
- 1-2 tablespoons of cooking oil (such as canola or olive oil)
- Seasonings of your choice (e.g., salt, pepper, paprika, garlic powder, thyme, rosemary)
- Optional: lemon or herbs for stuffing the chicken cavity

Instructions:

1. **Prep the Chicken:**
   - Remove the giblets and neck from the chicken cavity if they are included.
   - Pat the chicken dry with paper towels.
   - Season the chicken both inside and out with your preferred seasonings, including a light coating of oil to help the skin crisp up.
2. **Optional: Stuff the Cavity:**
   - You can add lemon wedges, garlic cloves, or fresh herbs like thyme or rosemary into the chicken cavity for added flavor.
3. **Preheat the Air Fryer:**
   - Preheat your air fryer to 350-375°F (175-190°C). The exact temperature may vary depending on your air fryer model, so consult your user manual for guidance.
4. **Truss the Chicken (Optional):**
   - Trussing is the process of tying the chicken's legs together to help it cook evenly. It's optional but can help maintain a more compact shape.
5. **Air Fry the Chicken:**
   - Place the chicken in the air fryer basket, breast side down. This will help the juices flow towards the breast meat and keep it moist.
   - Cook the chicken at the preheated temperature for 25-30 minutes per pound (45-60 minutes for a 3-4 pound chicken).
   - About halfway through the cooking time, flip the chicken over to breast side up.
   - Use a meat thermometer to check the internal temperature. The chicken is done when it reaches 165°F (74°C) in the thickest part of the breast and 175°F (80°C) in the thigh. Cooking times may vary depending on your air fryer's size and wattage.
6. **Rest and Serve:**
   - Allow the chicken to rest for about 10-15 minutes after cooking. This helps the juices redistribute and keeps the meat tender and juicy.
   - Carve the chicken and serve with your favorite sides.

Notes:

1. **Size Matters:** Adjust the cooking time according to the size of your chicken. Larger chickens will take longer to cook.
2. **Oil and Seasonings:** A light coating of oil and your favorite seasonings will help create a crispy, flavorful skin.
3. **Preheating:** Preheating the air fryer ensures that the chicken cooks evenly.
4. **Use a Meat Thermometer:** To guarantee a perfectly cooked chicken, invest in a good meat thermometer. It takes the guesswork out of determining if the chicken is done.
5. **Flipping the Chicken:** Flipping the chicken halfway through the cooking time helps ensure even browning and juiciness.
6. **Resting:** Allowing the chicken to rest before carving is crucial to retain its juices. It will be more tender and flavorful.

With these tips and this recipe, you can enjoy a juicy, flavorful, and crispy whole chicken prepared in your air fryer. Feel free to customize the seasonings to suit your taste preferences.

Certainly! Here are some additional tips and information to enhance your air fryer whole chicken experience:

7. Seasoning Ideas:

- Get creative with your seasonings. You can use a variety of herbs and spices like thyme, rosemary, paprika, garlic powder, onion powder, cayenne pepper, or even a dry rub of your choice.

8. Oil Choices:

- While a light coating of canola or olive oil works well, you can experiment with other oils like avocado oil, grapeseed oil, or even melted butter for added flavor.

9. Crispy Skin:

- For extra crispy skin, you can pat the chicken dry and refrigerate it, uncovered, for a few hours or overnight before cooking. This helps the skin dry out, leading to better crisping.

10. Basting (Optional):

- Some people like to baste the chicken with oil or melted butter during cooking to further enhance the skin's crispiness.

11. Air Fryer Size:

- The size and wattage of your air fryer can affect cooking times, so monitor the chicken's internal temperature and adjust as needed.

12. Safety Precautions:

- Make sure the chicken is fully thawed if it was frozen. Never put a frozen chicken directly into the air fryer.

13. Accompaniments:

- Serve your air-fried chicken with your favorite sides like roasted vegetables, mashed potatoes, or a fresh salad for a complete meal.

14. Gravy or Sauce:

- If you enjoy gravy, you can make it with the chicken drippings. Place the chicken on a plate, cover it with foil, and let it rest. Meanwhile, deglaze the air fryer basket with a bit of broth or white wine, scrape up the flavorful bits, and use this as the base for your gravy.

15. Leftovers:

- Leftover air-fried chicken is great for sandwiches, salads, or in other recipes like chicken pot pie.

16. Experiment:

- Don't be afraid to experiment with different flavor profiles and cooking temperatures to find the combination that suits your taste preferences best.

17. Cleaning:

- Clean your air fryer basket and accessories thoroughly after each use to prevent any buildup of grease or residue.

Remember that air fryers vary in performance, so it might take a couple of tries to find the perfect settings for your specific model. However, with practice and these tips, you can consistently create juicy and delicious air-fried whole chicken with crispy skin. Enjoy your homemade meal!

Perfect Air Fryer Salmon

Air frying salmon is a quick and healthy way to prepare this delicious fish. Here's a perfect air fryer salmon recipe along with some notes to help you get the best results:

Ingredients:

- 2 salmon fillets (6-8 ounces each)
- 2 tablespoons olive oil
- 1 teaspoon lemon juice

- 1 teaspoon minced garlic
- 1/2 teaspoon dried oregano
- 1/2 teaspoon dried thyme
- 1/2 teaspoon paprika
- Salt and pepper to taste
- Lemon wedges (for serving)

Notes:

1. **Preheat Your Air Fryer:** Preheat your air fryer to 375°F (190°C) for a few minutes before adding the salmon. This will ensure even cooking.
2. **Choose the Right Salmon:** Use fresh or thawed salmon fillets. You can choose skin-on or skinless salmon depending on your preference.
3. **Prepare the Marinade:** In a small bowl, mix the olive oil, lemon juice, minced garlic, dried oregano, dried thyme, paprika, salt, and pepper. This mixture will add flavor and help keep the salmon moist during cooking.
4. **Marinate the Salmon:** Place the salmon fillets in a shallow dish and brush both sides with the marinade. Allow them to marinate for 15-30 minutes in the refrigerator. This step is optional but will enhance the flavor.
5. **Spray or Grease the Air Fryer Basket:** Lightly grease the air fryer basket or use a non-stick cooking spray to prevent the salmon from sticking.
6. **Place the Salmon in the Air Fryer:** Place the salmon fillets in the preheated air fryer basket, skin-side down, or with the presentation side facing up. Make sure there is some space between them to allow for proper air circulation.
7. **Air Fry the Salmon:** Cook the salmon at 375°F (190°C) for about 10-12 minutes, depending on the thickness of the fillets. Check for doneness after 8 minutes by flaking the salmon with a fork. It's done when the salmon easily flakes and is opaque in the center.
8. **Adjust Cooking Time:** If your salmon is thicker, you may need to add a couple of minutes to the cooking time. Conversely, if it's thinner, reduce the cooking time to avoid overcooking.
9. **Serve Immediately:** Once the salmon is done, remove it from the air fryer and let it rest for a minute before serving. Squeeze fresh lemon juice over the top for an extra burst of flavor.
10. **Optional Crispy Skin:** If you have skin-on salmon and want crispy skin, you can cook the salmon skin-side up for the last few minutes of cooking. This will make the skin crispy, but be careful not to overcook the salmon in the process.

This air fryer salmon recipe is simple and yields a delicious, tender, and flavorful fish dish. It's a great way to enjoy a healthy meal in a short amount of time. You can pair it with your favorite sides like roasted vegetables, quinoa, or a fresh salad for a complete meal.

Certainly, here are some additional tips and variations to enhance your air fryer salmon experience:

Tips:

1. **Seasoning Variations:** Feel free to experiment with different seasonings and spices. You can use herbs like dill, basil, or cilantro for a fresh taste, or try Cajun seasoning for a bit of heat.
2. **Brush the Marinade:** Make sure to brush the salmon with the marinade rather than submerging it. Excess marinade can drip into the air fryer and cause smoking.
3. **Use a Meat Thermometer:** To ensure your salmon is cooked to the desired doneness, you can use a meat thermometer. Salmon is safe to eat at 145°F (63°C). Insert the thermometer into the thickest part of the fillet to check the internal temperature.
4. **Avoid Overcrowding:** If you're cooking multiple salmon fillets, ensure there's enough space around each fillet for air circulation. Overcrowding may lead to uneven cooking.

Variations:

1. **Honey Glazed Salmon:** Add a drizzle of honey on top of the salmon before air frying to create a sweet and savory glaze. It's a delightful combination with the natural richness of salmon.
2. **Teriyaki Salmon:** Marinate the salmon in a teriyaki sauce or make a homemade teriyaki marinade. Air fry the salmon until it's caramelized and glossy.
3. **Pesto Crusted Salmon:** Spread a layer of pesto sauce on top of the salmon fillets before air frying. It'll create a flavorful and aromatic crust.
4. **Lemon Butter Salmon:** Replace the olive oil with melted butter in the marinade for a richer flavor, and top the cooked salmon with a pat of lemon butter for extra indulgence.
5. **Crispy Salmon Skin Chips:** If you have skin-on salmon, you can separate the skin from the fillet, brush it with a little oil, season it, and air fry it separately until it's crispy. Use it as a delicious garnish.
6. **Serve with Sides:** Complement your salmon with sides like roasted asparagus, sautéed spinach, or a couscous salad. These side dishes pair well with the flavors of salmon.

Remember that air fryers can vary in cooking times and temperatures, so it's a good idea to keep an eye on your salmon during the cooking process, especially the first time you make it in your specific air fryer. With a little practice, you'll have perfectly cooked air fryer salmon every time. Enjoy your meal!

Crispy Air Fryer Fish (lemon parmesan breading!)

Crispy Air Fryer Fish with a lemon parmesan breading is a delicious and healthier alternative to traditional fried fish. The air fryer gives you that crispy texture without the need for excessive oil. Here's a simple recipe and some helpful notes to make it even better:

Ingredients:

- 4 fillets of white fish (such as cod, haddock, or tilapia)
- 1 cup breadcrumbs (Panko or regular)
- 1/2 cup grated Parmesan cheese
- Zest of one lemon
- 1 teaspoon dried oregano
- 1/2 teaspoon paprika
- Salt and pepper to taste
- 2 eggs, beaten
- Cooking spray or oil for the air fryer basket

Instructions:

1. **Prepare the Breading Mixture:** In a shallow bowl, combine the breadcrumbs, grated Parmesan cheese, lemon zest, dried oregano, paprika, salt, and pepper. Mix well to ensure even distribution of the flavors.
2. **Dip and Coat:** Dip each fish fillet in the beaten eggs, ensuring it's fully coated. Then, dredge the fillet in the breadcrumb mixture, pressing the crumbs onto the fish to adhere.
3. **Preheat the Air Fryer:** Preheat your air fryer to 375°F (190°C) for a few minutes. Some air fryers might not require preheating, so refer to your appliance's instructions.
4. **Spray the Basket:** Lightly grease the air fryer basket with cooking spray or a small amount of oil. This prevents the fish from sticking and helps in achieving a crispy texture.
5. **Air Fry the Fish:** Place the breaded fish fillets in a single layer in the air fryer basket. Depending on the size of your air fryer, you may need to cook them in batches. Cook the fish at 375°F (190°C) for about 10-15 minutes, or until they are golden brown and the internal temperature reaches 145°F (63°C).
6. **Serve:** Once the fish is cooked, carefully remove it from the air fryer and serve immediately. Squeeze some fresh lemon juice over the top for added flavor.

Notes:

- Make sure your fish fillets are of a similar thickness for even cooking. If they vary in thickness, some may cook faster or slower than others.
- You can adjust the seasoning in the breading mixture to your taste. Add more or less lemon zest, paprika, or oregano as you prefer.
- Be sure not to overcrowd the air fryer basket. Leaving space between the fillets allows for better air circulation and results in crispier fish.
- If your air fryer has different temperature and time settings, you can experiment with slightly higher or lower temperatures and times to find the perfect balance for your particular model.
- Serve your crispy air fryer fish with your favorite dipping sauce, such as tartar sauce or homemade aioli, and some side dishes like coleslaw, fries, or a salad. Enjoy!

Of course! Here are some additional tips and ideas to enhance your crispy air fryer fish with lemon parmesan breading:

1. Marinade: Consider marinating the fish fillets in a lemon and herb mixture before breading. This can infuse the fish with even more flavor. A simple marinade can consist of lemon juice, olive oil, garlic, and herbs like thyme or dill.

2. Season the Fish: Before you dip the fish in the beaten eggs and the breadcrumb mixture, season the fish fillets with salt and pepper. This adds an extra layer of flavor to the fish itself.

3. Customize the Breading: Get creative with the breading mixture. You can add ingredients like finely chopped fresh herbs (parsley, basil, or chives), crushed red pepper flakes for some heat, or even a touch of cayenne pepper for a spicy kick.

4. Dipping Sauces: Serve your air-fried fish with various dipping sauces. In addition to tartar sauce, consider serving it with remoulade, cocktail sauce, or a homemade lemon aioli for added zest.

5. Side Dish Options: Complement your crispy fish with a variety of side dishes. Classic choices include coleslaw, French fries, or a simple green salad. You can also try roasted vegetables, quinoa, or a serving of mashed potatoes for a heartier meal.

6. Air Fryer Maintenance: To keep your air fryer in good condition, remember to clean the basket and tray thoroughly after each use to prevent any residue buildup that can affect the cooking process. Refer to your air fryer's user manual for specific cleaning instructions.

7. Dietary Considerations: If you're looking for a lower-carb option, you can use almond meal or crushed pork rinds instead of breadcrumbs. This can make the dish keto-friendly.

8. Cooking Time Adjustments: Cooking times can vary depending on the thickness of the fish fillets and the specific air fryer model you're using. Be sure to monitor the cooking process and adjust the time as needed to prevent overcooking or undercooking.

9. Serving Presentation: To make your dish visually appealing, serve the crispy fish on a bed of fresh greens or with a colorful vegetable medley. Garnish with additional lemon slices or fresh herbs for a restaurant-quality presentation.

10. Experiment: Don't be afraid to experiment with different types of fish. While white fish like cod and haddock are popular choices, you can also try salmon, trout, or other varieties to discover new flavors.

Crispy air fryer fish with lemon parmesan breading is a versatile and delicious dish that you can customize to suit your taste. Enjoy your culinary adventure as you explore various flavors and side dishes to complement this delectable main course.

Air Fryer Chicken Nuggets

Air fryer chicken nuggets are a delicious and healthier alternative to traditional fried chicken nuggets. They're crispy on the outside and tender on the inside, and you can customize the seasonings to your liking. Here's a basic recipe along with some notes to help you make the perfect air fryer chicken nuggets:

Ingredients:

- 1 pound boneless, skinless chicken breasts or thighs, cut into bite-sized pieces
- 1 cup all-purpose flour (you can also use breadcrumbs or panko for added crispiness)
- 2 eggs, beaten
- 1 teaspoon salt
- 1/2 teaspoon black pepper
- 1/2 teaspoon paprika (adjust to taste)
- 1/2 teaspoon garlic powder (adjust to taste)
- Cooking spray (preferably oil spray, for coating the nuggets)

Instructions:

1. **Preheat the Air Fryer:** Preheat your air fryer to 400°F (200°C) for about 5 minutes.
2. **Prepare the Breading Station:** In one shallow dish, place the flour. In another dish, beat the eggs with a pinch of salt and pepper. In a third dish, mix the remaining salt, black pepper, paprika, and garlic powder.
3. **Coat the Chicken:** Dip each piece of chicken into the flour, ensuring it's well coated. Then, dip it into the beaten eggs, and finally, coat it with the seasoned breadcrumb mixture.
4. **Arrange in the Air Fryer:** Lightly spray the air fryer basket with cooking spray to prevent sticking. Arrange the coated chicken nuggets in a single layer in the basket. Do not overcrowd the basket; you may need to cook them in batches.
5. **Cook in the Air Fryer:** Place the basket in the preheated air fryer and cook for 12-15 minutes, flipping the nuggets halfway through the cooking time. Cooking times may vary depending on the size and thickness of your nuggets, so use a meat thermometer to ensure the internal temperature reaches 165°F (74°C).
6. **Serve:** Once the chicken nuggets are golden brown and cooked through, remove them from the air fryer and let them cool for a minute or two before serving.

Notes:

1. **Cutting the Chicken:** Try to cut the chicken into uniform-sized pieces to ensure even cooking.
2. **Breading Options:** You can use flour, breadcrumbs, or panko breadcrumbs for coating the chicken. Panko breadcrumbs tend to make the nuggets extra crispy.
3. **Seasonings:** Feel free to adjust the seasonings to suit your taste. You can add herbs, cayenne pepper, or other spices for extra flavor.
4. **Preheating:** Preheating the air fryer is essential for achieving crispy results. It's similar to preheating an oven.

5. **Don't Overcrowd:** Avoid overcrowding the air fryer basket, as it can lead to uneven cooking and less crispy results. Cook in batches if necessary.
6. **Cooking Time:** The cooking time can vary depending on the air fryer model and the size of the chicken pieces. Always check for doneness with a meat thermometer.
7. **Serve with Dipping Sauces:** Serve your air fryer chicken nuggets with your favorite dipping sauces, like ketchup, honey mustard, or barbecue sauce.

Enjoy your homemade air fryer chicken nuggets as a tasty and healthier snack or meal!

Certainly, here are some additional tips and variations for making air fryer chicken nuggets:

Additional Tips:

1. **Marination:** For even more flavor, consider marinating the chicken pieces in buttermilk or a seasoned brine for a few hours or overnight before breading and air frying. This will make the nuggets even juicier and flavorful.
2. **Use Cooking Spray:** When spraying the nuggets with cooking spray before air frying, it helps them become extra crispy and golden. You can use an oil spray or a non-stick cooking spray.
3. **Check for Doneness:** To ensure your chicken nuggets are thoroughly cooked, use a meat thermometer to verify that the internal temperature reaches 165°F (74°C). This is especially important to avoid undercooked chicken.
4. **Shake or Flip:** Depending on your air fryer model, you may want to shake the basket or flip the nuggets halfway through the cooking time to ensure even browning and crispiness.

Variations:

1. **Spicy Chicken Nuggets:** Add cayenne pepper, hot sauce, or chili powder to the breadcrumb mixture to make spicy chicken nuggets.
2. **Parmesan-Crusted Nuggets:** Mix grated Parmesan cheese with breadcrumbs to create a cheesy crust for your chicken nuggets.
3. **Asian-Style Nuggets:** Season the chicken with soy sauce, ginger, and garlic, and coat them in panko breadcrumbs with sesame seeds for an Asian twist.
4. **Gluten-Free Nuggets:** If you're gluten-sensitive, you can use gluten-free flour and breadcrumbs for the breading.
5. **Sweet Potato or Zucchini Nuggets:** Experiment with different vegetables, such as sweet potatoes or zucchini, to create vegetable-based nuggets.
6. **Tofu Nuggets:** For a vegetarian option, use tofu cut into nugget-sized pieces and follow a similar breading and air frying process.
7. **Serving Ideas:** Serve your chicken nuggets with a variety of side dishes like coleslaw, sweet potato fries, or a fresh green salad for a complete meal.
8. **Homemade Sauces:** Make your own dipping sauces like honey mustard, buffalo sauce, or garlic aioli for a unique flavor experience.

Remember that the exact cooking time and temperature can vary between different air fryer models, so it's essential to keep an eye on the nuggets as they cook and adjust the settings as needed. With these tips and variations, you can create delicious air fryer chicken nuggets to suit your taste and dietary preferences.

Air Fryer Chicken Thighs

Air frying chicken thighs is a great way to enjoy crispy, flavorful chicken without the excess oil and calories associated with traditional frying. Here's a simple recipe for air fryer chicken thighs, along with some notes:

Ingredients:

- 4-6 bone-in, skin-on chicken thighs
- 1 tablespoon olive oil or cooking spray
- 1 teaspoon salt (adjust to taste)
- 1/2 teaspoon black pepper
- 1/2 teaspoon paprika
- 1/2 teaspoon garlic powder
- 1/2 teaspoon onion powder
- 1/2 teaspoon dried thyme (optional)
- 1/2 teaspoon dried rosemary (optional)

Instructions:

1. **Preheat the Air Fryer:** Preheat your air fryer to 375°F (190°C). This step ensures that the chicken thighs start cooking immediately when you place them in the basket.
2. **Prepare the Chicken:** Pat the chicken thighs dry with paper towels. This helps the skin crisp up nicely. You can trim any excess skin or fat if desired.
3. **Season the Chicken:** In a small bowl, mix together the salt, pepper, paprika, garlic powder, onion powder, and any optional herbs (thyme and rosemary). Rub this seasoning mixture all over the chicken thighs, ensuring they are well-coated on all sides. You can also marinate the chicken for a few hours or overnight in the refrigerator for even more flavor.
4. **Oil or Cooking Spray:** Lightly brush or spray the chicken skin with olive oil or cooking spray. This helps the skin turn golden brown and crispy.
5. **Air Fry the Chicken:** Place the seasoned chicken thighs in the air fryer basket, skin side up, making sure they are not overcrowded. You may need to cook them in batches if your air fryer is small. Cooking times may vary based on the size of the thighs and the specific air fryer model, but typically, you can start with 25-30 minutes. Check the internal temperature with a meat thermometer; the chicken is done when it reaches 165°F (74°C).

6. **Flip (Optional):** If you want extra crispy skin, you can flip the chicken thighs halfway through the cooking time. This isn't necessary but can yield better results.
7. **Rest and Serve:** Once the chicken is cooked through, remove it from the air fryer and let it rest for a few minutes before serving. This allows the juices to redistribute, keeping the meat moist.

Notes:

1. **Chicken Thigh Variations:** You can adjust the seasoning to your liking. Try different spice blends, herbs, or sauces for a variety of flavors.
2. **Crispy Skin:** The key to achieving crispy skin is to ensure the chicken is dry before seasoning and to use a bit of oil or cooking spray. Flipping the chicken halfway through the cooking time can also help with achieving an evenly crispy skin.
3. **Cooking Times:** Cooking times may vary depending on your air fryer model and the size of the chicken thighs. It's important to use a meat thermometer to ensure the chicken is cooked to a safe internal temperature of 165°F (74°C).
4. **Side Dishes:** Serve your air fryer chicken thighs with your favorite sides, such as roasted vegetables, a salad, or mashed potatoes.

Enjoy your delicious and crispy air fryer chicken thighs!

Certainly! Here are some additional tips and ideas for making the most of your air fryer chicken thighs:

1. **Brining:** To further enhance the flavor and juiciness of your chicken thighs, consider brining them before cooking. A simple brine can be made with water, salt, and sugar. Soak the chicken thighs in the brine for a few hours or overnight in the refrigerator.
2. **Breading or Coating:** If you want an even crispier texture, you can dip the chicken thighs in flour, egg, and breadcrumbs or panko before air frying. This will create a delicious, crunchy coating.
3. **Herb Butter:** After cooking, you can baste the chicken thighs with melted herb butter for extra flavor. Simply mix melted butter with minced herbs like parsley, thyme, and rosemary and drizzle it over the cooked chicken.
4. **Cooking Time:** Keep an eye on your chicken thighs while they're cooking. The cooking time may vary depending on their size and your air fryer's performance. Adjust the time as needed to ensure they are cooked through without overcooking.
5. **Rack or Basket:** Some air fryers come with a rack or grill pan. Using the rack can help the hot air circulate around the chicken thighs more effectively, resulting in even crispiness. If your air fryer has this option, give it a try.
6. **Preheating:** Preheating your air fryer is crucial for even cooking and crisping. It's a good practice to follow, but some modern air fryers preheat quickly, so you might not need to wait as long as you would with an oven.
7. **Leftovers:** If you have leftover cooked chicken thighs, they can be reheated in the air fryer for a few minutes to regain their crispiness. This works well for reviving the texture of refrigerated or frozen leftovers.

8. **Serving Ideas:** Consider serving your air fryer chicken thighs with a variety of side dishes, such as coleslaw, rice, quinoa, or a fresh green salad. Sauces like barbecue, honey mustard, or tzatziki can also be great accompaniments.
9. **Experiment:** Don't be afraid to experiment with different seasonings and marinades. You can customize the flavors to match your preferences or try international spice blends for unique twists.
10. **Safety:** Always ensure that your chicken is fully cooked to a safe internal temperature of 165°F (74°C) to avoid foodborne illnesses.

Air frying is a versatile cooking method, and you can use these tips and ideas to create a variety of chicken thigh dishes that suit your taste and dietary preferences. Enjoy your air fryer culinary adventures!

Air Fryer Meatballs (fresh, frozen)

Air fryer meatballs are a delicious and healthier alternative to traditional fried meatballs. They come out crispy on the outside and tender on the inside. You can make them using fresh or frozen meatballs. Here's a basic recipe for air fryer meatballs along with some notes:

Ingredients:

- 1 pound of ground meat (beef, pork, turkey, chicken, or a combination)
- 1/4 cup breadcrumbs
- 1/4 cup grated Parmesan cheese (optional)
- 1/4 cup finely chopped onions (optional)
- 1/4 cup milk
- 1 egg
- 1 teaspoon salt
- 1/2 teaspoon black pepper
- 1/2 teaspoon garlic powder (optional)
- 1/2 teaspoon Italian seasoning (optional)
- Cooking spray or oil (for the air fryer basket)

Instructions:

1. In a mixing bowl, combine the ground meat, breadcrumbs, grated Parmesan cheese, finely chopped onions, milk, egg, salt, pepper, and any optional seasonings you prefer. Mix well until all the ingredients are evenly incorporated.
2. Shape the mixture into meatballs. You can make them any size you prefer, but smaller meatballs will cook faster in the air fryer.
3. Preheat your air fryer to 375°F (190°C) for a few minutes.
4. Lightly grease the air fryer basket with cooking spray or a small amount of oil to prevent the meatballs from sticking.

5. Place the meatballs in the air fryer basket, leaving some space between them to allow for even cooking.
6. Cook the meatballs in the preheated air fryer at 375°F (190°C) for about 12-15 minutes for fresh meatballs, or 15-20 minutes for frozen meatballs, shaking the basket or turning them halfway through to ensure even cooking. Cooking times may vary based on the size and type of meat used, so it's essential to check for doneness.
7. The meatballs are done when they are golden brown and reach an internal temperature of at least 165°F (74°C) for beef and pork, or 170°F (77°C) for poultry.
8. Serve the air-fried meatballs with your favorite sauce, such as marinara, barbecue, or a dipping sauce of your choice.

Notes:

1. If using frozen meatballs, there's no need to defrost them before air frying. You can cook them straight from the freezer, but they may take a little longer to cook than fresh meatballs.
2. You can customize the seasonings and ingredients to suit your taste. Feel free to add herbs, spices, or other ingredients like chopped herbs, grated garlic, or red pepper flakes.
3. Make sure not to overcrowd the air fryer basket. If you're making a large batch, cook the meatballs in batches for the best results.
4. Be cautious with the cooking time, as it can vary depending on your air fryer's brand and model. It's essential to check the meatballs' internal temperature to ensure they're fully cooked.
5. Leftover meatballs can be refrigerated and reheated in the air fryer for a few minutes to maintain their crispy texture.

Certainly! Here are some additional tips and variations for making air fryer meatballs:

Tips:

1. **Preheat the Air Fryer**: Preheating your air fryer for a few minutes before cooking the meatballs helps ensure even cooking and a crispier exterior.
2. **Use Lean Meat**: If you're looking for a healthier option, use lean ground meat like turkey or chicken. You can also mix different types of ground meat for a unique flavor.
3. **Don't Overmix**: When mixing the meatball ingredients, avoid overmixing the meat, as it can make the meatballs tough. Mix until the ingredients are just combined.
4. **Basting**: You can baste the meatballs with a little oil or cooking spray halfway through cooking to help them brown and crisp up more.
5. **Air Fryer Accessories**: Some air fryers come with accessories like grill pans, which can be used to cook meatballs. These can help with even cooking and allow for more meatballs in one batch.

Variations:

1. **Saucy Meatballs**: After the meatballs are cooked, toss them in your favorite sauce to coat them evenly. BBQ sauce, sweet and sour sauce, and teriyaki sauce are excellent options.
2. **Stuffed Meatballs**: Make your meatballs even more exciting by stuffing them with mozzarella cheese, spinach, or other fillings. Just shape the meatball around the filling before air frying.
3. **Different Seasonings**: Experiment with various seasonings and herbs. For a Mediterranean twist, use oregano, cumin, and coriander. For a Mexican flavor, try chili powder and cumin.
4. **Mini Meatballs**: Make mini meatballs for a party or appetizer. They cook even faster in the air fryer and are perfect for dipping in sauces.
5. **Vegetarian Meatballs**: If you prefer a vegetarian option, you can make meatballs using ingredients like lentils, mushrooms, or plant-based meat substitutes.
6. **Gluten-Free Meatballs**: If you're following a gluten-free diet, use gluten-free breadcrumbs or almond flour as a substitute for regular breadcrumbs.
7. **Herbed Meatballs**: Add fresh herbs like parsley, basil, or cilantro to the meat mixture for a burst of freshness and flavor.
8. **Sweet and Sour Meatballs**: Make a sweet and sour glaze using pineapple juice, ketchup, brown sugar, and vinegar. Toss the cooked meatballs in the sauce for a sweet and tangy treat.
9. **Asian Meatballs**: Season the meatballs with soy sauce, ginger, and garlic, and serve with a dipping sauce made from soy sauce, rice vinegar, and sesame oil.
10. **Keto Meatballs**: If you're following a ketogenic diet, you can omit breadcrumbs altogether or use almond flour as a low-carb alternative.

Air fryer meatballs are a versatile dish that can be customized to suit your taste and dietary preferences. Enjoy them as a snack, appetizer, or as part of a meal with pasta, rice, or vegetables.

Air Fryer Salmon Patties (Golden + Crispy)

Air fryer salmon patties are a delicious and healthier alternative to traditional fried salmon patties. They come out golden and crispy on the outside while remaining tender and flavorful on the inside. Here's a recipe and some notes to help you make these mouthwatering salmon patties in your air fryer:

Ingredients:

- 1 pound fresh or canned salmon (drained and flaked)
- 1/2 cup breadcrumbs (panko or regular)
- 1/4 cup mayonnaise
- 1/4 cup chopped green onions

- 1/4 cup chopped red bell pepper
- 1/4 cup chopped fresh parsley
- 1 egg
- 1 tablespoon Dijon mustard
- 1 tablespoon lemon juice
- 1/2 teaspoon garlic powder
- 1/2 teaspoon dried dill (or 1 tablespoon fresh dill)
- Salt and black pepper to taste
- Cooking spray or oil for the air fryer basket

Instructions:

1. **Prepare the salmon:** If using fresh salmon, cook it by poaching, baking, or grilling until it's fully cooked and flakey. Allow it to cool and then remove the skin and any bones. If using canned salmon, make sure it's drained and flaked.
2. **Combine ingredients:** In a large mixing bowl, combine the flaked salmon, breadcrumbs, mayonnaise, green onions, red bell pepper, parsley, egg, Dijon mustard, lemon juice, garlic powder, dill, salt, and pepper. Mix everything together until well combined.
3. **Shape the patties:** Divide the mixture into 4-6 equal portions and shape them into patties. Make sure they're not too thick to ensure even cooking.
4. **Preheat the air fryer:** Preheat your air fryer to 375°F (190°C). This usually takes 3-5 minutes.
5. **Air fry the salmon patties:** Lightly grease the air fryer basket or tray with cooking spray or oil. Place the salmon patties in the basket or on the tray, making sure there is some space between them. You may need to cook them in batches if your air fryer is small. Cook for 8-10 minutes, flipping them halfway through the cooking time. They should be golden brown and crispy on the outside.
6. **Serve:** Once the salmon patties are cooked, remove them from the air fryer, and let them cool for a minute before serving. You can serve them on buns as sandwiches, on a bed of salad, or with your favorite dipping sauce.

Notes:

1. **Variations:** Feel free to customize the recipe by adding ingredients like capers, diced pickles, or different herbs and spices to suit your taste.
2. **Panko breadcrumbs:** Panko breadcrumbs are preferred for their extra crispiness, but you can use regular breadcrumbs if that's what you have on hand.
3. **Oil or cooking spray:** Using a bit of oil or cooking spray on the patties helps them become crispy in the air fryer.
4. **Don't overcrowd the air fryer:** Make sure there's enough space between the salmon patties in the air fryer to allow for proper air circulation and even cooking.
5. **Serve with dipping sauce:** Consider serving your salmon patties with a dipping sauce like tartar sauce, aioli, or a lemon-dill sauce for extra flavor.

Enjoy your air fryer salmon patties! They're a tasty and healthier option for a quick and satisfying meal.

Certainly, here are some additional tips and ideas for your air fryer salmon patties:

1. Cooking time: The cooking time may vary depending on the thickness of your salmon patties and the specific model of your air fryer. Keep an eye on them, and adjust the cooking time as needed to ensure they are cooked to your desired level of crispiness and doneness.

2. Preheating: Preheating the air fryer is essential for even cooking and achieving that crispy exterior. Don't skip this step.

3. Temperature: You can experiment with the cooking temperature. Some people prefer cooking salmon patties at a slightly higher temperature, around 400°F (200°C), for a shorter time to get an even crispier exterior.

4. Use an air fryer parchment liner: To prevent the salmon patties from sticking to the air fryer basket or tray, you can use air fryer parchment liners. They make cleanup easier, too.

5. Frozen salmon patties: If you're using frozen pre-made salmon patties, you can still air fry them. Just follow the package instructions, but typically, it's around 12-15 minutes at 375°F (190°C), flipping halfway through.

6. Doneness: The internal temperature of your salmon patties should reach 145°F (63°C) to ensure they are fully cooked. Use a meat thermometer to check if you're unsure.

7. Sides: Salmon patties pair well with a variety of side dishes such as coleslaw, sweet potato fries, roasted vegetables, or a simple green salad.

8. Leftovers: If you have leftover salmon patties, they can be refrigerated for a day or two and reheated in the air fryer to maintain their crispiness. Just reheat at a lower temperature for a shorter time to avoid overcooking.

9. Dietary considerations: You can adapt the recipe to suit dietary preferences. For a gluten-free version, use gluten-free breadcrumbs. To make them keto-friendly, use almond flour or crushed pork rinds instead of breadcrumbs.

10. Seasoning: Feel free to adjust the seasonings to your taste. You can add a pinch of cayenne pepper for some heat or use different herbs and spices for a unique flavor profile.

Experiment with these ideas and make the recipe your own. Air fryer salmon patties are a versatile and delicious dish that can be tailored to your preferences and dietary needs. Enjoy your crispy, golden salmon patties!

Air Fryer Shrimp (Honey Lime)

Sure, here's a recipe for Honey Lime Air Fryer Shrimp along with some notes:

Ingredients:

- 1 pound large shrimp, peeled and deveined
- 2 tablespoons honey
- 2 tablespoons fresh lime juice
- 2 cloves garlic, minced
- 1 teaspoon soy sauce
- 1 teaspoon olive oil
- 1/2 teaspoon ground cumin
- 1/2 teaspoon paprika
- 1/2 teaspoon salt
- 1/4 teaspoon black pepper
- Cooking spray

Instructions:

1. **Marinate the Shrimp:** In a mixing bowl, combine the honey, lime juice, minced garlic, soy sauce, olive oil, ground cumin, paprika, salt, and black pepper. Mix well to create a marinade.
2. **Coat the Shrimp:** Add the peeled and deveined shrimp to the marinade. Toss to coat the shrimp thoroughly. Allow the shrimp to marinate for about 15-20 minutes in the refrigerator.
3. **Preheat the Air Fryer:** Preheat your air fryer to 375°F (190°C). Some air fryers may not require preheating, so check your appliance's manual for guidance.
4. **Air Fry the Shrimp:** While the air fryer is preheating, lightly grease the air fryer basket with cooking spray. Then, arrange the marinated shrimp in a single layer in the basket. Make sure the shrimp are not overcrowded; you may need to cook them in batches if necessary.
5. **Cook the shrimp:** Air fry the shrimp at 375°F (190°C) for about 5-7 minutes, flipping them halfway through the cooking time, until they are pink and opaque. The exact cooking time may vary depending on the size of your shrimp and the specific air fryer model, so keep an eye on them.
6. **Serve:** Once the shrimp are cooked, remove them from the air fryer and serve immediately. You can garnish them with some extra lime wedges and chopped fresh cilantro if desired.

Recipe Notes:

- Be sure to not overcook the shrimp, as they can become rubbery. Cooking time may vary based on the size of the shrimp, so it's essential to monitor them closely.
- You can adjust the sweetness and acidity of the dish by altering the amount of honey and lime juice to suit your taste.

- If your air fryer has a non-stick coating, you might not need to use cooking spray, but it can help prevent sticking and make cleanup easier.
- This recipe is versatile, and you can customize the seasonings to your liking. You can add a pinch of chili powder for some heat or use different spices to change the flavor profile.

Enjoy your Honey Lime Air Fryer Shrimp as a delicious and quick meal or appetizer!

Certainly, here are some additional tips and ideas to enhance your Honey Lime Air Fryer Shrimp recipe:

1. **Serving Suggestions:**
   - Serve the shrimp over a bed of cooked rice, a salad, or as a filling for tacos or wraps.
   - Drizzle any leftover marinade over the cooked shrimp for extra flavor.
   - For a refreshing contrast, serve the shrimp with a side of coleslaw or a cucumber salad.
2. **Garnish Options:**
   - Garnish the shrimp with chopped fresh cilantro, chopped green onions, or sesame seeds for added color and flavor.
   - A squeeze of extra lime juice just before serving can brighten up the dish.
3. **Customize the Marinade:**
   - Experiment with different ingredients in the marinade, such as minced ginger or a touch of red pepper flakes for some heat.
   - If you like a stronger lime flavor, add some lime zest to the marinade.
4. **Cooking Variations:**
   - Instead of shrimp, you can try this recipe with other seafood like scallops, or even with chicken strips for a different twist.
   - If you prefer a crispy coating on your shrimp, you can dip the marinated shrimp in a light batter or breadcrumb mixture before air frying.
5. **Dipping Sauces:**
   - Serve the shrimp with a dipping sauce, such as a sweet chili sauce, a cilantro-lime aioli, or a creamy avocado dip for extra flavor.
6. **Crispiness Tips:**
   - To ensure your shrimp turns out crispy, make sure they are not overcrowded in the air fryer basket. If necessary, cook them in batches.
   - You can give the shrimp a light spray of cooking oil before air frying for an extra crispy texture.
7. **Healthier Option:**
   - If you're looking for a lower-calorie version, you can reduce the amount of honey in the marinade or substitute it with a natural sweetener like maple syrup or agave nectar.
8. **Side Dish Pairings:**
   - Pair your Honey Lime Air Fryer Shrimp with a side of roasted vegetables, sautéed greens, or quinoa for a balanced meal.

Remember, the beauty of cooking is the ability to tailor recipes to your personal taste, so feel free to experiment and make this dish your own. Enjoy your delicious Honey Lime Air Fryer Shrimp!

Crispy Air Fryer Chicken Tenders

Crispy Air Fryer Chicken Tenders are a delicious and healthier alternative to traditional fried chicken tenders. They are quick and easy to make, and the air fryer gives them a satisfyingly crispy texture without the need for a lot of oil. Here's a simple recipe along with some notes to help you make the best chicken tenders:

Ingredients:

- 1 pound chicken tenders (or boneless, skinless chicken breasts cut into strips)
- 1 cup all-purpose flour
- 2 large eggs
- 1 cup breadcrumbs (panko or regular)
- 1/2 cup grated Parmesan cheese (optional)
- 1 teaspoon paprika
- 1/2 teaspoon garlic powder
- 1/2 teaspoon onion powder
- 1/2 teaspoon salt
- 1/4 teaspoon black pepper
- Cooking spray or oil (for the air fryer basket)

Instructions:

1. **Prepare the Coating**: In one bowl, add the flour. In another bowl, whisk the eggs. In a third bowl, combine the breadcrumbs, Parmesan cheese (if using), paprika, garlic powder, onion powder, salt, and black pepper. This mixture will be your coating.
2. **Coat the Chicken**: Dip each chicken tender into the flour, ensuring it's fully coated. Then, dip it into the beaten eggs, allowing any excess to drip off. Finally, coat it in the breadcrumb mixture, pressing the crumbs onto the chicken to adhere well. Repeat this process for all the chicken tenders.
3. **Preheat the Air Fryer**: Preheat your air fryer to 375°F (190°C) for a few minutes.
4. **Cook the Chicken Tenders**: Lightly grease the air fryer basket with cooking spray or oil to prevent sticking. Place the coated chicken tenders in a single layer in the basket, making sure they are not overcrowded. You may need to cook them in batches if your air fryer is small.
5. **Air Fry**: Cook the chicken tenders at 375°F (190°C) for 10-12 minutes, flipping them halfway through the cooking time. The exact cooking time may vary based on the thickness of your chicken tenders and the brand of your air fryer. Make sure the chicken reaches an internal temperature of 165°F (74°C) to ensure it's fully cooked.

6. **Serve**: Once the chicken tenders are golden brown and crispy, remove them from the air fryer and let them rest for a few minutes. Serve them with your favorite dipping sauces, such as ketchup, BBQ sauce, or ranch dressing.

Notes:

1. **Preheating**: Preheating your air fryer helps ensure even cooking and crispiness, so don't skip this step.
2. **Oil**: You can use a cooking spray or lightly brush the chicken tenders with oil before air frying to help them achieve a crispy texture.
3. **Variations**: Feel free to customize the seasoning and spices to suit your taste. You can add herbs like thyme, rosemary, or oregano for extra flavor.
4. **Dipping Sauces**: These chicken tenders go great with various dipping sauces, such as honey mustard, buffalo sauce, or sweet and sour sauce.
5. **Leftovers**: Store any leftovers in an airtight container in the refrigerator. You can reheat them in the air fryer for a few minutes to restore their crispiness.

Certainly! Here are some additional tips and ideas for making delicious and crispy air fryer chicken tenders:

1. Marinating: For extra flavor, you can marinate the chicken tenders in buttermilk or a seasoned brine for a few hours before coating them. This will not only add flavor but also help keep the chicken moist.

2. Double Coating: To achieve an even thicker and crispier coating, you can double-dip the chicken tenders. After the first coating, dip them again in the egg and breadcrumb mixture before air frying.

3. Seasoning: Experiment with different seasonings and spices to create unique flavor profiles. Cajun seasoning, Italian herbs, or a touch of cayenne pepper can give your chicken tenders a kick.

4. Temperature and Time: Keep an eye on the cooking time and temperature, as every air fryer can vary. Check the chicken's internal temperature to ensure it's fully cooked. If your chicken is browning too quickly, you can reduce the temperature and cook for a longer time.

5. Panko Breadcrumbs: Panko breadcrumbs tend to result in an even crispier texture, so consider using them for your coating.

6. Warming Drawer: If you're making multiple batches of chicken tenders and want to keep them warm while the others cook, you can use a warming drawer or a low-temperature oven to maintain their crispiness.

7. Air Fryer Basket Space: Don't overcrowd the air fryer basket. If the chicken tenders are too close together, they won't cook evenly or become as crispy.

8. Clean the Air Fryer: Make sure to clean your air fryer regularly to prevent smoke and odors from old food residue affecting the taste of your chicken tenders.

9. Gluten-Free Option: If you're looking for a gluten-free version, use gluten-free flour and breadcrumbs. You can also make a coating with crushed gluten-free cornflakes or rice cereal for added crunch.

10. Sides: Serve your crispy chicken tenders with a variety of sides like coleslaw, french fries, or a fresh salad for a complete meal.

11. Dipping Ideas: Get creative with your dipping sauces. Try homemade sauces like honey sriracha, garlic aioli, or tzatziki for a unique twist.

Remember, the key to perfect air fryer chicken tenders is to customize the recipe to your liking and make adjustments based on your specific air fryer model. With these tips and ideas, you'll be able to create crispy, flavorful chicken tenders that everyone will enjoy.

20 Minute Air Fryer Chicken Breast

Here's a simple 20-minute air fryer chicken breast recipe along with some notes to help you make a delicious and quick meal. This recipe is for boneless, skinless chicken breasts.

Ingredients:

- 2 boneless, skinless chicken breasts
- 1 tablespoon olive oil
- 1 teaspoon paprika
- 1 teaspoon garlic powder
- 1 teaspoon onion powder
- 1/2 teaspoon salt
- 1/4 teaspoon black pepper
- Optional: Your favorite seasoning or herbs for added flavor

Instructions:

1. **Preheat your air fryer**: Set the air fryer to 375°F (190°C) and allow it to preheat for a few minutes.
2. **Prepare the chicken**: Pat the chicken breasts dry with a paper towel. This helps to ensure they get crispy in the air fryer.
3. **Season the chicken**: In a bowl, mix the olive oil with the paprika, garlic powder, onion powder, salt, and black pepper. You can also add any additional seasonings or herbs you like. Coat the chicken breasts with this mixture, making sure they are well-seasoned on all sides.

4. **Air fry the chicken**: Place the seasoned chicken breasts in the air fryer basket in a single layer, making sure they don't touch each other. If your air fryer is small, you may need to cook them one at a time.
5. **Cook the chicken**: Cook the chicken at 375°F (190°C) for about 10 minutes. After 10 minutes, flip the chicken breasts over and continue cooking for another 8-10 minutes or until the internal temperature of the chicken reaches 165°F (74°C). Cooking times may vary depending on the thickness of the chicken breasts and your specific air fryer model, so it's a good idea to check the internal temperature for doneness.
6. **Rest and serve**: Once the chicken is done, let it rest for a few minutes before slicing and serving. Resting the chicken allows the juices to redistribute and keeps it moist.
7. **Optional: Make a sauce**: While the chicken is resting, you can prepare a sauce or glaze to drizzle over the chicken if desired. Some options include a honey mustard glaze, barbecue sauce, or a lemon butter sauce.

Notes:

- Make sure not to overcrowd the air fryer basket. Cook the chicken in a single layer, so it cooks evenly and gets crispy.
- If you have thicker chicken breasts, you may need to adjust the cooking time. You can also flatten the chicken breasts to ensure even cooking.
- Always use an instant-read meat thermometer to check the internal temperature of the chicken. It should reach 165°F (74°C) to be considered safe to eat.
- Feel free to customize the seasonings to your liking. You can use different spices and herbs based on your preferences.
- Don't forget to preheat the air fryer to ensure consistent cooking.

This recipe provides a basic guideline, but you can get creative and experiment with different flavors and coatings to suit your taste. Enjoy your air fryer chicken breast!

Certainly, here are some additional tips and ideas for making the perfect air fryer chicken breast:

Tips:

1. **Marinate the chicken:** For extra flavor and juiciness, you can marinate the chicken breasts in your favorite marinade for at least 30 minutes or even overnight in the refrigerator. Just be sure to pat them dry before air frying to prevent excess moisture.
2. **Coating options:** Instead of a wet marinade, you can also coat the chicken with a dry rub. Use a variety of spices, herbs, or even crushed nuts for a crunchy coating. The air fryer will still give you a crispy result.
3. **Spray with oil:** If you're trying to reduce the amount of oil used, you can use a cooking spray to lightly coat the chicken before air frying. This will help with crisping and browning.
4. **Use a meat thermometer:** Investing in an instant-read meat thermometer is crucial for achieving perfectly cooked chicken. It takes the guesswork out of determining doneness.

5. **Let it rest:** Allowing the cooked chicken to rest for a few minutes before slicing helps the juices redistribute and ensures a moist result.
6. **Sauce and toppings:** After cooking, consider adding some sauce or toppings. Try adding a squeeze of lemon juice, a sprinkle of fresh herbs, or some grated Parmesan cheese for extra flavor.

Variations:

1. **Stuffed chicken breast:** Slice a pocket into the chicken breast and stuff it with ingredients like spinach, cheese, or sun-dried tomatoes before air frying. This adds an extra layer of flavor.
2. **Buffalo chicken:** Coat the chicken in buffalo sauce or a mixture of hot sauce and butter for a spicy kick.
3. **Parmesan-crusted chicken:** After seasoning, coat the chicken with breadcrumbs mixed with grated Parmesan cheese for a crispy, cheesy crust.
4. **Teriyaki chicken:** Marinate the chicken in teriyaki sauce for an Asian-inspired flavor.
5. **Pesto chicken:** Brush the chicken with pesto sauce before or after air frying for a burst of herb and garlic flavor.
6. **Lemon garlic chicken:** Season with lemon juice, garlic, and rosemary for a zesty and aromatic taste.
7. **Barbecue chicken:** Brush the chicken with your favorite barbecue sauce for a smoky and sweet finish.

Remember that cooking times may vary based on the size and thickness of your chicken breasts, as well as the specific air fryer model you're using. Always use the meat thermometer to ensure safe and perfectly cooked chicken. With some creativity and experimentation, you can create a variety of delicious air fryer chicken breast recipes to suit your taste preferences.

Air Fryer Chicken Wings

Air fryer chicken wings are a delicious and healthier alternative to traditional fried chicken wings. They come out crispy on the outside and tender on the inside, and you can customize them with your favorite sauces or seasonings. Here's a basic recipe and some notes for making air fryer chicken wings:

Ingredients:

- Chicken wings (fresh or frozen)
- Olive oil or cooking spray
- Salt and pepper (or your preferred seasoning)

Instructions:

1. **Preheat the Air Fryer:** Preheat your air fryer to around 375°F (190°C) for about 5 minutes.
2. **Prepare the Chicken Wings:** If using frozen chicken wings, make sure they are thawed and dry them with paper towels. You can also use fresh chicken wings. Trim off any excess skin and separate the wings into drumettes and flats. Pat them dry with paper towels to remove excess moisture. This helps in achieving a crispy skin.
3. **Season the Wings:** Drizzle a little olive oil over the chicken wings or use a cooking spray to lightly coat them. Season the wings with salt and pepper, or your preferred seasoning mix. You can get creative here by using a variety of spices, herbs, or even marinating the wings for a few hours in your favorite sauce.
4. **Arrange in the Air Fryer:** Place the seasoned chicken wings in a single layer in the air fryer basket. Don't overcrowd them, as this can prevent even cooking and crispiness. You may need to cook them in batches.
5. **Air Fry the Wings:** Cook the chicken wings at 375°F (190°C) for about 25-30 minutes. Halfway through the cooking time, pause the air fryer and shake the basket or flip the wings to ensure even cooking. Cooking times may vary depending on the size of the wings and the specific air fryer model, so it's a good idea to check the wings' internal temperature using a meat thermometer. The wings are done when they reach an internal temperature of 165°F (74°C).
6. **Optional Extra Crispiness:** If you want the wings even crispier, you can increase the temperature or cooking time by a few minutes. Just be sure not to overcook them, as they can become dry.
7. **Serve:** Once the wings are done, remove them from the air fryer and let them rest for a minute before serving. You can toss them in your favorite sauce, like buffalo, barbecue, honey mustard, or teriyaki, for added flavor.

Notes:

- Make sure your chicken wings are dry before seasoning and cooking. This helps achieve the desired crispy texture.
- Don't overcrowd the air fryer basket. It's better to cook the wings in batches if necessary to allow proper air circulation.
- Cooking times can vary, so it's essential to check the internal temperature with a meat thermometer to ensure the wings are cooked through.
- Experiment with different seasonings and sauces to customize the flavor to your liking.
- Be mindful of your air fryer's cooking guidelines, as some models may have slightly different temperature and time recommendations.

Enjoy your air fryer chicken wings as a tasty and healthier snack or meal!

Certainly! Here are some additional tips and variations to enhance your air fryer chicken wings:

1. Crispy Coating Options:

- To achieve an even crispier texture, you can coat the seasoned wings with a thin layer of cornstarch or baking powder before air frying. This helps create a crunchier crust.

2. Sauce and Flavor Variations:

- After air frying, you can toss the wings in a variety of sauces or seasonings to suit your taste. Some popular options include barbecue sauce, buffalo sauce, honey mustard, garlic parmesan, teriyaki, or a combination of your favorite spices.

3. Dipping Sauces:

- Serve your air fryer chicken wings with a selection of dipping sauces. Classic choices include blue cheese dressing, ranch dressing, or a yogurt-based tzatziki sauce. These can complement the flavors of your wings nicely.

4. Temperature and Time Adjustments:

- Air fryer models may vary in their cooking times and temperatures. You can experiment with different settings to find the perfect balance between crispy skin and tender meat. Just keep an eye on them to avoid overcooking.

5. Preheat for Crispiness:

- Preheating your air fryer is essential for achieving a crispy exterior. The initial blast of heat helps seal in the juices and ensures a golden and crispy texture.

6. Cooking Frozen Wings:

- If using frozen wings, it's a good idea to add a few extra minutes to the cooking time. Make sure to check the internal temperature to ensure they're thoroughly cooked.

7. Keep Warm Feature:

- Many air fryers have a "keep warm" function, which can be helpful if you're cooking wings in batches. It allows you to keep the first batch warm while you cook the second one.

8. Serve with Fresh Vegetables:

- To balance the meal and add freshness, consider serving your chicken wings with celery sticks, carrot sticks, and cucumber slices.

9. Don't Overcrowd the Basket:

- It's worth reiterating that overcrowding the air fryer basket can lead to uneven cooking. Make sure there's some space between the wings for the hot air to circulate.

10. Custom Seasoning Blends: - Get creative with your seasoning blends. Mix your favorite herbs, spices, and even a touch of grated Parmesan or grated lemon zest for a unique flavor profile.

Air fryer chicken wings are a versatile and customizable dish. Feel free to experiment and adapt the recipe to your liking, and don't be afraid to try out different sauces and seasonings to create your own signature wings. Enjoy!

Lemon Pepper Air Fryer Chicken and Broccoli

Sure, here's a simple recipe for Lemon Pepper Air Fryer Chicken and Broccoli, along with some notes:

Ingredients:

For the Lemon Pepper Chicken:

- 2 boneless, skinless chicken breasts
- 2 tablespoons olive oil
- 1 tablespoon lemon juice
- 1 teaspoon lemon zest
- 1 teaspoon black pepper
- 1/2 teaspoon salt
- 1/2 teaspoon garlic powder
- 1/2 teaspoon onion powder
- 1/2 teaspoon dried thyme (optional)

For the Broccoli:

- 2 cups broccoli florets
- 1 tablespoon olive oil
- Salt and pepper to taste

Instructions:

1. Start by preheating your air fryer to 375°F (190°C) for a few minutes.
2. In a bowl, combine the olive oil, lemon juice, lemon zest, black pepper, salt, garlic powder, onion powder, and dried thyme (if using) to create a marinade for the chicken.
3. Place the chicken breasts in a resealable plastic bag or a shallow dish and pour the marinade over them. Seal the bag or cover the dish and let the chicken marinate for at least 15-20 minutes to soak up the flavors.
4. While the chicken is marinating, toss the broccoli florets with a tablespoon of olive oil and season with a pinch of salt and pepper.

5. Once the chicken has marinated, remove it from the bag or dish and place it in the air fryer basket. Cook the chicken at 375°F (190°C) for about 15-20 minutes or until the internal temperature reaches 165°F (74°C). The exact cooking time may vary depending on the thickness of your chicken breasts, so you may need to adjust it accordingly.
6. About 5 minutes before the chicken is done, add the seasoned broccoli to the air fryer basket. You can use a separate tray or basket for the broccoli if your air fryer has one. Cook the broccoli for 5-8 minutes or until it's tender and slightly crispy.
7. Once everything is cooked, remove the chicken and broccoli from the air fryer.
8. Slice the chicken into strips or cubes and serve it alongside the lemony air-fried broccoli.

Recipe Notes:

- You can adjust the seasoning and lemon flavor to your liking. If you prefer more or less lemon, adjust the lemon juice and zest accordingly.
- If your air fryer has different temperature and time settings, you may need to experiment a bit to find the perfect cooking time for your specific model. Cooking times can vary depending on the air fryer's size and wattage.
- You can add a sprinkle of grated Parmesan cheese or a drizzle of balsamic glaze for extra flavor.
- Make sure to monitor the cooking process to prevent overcooking, especially the chicken, as it can become dry if cooked for too long.

Enjoy your homemade Lemon Pepper Air Fryer Chicken and Broccoli!

Certainly! Here are some additional tips and variations for your Lemon Pepper Air Fryer Chicken and Broccoli recipe:

1. Crispy Coating: If you want a crispy coating on your chicken, you can coat the marinated chicken in breadcrumbs or panko before placing it in the air fryer. This will give your chicken a crunchy texture.

2. Seasoning Variations: Experiment with different seasonings to change up the flavor. For example, you can use Cajun seasoning for a spicy twist or Italian seasoning for a Mediterranean flavor.

3. Preheating: Preheating your air fryer is essential to ensure even cooking. Allow it to preheat for a few minutes before adding the chicken and broccoli.

4. Basket Shaking: Depending on your air fryer model, you may need to shake the basket or flip the chicken halfway through the cooking time to ensure even browning.

5. Serving Suggestions: You can serve your Lemon Pepper Air Fryer Chicken and Broccoli over cooked rice, quinoa, or pasta for a complete meal. A drizzle of lemon butter sauce can also add extra richness to the dish.

6. Vegetarian Option: For a vegetarian version, you can skip the chicken and make lemon pepper air-fried broccoli as a side dish.

7. Cooking Time for Broccoli: The cooking time for broccoli can vary depending on how crisp you like it. If you prefer it more tender, you can cook it for a bit longer.

8. Lemon Garnish: Consider adding some fresh lemon slices or wedges as a garnish for an extra burst of citrus flavor.

9. Meal Prep: This dish is suitable for meal prep. You can marinate the chicken in advance and store it in the fridge until you're ready to cook. Just remember to add the broccoli when you're ready to air fry.

10. Sides: To complement your meal, consider serving it with a fresh salad, garlic bread, or a simple sauce like tzatziki or hummus.

Feel free to customize this recipe to your taste and dietary preferences. It's a versatile and relatively quick meal to prepare in the air fryer, making it a great option for busy weeknight dinners. Enjoy your Lemon Pepper Air Fryer Chicken and Broccoli!

Air Fryer Burgers (Turkey or Beef)

Air fryer burgers are a quick and easy way to make delicious, juicy burgers without the need for a grill or stovetop pan. You can use either turkey or beef to make these burgers, and they will turn out great in the air fryer. Here's a simple recipe and some notes to help you make air fryer burgers:

Ingredients:

- 1 pound ground turkey or beef
- 1/2 teaspoon salt (adjust to taste)
- 1/4 teaspoon black pepper (adjust to taste)
- 1/2 teaspoon garlic powder (optional)
- 1/2 teaspoon onion powder (optional)
- 4 hamburger buns
- Your choice of burger toppings (lettuce, tomato, onion, cheese, ketchup, mayo, etc.)

Instructions:

1. **Preheat your air fryer:** Preheat your air fryer to 375°F (190°C) for a few minutes. This step is essential to ensure even cooking.
2. **Prepare the burger patties:** In a mixing bowl, combine the ground meat with salt, black pepper, and any optional seasonings (garlic powder and onion powder). Mix the

ingredients gently, taking care not to overwork the meat, as this can make the burgers tough. Form the mixture into 4 equally sized burger patties.

3. **Place the patties in the air fryer:** Carefully place the burger patties in the preheated air fryer basket. Make sure there's some space between them to allow for proper air circulation.

4. **Air fry the burgers:** Cook the burgers in the air fryer at 375°F (190°C) for about 12-15 minutes, flipping them halfway through the cooking time. Cooking times may vary depending on the thickness of the patties and the specific model of your air fryer. It's essential to cook them until they reach your desired level of doneness (medium-rare, medium, medium-well, or well-done). Use an instant-read meat thermometer to check the internal temperature. For medium-rare, aim for about 135°F (57°C), and then add a few degrees for each level of doneness.

5. **Toast the buns:** While the burgers are cooking, you can lightly toast the burger buns in the air fryer for a minute or two, or you can use a toaster or stovetop pan.

6. **Assemble the burgers:** Once the burgers are cooked to your liking, assemble them with your choice of toppings on the toasted buns. Serve hot.

Notes:

1. Don't overcrowd the air fryer basket. It's important to leave some space between the burger patties to allow air circulation and even cooking.

2. You can customize the seasoning to your liking. Feel free to add herbs, spices, or condiments of your choice to the ground meat mixture.

3. Use a meat thermometer to ensure your burgers reach the desired level of doneness to avoid overcooking or undercooking.

4. Keep an eye on the burgers as they cook. Cooking times can vary depending on the specific air fryer model and the thickness of the patties.

5. Be creative with your burger toppings. Add lettuce, tomato, onion, cheese, and any other condiments you enjoy.

Air fryer burgers are a convenient and healthy way to enjoy a classic meal. Experiment with different seasonings and toppings to make the perfect burger to suit your taste.

Certainly, here are some additional tips and ideas to make your air fryer burgers even more delicious and unique:

1. Seasoning Ideas:

- Mix in finely chopped herbs like parsley, cilantro, or chives for added flavor.
- Experiment with different spices such as paprika, cumin, or smoked paprika to give your burgers a unique twist.
- For a spicy kick, add some crushed red pepper flakes or a dash of hot sauce to the meat mixture.

2. Stuff Your Burgers:

- Consider making stuffed burgers by placing cheese, sautéed mushrooms, or caramelized onions inside the meat mixture before forming the patties.

3. Basting with Sauce:

- Brush your burgers with a flavorful sauce (like barbecue sauce, teriyaki, or Buffalo sauce) during the last few minutes of cooking to infuse them with extra flavor.

4. Customized Burger Blends:

- Combine different types of ground meat for a unique flavor. For instance, you can mix beef with ground pork, ground lamb, or even ground chicken.

5. Preheat the Air Fryer Basket:

- Preheating your air fryer basket not only ensures even cooking but also helps prevent the burgers from sticking to the basket.

6. Use Parchment Paper:

- Consider using parchment paper to line the air fryer basket for easier cleanup and to prevent the burgers from sticking.

7. Adjust Cooking Time:

- The cooking time will vary depending on the thickness and size of your burger patties. Smaller patties will cook faster, so adjust the cooking time accordingly.

8. Rest the Burgers:

- Allow the cooked burgers to rest for a few minutes before assembling your burger. This helps the juices redistribute and results in juicier burgers.

9. Get Creative with Toppings:

- Beyond the classic lettuce, tomato, and onion, you can add avocado, fried eggs, pickles, coleslaw, or even pineapple slices to your burgers.

10. Serve with Sides:

- Complete your meal with sides like sweet potato fries, coleslaw, potato salad, or a simple garden salad.

11. Don't Overdo It:

- Remember that air fryers work by circulating hot air, so there's no need to add too much oil or fat. A light spray of cooking oil on the burger patties can help them brown nicely.

Experiment with different combinations of seasonings, fillings, and toppings to create your signature air fryer burgers. Whether you prefer a classic cheeseburger or something more gourmet, the air fryer can help you achieve fantastic results in a short amount of time.

Crispy Air Fryer Chicken Taquitos

Crispy Air Fryer Chicken Taquitos are a delicious and easy-to-make snack or appetizer. They're filled with seasoned shredded chicken, cheese, and rolled in tortillas, then air-fried until golden and crispy. Here's a recipe for you:

Ingredients:

- 2 cups cooked and shredded chicken (rotisserie or boiled)
- 1 cup shredded cheddar cheese (or your choice of cheese)
- 1/2 cup cream cheese, softened
- 1/4 cup sour cream
- 1/4 cup diced green onions
- 2 cloves garlic, minced
- 1 teaspoon chili powder
- 1/2 teaspoon cumin
- 1/2 teaspoon paprika
- 1/4 teaspoon cayenne pepper (adjust to your spice preference)
- Salt and pepper to taste
- 10-12 small flour tortillas
- Cooking spray or oil for the air fryer

Instructions:

1. **Prepare the Filling:**
   - In a mixing bowl, combine the shredded chicken, shredded cheddar cheese, softened cream cheese, sour cream, diced green onions, minced garlic, and the spices (chili powder, cumin, paprika, cayenne pepper, salt, and pepper). Mix until everything is well combined.
2. **Fill the Tortillas:**
   - Place a tortilla on a clean surface.
   - Spoon a generous amount of the chicken mixture onto the center of the tortilla.
   - Roll up the tortilla tightly, making sure to tuck in the sides to encase the filling. Secure the taquito with a toothpick if needed.
   - Repeat the process with the remaining tortillas and filling.
3. **Preheat the Air Fryer:**
   - Preheat your air fryer to 375°F (190°C).
4. **Air Fry the Taquitos:**

- Lightly grease the air fryer basket with cooking spray or oil to prevent sticking.
- Place the taquitos in the air fryer basket, making sure they are not touching each other.
- Cook for about 8-10 minutes or until the taquitos are golden brown and crispy. You may need to flip them halfway through to ensure even cooking.

5. **Serve:**
   - Remove the crispy taquitos from the air fryer and let them cool for a minute or two before serving.
   - Serve with your favorite dipping sauces, such as salsa, guacamole, sour cream, or ranch dressing.

Notes:

- Feel free to customize the filling with your favorite ingredients. You can add diced bell peppers, jalapeños, or black beans for extra flavor and texture.
- Make sure to tightly roll the taquitos to prevent the filling from spilling out during air frying.
- Cooking times may vary slightly depending on the size and brand of your air fryer. Keep an eye on the taquitos to avoid overcooking or undercooking.
- You can make a large batch of taquitos and freeze them before air frying. Just place them in a single layer on a baking sheet, freeze until firm, and then transfer to a freezer-safe bag or container. When you're ready to enjoy them, you can cook them from frozen in the air fryer, but you may need to add a couple of extra minutes to the cooking time.

These crispy air fryer chicken taquitos make for a great snack, party appetizer, or even a quick and easy weeknight dinner. Enjoy!

Certainly! Here are some additional tips and variations for making crispy air fryer chicken taquitos:

Tips:

1. **Tortilla Variations:** You can use corn tortillas or flour tortillas, depending on your preference. Corn tortillas tend to have a slightly different texture when air-fried, but they can still be delicious.
2. **Prevent Stickiness:** To prevent the taquitos from sticking to the air fryer basket, you can place a piece of parchment paper or aluminum foil at the bottom of the basket. Make sure to poke a few holes in it to allow air circulation.
3. **Dipping Sauces:** These taquitos pair well with a variety of dipping sauces. Consider options like queso dip, chipotle mayo, or a homemade salsa for added flavor.
4. **Spice Level:** Adjust the amount of cayenne pepper to control the spiciness of the filling. If you prefer milder taquitos, you can omit it altogether.

Variations:

1. **Vegetarian Taquitos:** If you're looking for a meatless option, you can substitute the chicken with sautéed vegetables like bell peppers, onions, and mushrooms. Add some black beans or refried beans for extra protein.
2. **Tex-Mex Flavors:** Experiment with Tex-Mex seasonings like taco seasoning or fajita seasoning for a different flavor profile.
3. **Breakfast Taquitos:** Try making breakfast taquitos by filling them with scrambled eggs, cheese, and crumbled breakfast sausage. Serve with salsa or hot sauce for an extra kick.
4. **Dessert Taquitos:** Sweet taquitos can be made by filling the tortillas with a mixture of cream cheese, sugar, and cinnamon, along with fruit like sliced bananas or strawberries. After air frying, dust them with powdered sugar for a delicious dessert.
5. **Healthier Options:** For a healthier version, use whole wheat or low-carb tortillas, and consider using leaner proteins like grilled chicken breast or turkey. You can also reduce the amount of cheese and opt for low-fat cream cheese and Greek yogurt instead of sour cream.
6. **Gluten-Free:** If you need a gluten-free version, use gluten-free tortillas and ensure that your seasonings and ingredients are gluten-free as well.

Experiment with these ideas and tailor your air fryer chicken taquitos to your liking. They're versatile and can be adapted to suit different dietary preferences and occasions. Enjoy your crispy, flavorful taquitos!

Herb Crusted Air Fryer Pork Tenderloin

Herb-Crusted Air Fryer Pork Tenderloin is a delicious and relatively quick dish to prepare. The air fryer gives it a nice crispy exterior while keeping the inside tender and juicy. Here's a recipe and some notes to help you make it:

Ingredients:

- 1 pork tenderloin (about 1 to 1.5 pounds)
- 2 tablespoons olive oil
- 2 cloves garlic, minced
- 1 teaspoon dried rosemary (or 1 tablespoon fresh, finely chopped)
- 1 teaspoon dried thyme (or 1 tablespoon fresh, finely chopped)
- 1 teaspoon dried sage (or 1 tablespoon fresh, finely chopped)
- 1/2 teaspoon salt
- 1/4 teaspoon black pepper
- 1/2 cup breadcrumbs (Panko or regular)
- Cooking spray (for the air fryer basket)

Instructions:

1. **Prepare the Pork Tenderloin:**
   - Preheat your air fryer to 375°F (190°C).
   - Trim the silver skin and excess fat from the pork tenderloin if needed. Pat it dry with paper towels.
2. **Create the Herb Crust:**
   - In a small bowl, mix together the olive oil, minced garlic, rosemary, thyme, sage, salt, and black pepper. This will be the herb crust for your pork.
3. **Coat the Pork Tenderloin:**
   - Rub the herb mixture all over the pork tenderloin, ensuring it's evenly coated.
4. **Coat with Breadcrumbs:**
   - Spread the breadcrumbs on a plate. Roll the coated pork tenderloin in the breadcrumbs, pressing them onto the surface to create a nice crust.
5. **Air Fry the Pork:**
   - Lightly grease the air fryer basket with cooking spray to prevent sticking.
   - Place the pork tenderloin in the air fryer basket.
   - Air fry at 375°F (190°C) for 20-25 minutes, turning the tenderloin halfway through the cooking time, until the internal temperature reaches 145°F (63°C). The exact time may vary depending on your air fryer, so use a meat thermometer to be sure.
6. **Rest and Slice:**
   - Remove the pork from the air fryer and let it rest for a few minutes before slicing. This will help the juices redistribute for a more tender result.
7. **Serve:**
   - Slice the pork tenderloin into medallions and serve. It goes well with a variety of side dishes like roasted vegetables, mashed potatoes, or a simple salad.

Recipe Notes:

- Make sure to preheat your air fryer to ensure even cooking.
- You can customize the herbs and seasonings to your preference. Try using fresh herbs for a more intense flavor.
- If your air fryer has a larger capacity, you can cook two pork tenderloins at once, just make sure they're not overcrowded in the basket.
- Using a meat thermometer is crucial to ensure your pork is cooked to the right temperature without overcooking.

This Herb-Crusted Air Fryer Pork Tenderloin is a fantastic and healthy dish that's perfect for a quick weeknight dinner or a special occasion. Enjoy!

Certainly! Here are some additional tips and ideas to enhance your Herb-Crusted Air Fryer Pork Tenderloin experience:

1. Marinade: Marinating the pork tenderloin for a few hours or even overnight before applying the herb crust can add extra flavor. A simple marinade with olive oil, garlic, and some of the same herbs you'll use in the crust can do wonders.

2. Pork Seasoning Variations: Experiment with different herb combinations and seasonings. For example, you can try using fresh or dried oregano, basil, or even a touch of smoked paprika for a unique flavor profile.

3. Sauce or Gravy: Serve the pork tenderloin with a delicious sauce or gravy. A classic option is a pan sauce made from the drippings in the air fryer basket, along with some chicken broth and a splash of white wine or vinegar.

4. Sides: Pair your pork tenderloin with a variety of sides such as roasted vegetables, mashed potatoes, couscous, or a fresh garden salad. These side dishes can complement the flavors of the pork.

5. Temperature and Doneness: The recommended safe internal temperature for pork tenderloin is 145°F (63°C). However, you can cook it to your preferred level of doneness. Cooking it to 135-140°F (57-60°C) will result in a slightly pink and more tender interior, while going closer to 150°F (65°C) will be well-done.

6. Resting Time: Allowing the pork to rest for 5-10 minutes after cooking is essential. This helps the juices redistribute and keeps the meat moist.

7. Breadcrumb Variations: Instead of regular breadcrumbs, try using panko breadcrumbs for an even crispier crust. You can also mix the breadcrumbs with grated Parmesan cheese for added flavor.

8. Cooking Time Adjustments: The air fryer cooking time may vary depending on the thickness of the pork tenderloin and your specific air fryer model. It's crucial to use a meat thermometer to ensure it's cooked to your desired level of doneness.

9. Leftovers: If you have any leftovers, you can use the sliced pork tenderloin for sandwiches, wraps, or salads the next day. It's versatile and delicious in various dishes.

Feel free to get creative with your Herb-Crusted Air Fryer Pork Tenderloin and adapt it to your taste preferences. Enjoy your cooking adventure!

Air Fryer Grilled Cheese (SO crispy!)

Air fryer grilled cheese is a delightful twist on the classic grilled cheese sandwich. It offers a crispy and crunchy exterior with gooey, melted cheese on the inside. Here's a simple recipe and some notes to help you make the perfect air fryer grilled cheese:

Ingredients:

- 2 slices of your favorite bread

- 2-4 slices of your preferred cheese (e.g., cheddar, Swiss, American)
- Butter or margarine, softened
- Optional: condiments (mayonnaise, mustard, or ketchup)

Instructions:

1. **Preheat the Air Fryer:** Preheat your air fryer to 350°F (180°C). This will ensure even cooking and a crispy result.
2. **Butter the Bread:** Spread a thin layer of softened butter or margarine on one side of each slice of bread. You can also use mayonnaise for a different flavor and extra crispiness.
3. **Add Condiments (Optional):** If you like, spread condiments like mustard or mayonnaise on the unbuttered side of the bread slices.
4. **Assemble the Sandwich:** Place the cheese slices between the slices of bread with the buttered sides facing out. This will help create a golden, crispy exterior.
5. **Air Fry the Grilled Cheese:** Carefully place the assembled sandwich in the preheated air fryer basket. Cook for about 6-8 minutes at 350°F (180°C), flipping the sandwich halfway through. Cooking times may vary depending on your air fryer model, so keep an eye on it. The sandwich is ready when it's golden brown and the cheese is melted to your liking.
6. **Serve:** Remove the air-fried grilled cheese from the air fryer and let it cool for a minute before cutting it in half. The cheese will be hot and gooey, so exercise caution. Enjoy!

Recipe Notes:

1. **Butter vs. Mayonnaise:** Using mayonnaise on the outer sides of the bread can create an exceptionally crispy and golden crust, but butter works just as well and adds a classic flavor.
2. **Condiments:** Feel free to experiment with your favorite condiments, including ketchup, sriracha, or pesto, for added flavor.
3. **Cheese Selection:** Mix and match your favorite cheese varieties for a more complex flavor. A combination of cheddar and mozzarella or Swiss and provolone can be delicious.
4. **Bread Choice:** Opt for your preferred bread, whether it's white, whole wheat, sourdough, or any other type. Thicker slices will result in a heartier sandwich.
5. **Don't Overcrowd:** Make sure there's enough space around the sandwich in the air fryer basket for proper air circulation. If you're making multiple sandwiches, cook them in batches.
6. **Flipping:** Flipping the sandwich halfway through the cooking time ensures even crispiness on both sides.
7. **Adjust Cooking Time:** The cooking time may vary depending on your specific air fryer, so it's best to check the sandwich's progress to prevent burning.

Air fryer grilled cheese is a quick and convenient way to make this classic comfort food. You'll love the crispy exterior and gooey interior of this delicious sandwich!

Certainly! Here are some additional tips and variations to consider when making air fryer grilled cheese:

Tips:

8. **Preheat for Even Cooking:** Preheating your air fryer is essential. It helps ensure that your grilled cheese cooks evenly and gets that crispy texture you desire.
9. **Avoid Soggy Sandwiches:** To prevent your sandwich from becoming soggy, you can layer your cheese between slices of other ingredients like deli meats, vegetables, or even bacon. Just make sure everything is cooked or heated through before assembling the sandwich.
10. **Custom Seasonings:** Add extra flavor by sprinkling your favorite seasonings on the buttered sides of the bread. Herbs like rosemary, thyme, or garlic powder can enhance the taste.
11. **Use Parchment Paper:** Placing a small piece of parchment paper underneath your sandwich can make it easier to remove from the air fryer and prevent any cheese or butter from sticking to the basket.
12. **Temperature and Time Adjustments:** Air fryer models can vary, so you might need to experiment with the temperature and cooking time. You can adjust the temperature higher for a quicker, crispier result or lower for a softer sandwich.

Variations:

13. **Add Bacon:** Crispy bacon can be a fantastic addition to your grilled cheese. Cook the bacon separately in the air fryer or stovetop until it's crispy, then add it to your sandwich.
14. **Tomato and Basil:** Add a slice of ripe tomato and some fresh basil leaves for a caprese-style grilled cheese. This is a delicious twist with an Italian flair.
15. **Sweet and Savory:** For a sweet and savory combination, spread some fig jam or apple butter on the bread before assembling your sandwich. This pairs wonderfully with a mild cheese like brie.
16. **Spicy Kick:** If you like it spicy, consider adding sliced jalapeños, hot sauce, or a sprinkle of red pepper flakes to your grilled cheese.
17. **Gourmet Grilled Cheese:** Elevate your grilled cheese by using artisanal bread and high-quality cheeses like Gruyère, Gouda, or goat cheese. You can also experiment with ingredients like caramelized onions, arugula, or truffle oil.
18. **Dipping Sauces:** Serve your air fryer grilled cheese with dipping sauces like tomato soup, marinara, or ranch dressing for an extra layer of flavor.
19. **Mini Grilled Cheese:** Make bite-sized grilled cheese by cutting your sandwich into smaller pieces or using slider-sized buns. These are great for parties and appetizers.

Air fryer grilled cheese is highly versatile, allowing you to get creative with flavors and ingredients. You can adapt the recipe to your preferences and explore a wide range of delicious combinations. Enjoy your crispy, gooey, and flavorful creations!

Crispy Air Fryer Falafels

Crispy Air Fryer Falafels are a healthier alternative to traditional deep-fried falafels. They're packed with flavor and have a delightful crunch while being lower in oil and calories. Here's a recipe and some notes to help you make delicious falafels in your air fryer:

Ingredients:

- 1 1/2 cups dried chickpeas (or 2 cans of chickpeas, drained and rinsed)
- 1/2 large onion, roughly chopped
- 2-3 cloves of garlic
- 2 tablespoons fresh parsley, chopped
- 2 tablespoons fresh cilantro, chopped
- 1 teaspoon cumin
- 1 teaspoon coriander
- 1/4 teaspoon cayenne pepper (adjust to taste)
- 1 teaspoon salt, or to taste
- 1/2-1 teaspoon baking powder
- 4-5 tablespoons all-purpose flour or chickpea flour (for binding)

Instructions:

1. **Prepare Chickpeas:** If using dried chickpeas, soak them in water for at least 12 hours or overnight. Drain them before using. Canned chickpeas should be rinsed and drained.
2. **Mix Ingredients:** In a food processor, combine the chickpeas, onion, garlic, parsley, cilantro, cumin, coriander, cayenne, and salt. Blend until the mixture is finely chopped but not pureed. You may need to scrape down the sides of the bowl during processing.
3. **Check Consistency:** The mixture should be coarse and not too wet. If it's too wet, your falafels may not hold their shape. Add the baking powder and 4 tablespoons of flour and pulse to combine. Check the consistency again. If it's still too wet, add more flour, one tablespoon at a time, until the mixture is easy to shape into patties.
4. **Shape Falafels:** Form the mixture into small, golf ball-sized patties, using your hands. You can make them as big or as small as you like. Place them on a baking sheet lined with parchment paper.
5. **Air Fry:** Preheat your air fryer to 370°F (190°C). Lightly brush or spray the falafels with oil to help them crisp up. Place them in the air fryer basket in a single layer, leaving some space between them.
6. **Cook:** Air fry the falafels for 12-15 minutes, or until they are golden brown and crispy. You may need to flip them halfway through the cooking time to ensure even browning.
7. **Serve:** Serve your crispy air fryer falafels with pita bread, hummus, tahini sauce, fresh vegetables, and your favorite toppings like tomatoes, cucumbers, and lettuce.

Notes:

- You can use either dried chickpeas or canned chickpeas. If using canned, make sure to rinse and drain them thoroughly before using.
- If the falafel mixture is too wet and doesn't hold together, add more flour, a tablespoon at a time, until it reaches the right consistency.
- To make the falafels even crispier, you can lightly spray or brush them with oil before air frying.
- The cooking time may vary depending on your air fryer model, so keep an eye on them and adjust the time if needed.
- Feel free to customize your falafels with additional spices or herbs according to your taste. You can also make them spicy by adding more cayenne pepper or red pepper flakes.
- These falafels can be frozen before or after air frying. Just thaw and reheat them in the air fryer when you're ready to enjoy them.

Certainly, here are some additional tips and variations for making crispy air fryer falafels:

Tips:

1. **Use Dry Chickpeas:** If possible, use dried chickpeas instead of canned for the best texture. Soak them for at least 12 hours, and they should swell up to twice their size.
2. **Don't Overprocess:** Be cautious not to overprocess the falafel mixture. You want it to be finely chopped but not a puree. A little texture is good for the final result.
3. **Chill the Mixture:** After shaping the falafel patties, refrigerate them for 15-30 minutes. Chilled falafels hold their shape better during cooking.
4. **Grease the Basket:** Even though air frying uses less oil, it's a good idea to lightly grease the air fryer basket or tray to prevent sticking.
5. **Temperature and Time:** Cooking time and temperature can vary between air fryer models. Start with the recommended temperature and time, but be prepared to adjust as needed. You may need to experiment a bit to find the perfect settings for your specific air fryer.

Variations:

1. **Baked Falafels:** If you don't have an air fryer, you can also bake the falafels in a preheated oven at 375°F (190°C) for about 25-30 minutes or until they're crispy and golden brown.
2. **Gluten-Free Falafels:** Use chickpea flour or a gluten-free flour blend instead of regular all-purpose flour to make the falafels gluten-free.
3. **Herb Variations:** You can customize the falafel flavor by adding fresh herbs like mint, dill, or basil to the mixture. These herbs can impart a unique and refreshing taste.
4. **Vegan Falafels:** This recipe is already vegan, but if you want a more egg-free version, you can replace the baking powder with a flax or chia seed egg (1 tablespoon ground flax or chia seeds mixed with 3 tablespoons water).
5. **Spicy Falafels:** Increase the amount of cayenne pepper, or add chopped jalapeños or red pepper flakes for an extra kick.

6. **Nutty Twist:** Add a handful of chopped nuts like walnuts or almonds to the mixture for a nutty crunch.
7. **Grainy Falafels:** Mix in cooked quinoa, bulgur, or farro for added texture and flavor.
8. **Sweet Potato Falafels:** For a unique twist, replace a portion of the chickpeas with mashed sweet potatoes. This will add a hint of sweetness and extra creaminess to the falafels.

Experiment with these variations to create falafels that suit your taste preferences. Crispy air fryer falafels make a versatile and satisfying meal, whether in a pita sandwich, on a salad, or as a delicious appetizer with your favorite dipping sauce.

Air Fryer Cauliflower Chickpea Tacos

Air Fryer Cauliflower Chickpea Tacos are a delicious and healthy alternative to traditional meat tacos. They are perfect for vegetarians and vegans, and they're packed with flavor and texture. Here's a recipe along with some notes to make these tacos:

Ingredients:

For the Cauliflower Chickpea Filling:

- 1 small head of cauliflower, cut into small florets
- 1 can of chickpeas (15 oz), drained and rinsed
- 2 tablespoons olive oil
- 1 teaspoon chili powder
- 1/2 teaspoon cumin
- 1/2 teaspoon smoked paprika
- 1/2 teaspoon garlic powder
- Salt and pepper to taste

For the Air Fryer Tacos:

- 8 small taco-sized tortillas (corn or flour)
- 1 cup shredded red cabbage
- 1 cup diced tomatoes
- 1/2 cup diced red onion
- 1/2 cup chopped fresh cilantro
- 1 cup vegan sour cream or your favorite taco sauce
- Lime wedges for serving

Instructions:

1. Preheat your air fryer to 375°F (190°C).

2. In a large mixing bowl, combine the cauliflower florets and chickpeas.
3. Drizzle olive oil over the cauliflower and chickpeas. Sprinkle with chili powder, cumin, smoked paprika, garlic powder, salt, and pepper. Toss everything to coat evenly with the spices and oil.
4. Place the seasoned cauliflower and chickpea mixture in the air fryer basket in a single layer, making sure not to overcrowd. You may need to cook them in batches depending on the size of your air fryer.
5. Cook the cauliflower and chickpea mixture in the air fryer for 15-20 minutes, shaking the basket or tossing the mixture with a spatula halfway through, until the cauliflower is tender and browned.
6. While the filling is cooking, warm the tortillas in a dry skillet or microwave them for a few seconds until they are pliable.
7. Assemble your tacos: Place a generous spoonful of the cauliflower chickpea filling in each tortilla. Top with shredded red cabbage, diced tomatoes, red onions, and fresh cilantro.
8. Drizzle with vegan sour cream or your favorite taco sauce.
9. Serve your air fryer cauliflower chickpea tacos with lime wedges on the side for extra flavor.

Notes:

- You can customize your tacos with additional toppings like avocado slices, shredded vegan cheese, or hot sauce, according to your preferences.
- If you don't have an air fryer, you can roast the cauliflower and chickpea mixture in a preheated oven at 425°F (220°C) for about 25-30 minutes, tossing them once or twice during cooking until they're tender and crispy.
- Make sure not to overcrowd the air fryer basket. If it's too full, the cauliflower and chickpeas won't cook evenly, and you won't get that crispy texture.
- Adjust the seasonings to your taste. If you like your tacos spicier, you can add more chili powder or hot sauce.

Enjoy your delicious and nutritious Air Fryer Cauliflower Chickpea Tacos!

Certainly! Here are some additional tips and ideas to enhance your Air Fryer Cauliflower Chickpea Tacos:

1. **Sauce Variations:** Experiment with different sauces to drizzle on your tacos. Try a tangy vegan tahini sauce, a smoky chipotle aioli, or a classic salsa verde for added flavor.
2. **Add Guacamole:** A dollop of homemade guacamole or sliced avocado can bring a creamy and healthy element to your tacos. The richness of avocado pairs wonderfully with the roasted cauliflower and chickpeas.
3. **Pickled Red Onions:** For an extra burst of flavor, make quick-pickled red onions. Simply soak thinly sliced red onions in a mixture of vinegar, sugar, and salt for about 15-20 minutes. Drain and use them as a zesty topping.

4. **Spice It Up:** If you like it spicy, add some sliced jalapeños or a dash of hot sauce to your tacos. You can also increase the amount of chili powder or cayenne pepper in the seasoning mix for an extra kick.
5. **Cheese Options:** If you're not vegan, consider adding shredded cheese to your tacos. Options like crumbled queso fresco or shredded cheddar can be delicious complements to the roasted cauliflower and chickpeas.
6. **Grilled Tortillas:** Give your tortillas a smoky flavor by lightly grilling them on a stovetop grill or in a skillet. It adds a nice char and enhances the overall taste of the tacos.
7. **Serve with Lime Wedges:** Don't forget the lime wedges! Squeezing fresh lime juice over your tacos just before eating adds a bright, citrusy contrast to the earthy flavors of the cauliflower and chickpeas.
8. **Serving Suggestion:** Accompany your tacos with a side of Mexican rice, black beans, or a fresh salad for a complete and satisfying meal.
9. **Leftovers:** If you have leftover cauliflower chickpea filling, it can be used in various ways. Try it in a burrito, on a salad, or as a topping for a loaded baked potato.
10. **Taco Bar:** Set up a taco bar with a variety of toppings and sauces, allowing your family or guests to build their tacos according to their preferences.

Remember, tacos are highly customizable, so feel free to get creative and adjust the recipe to suit your tastes. Enjoy your Air Fryer Cauliflower Chickpea Tacos!

Crispy Seasoned Air Fryer Tofu

Crispy seasoned air fryer tofu is a delicious and healthy alternative to deep-fried tofu. It's easy to make and can be used in a variety of dishes as a protein source or as a crunchy snack. Here's a basic recipe and some notes to help you make the most of your air-fried tofu:

Ingredients:

- 1 block of extra-firm tofu
- 2-3 tablespoons of your favorite seasoning (e.g., paprika, garlic powder, onion powder, cayenne pepper, or a premade seasoning blend)
- 1-2 tablespoons of olive oil or cooking spray (for added crispiness)
- Salt and pepper to taste

Instructions:

1. **Prepare the Tofu:**
   - Start by pressing the tofu to remove excess moisture. Place the block of tofu on a plate and cover it with another plate. Put something heavy on top, like a can or a cast-iron skillet, to help press the water out. Press it for at least 15-30 minutes, but longer if possible. You can even press it in the refrigerator for a few hours for the best results.

2. **Cut the Tofu:**
   - Once the tofu is pressed, cut it into small cubes or strips of your desired size. Thinner pieces will become crispier in the air fryer.
3. **Season the Tofu:**
   - In a mixing bowl, toss the tofu with your choice of seasoning, salt, and pepper. You can use a pre-made spice blend or create your own combination.
4. **Preheat the Air Fryer:**
   - Preheat your air fryer to 375-400°F (190-200°C) for a few minutes.
5. **Air Fry the Tofu:**
   - Lightly grease the air fryer basket or tray with a small amount of oil or cooking spray to prevent sticking. Place the seasoned tofu cubes or strips in a single layer in the air fryer. Avoid overcrowding the basket, as this can affect the crispiness.
6. **Cook the Tofu:**
   - Air fry the tofu for about 15-20 minutes, flipping or shaking the basket every 5-10 minutes to ensure even cooking. Cooking times may vary depending on your specific air fryer and the thickness of the tofu, so keep an eye on it.
7. **Check for Crispiness:**
   - The tofu is ready when it's golden brown and crispy on the outside. If you want it even crispier, you can cook it for a few more minutes.
8. **Serve:**
   - Serve your crispy air fryer tofu as a snack, in salads, as a topping for rice or noodles, or in any dish you like.

Notes:

- Extra-firm tofu works best for this recipe because it holds its shape and gets crispy.
- Pressing the tofu is crucial to remove excess moisture and allow it to crisp up better in the air fryer.
- Don't skip the step of lightly greasing the air fryer basket to prevent sticking, even if you use a non-stick air fryer.
- Experiment with different seasonings to create various flavor profiles, such as teriyaki, barbecue, or a simple salt and pepper seasoning.
- Use a food thermometer to ensure the tofu reaches an internal temperature of 165°F (74°C) for food safety.
- Leftover crispy tofu can be stored in the refrigerator and reheated in the air fryer or oven for a quick snack or meal addition.

Certainly, here are some additional tips and variations for making crispy seasoned air fryer tofu:

Additional Tips:

1. **Cornstarch Coating:** For an extra crispy exterior, you can toss the tofu cubes in cornstarch or arrowroot powder before air frying. This creates a light, crunchy coating.

2. **Marinating:** Marinating the tofu before air frying can infuse it with extra flavor. You can marinate it in a sauce of your choice for at least 30 minutes or overnight in the refrigerator.
3. **Cooking Time:** Keep an eye on the tofu while it's cooking. Cooking times can vary depending on the air fryer's make and model. Adjust the cooking time to achieve your desired level of crispiness.
4. **Flipping or Shaking:** Regularly flipping or shaking the tofu during cooking ensures that all sides get evenly crispy. If you have a larger air fryer, you might not need to do this as often.
5. **Oil Choices:** Instead of olive oil, you can use other high-heat cooking oils like canola, vegetable, or peanut oil. Alternatively, use cooking spray to keep the tofu lightly oiled.

Variations:

1. **Saucy Tofu:** After the tofu is crispy, you can toss it in your favorite sauce, such as barbecue, teriyaki, buffalo, or sweet chili, and then return it to the air fryer for a couple of minutes to caramelize the sauce.
2. **Tofu Nuggets:** Cut the tofu into small bite-sized nuggets for a fun and kid-friendly snack. Kids often love crispy tofu nuggets, and they're a great alternative to chicken nuggets.
3. **Asian-Inspired Tofu:** Season the tofu with a mix of soy sauce, ginger, garlic, and sesame oil for an Asian flair. You can also serve it with a side of stir-fried vegetables and rice.
4. **Spicy Tofu:** If you like heat, add some cayenne pepper, crushed red pepper flakes, or sriracha to your seasoning mix for a spicy kick.
5. **Sesame-Crusted Tofu:** Add a layer of sesame seeds to the tofu cubes for a unique flavor and added crunch.
6. **Herb-Crusted Tofu:** Mix dried herbs like rosemary, thyme, or basil into your seasoning for a savory, herbaceous flavor.
7. **Tofu Fries:** Cut the tofu into long, thin strips to make tofu fries, perfect for dipping in your favorite sauces.

Crispy seasoned air fryer tofu is a versatile and healthy addition to many dishes or as a snack on its own. Don't be afraid to get creative with your seasonings and flavor profiles to suit your tastes and complement the dishes you plan to prepare. Enjoy your crispy tofu!

Air Fryer Baked Potatoes

Air fryer baked potatoes are a delicious and easy-to-make side dish. They come out with a crispy skin and a fluffy interior, and you can customize them with your favorite toppings. Here's a basic recipe and some notes to help you make the perfect air fryer baked potatoes:

Ingredients:

- 4 medium-sized russet potatoes
- 1-2 tablespoons of olive oil
- Salt and pepper, to taste
- Toppings of your choice (sour cream, cheddar cheese, chives, bacon bits, etc.)

Instructions:

1. **Prep the Potatoes:**
   - Wash and scrub the potatoes thoroughly to remove any dirt.
   - Dry the potatoes with a paper towel.
   - Prick the potatoes with a fork or knife a few times to allow steam to escape while cooking.
2. **Coat with Oil:**
   - Lightly coat each potato with olive oil. You can use your hands or a brush to do this.
3. **Season:**
   - Season the potatoes with salt and pepper to taste. You can also add other seasonings like garlic powder, paprika, or rosemary for extra flavor.
4. **Preheat the Air Fryer:**
   - Preheat your air fryer to 400°F (200°C) for a few minutes.
5. **Air Fry:**
   - Place the seasoned potatoes in the air fryer basket or tray in a single layer. Don't overcrowd them; you may need to cook in batches if necessary.
   - Cook at 400°F (200°C) for 40-50 minutes, depending on the size of your potatoes. Flip the potatoes halfway through the cooking time to ensure even cooking. Check for doneness by inserting a fork or knife into the potato; it should slide in easily when they're done.
6. **Serve:**
   - Once the potatoes are cooked to your desired level of crispiness and tenderness, remove them from the air fryer.
7. **Toppings:**
   - Serve the air fryer baked potatoes with your favorite toppings, such as sour cream, cheddar cheese, chives, bacon bits, or any other toppings you like.

Notes:

1. **Potato Selection:** Choose russet potatoes for the best results as they have a high starch content and yield a fluffy interior. You can also use other varieties like Yukon Gold or red potatoes.
2. **Pricking the Potatoes:** Pricking the potatoes before cooking helps to prevent them from bursting open due to steam buildup.
3. **Seasoning:** Feel free to get creative with your seasonings. You can use various herbs and spices to suit your taste.

4. **Cooking Time:** Cooking time may vary depending on your air fryer model and the size of your potatoes. Adjust the cooking time accordingly. Smaller potatoes will cook faster, while larger ones may take longer.
5. **Overcrowding:** It's essential not to overcrowd the air fryer basket, as this can lead to uneven cooking. Make sure there's some space between the potatoes.
6. **Cleaning:** Clean your air fryer basket or tray after use to remove any oil and potato residue.

Air fryer baked potatoes are a quick and convenient side dish, perfect for serving with your favorite entrees. Enjoy customizing them with your preferred toppings for a delicious and satisfying meal.

Certainly! Here are some additional tips and variations to enhance your air fryer baked potatoes:

1. Potato Variations:

- Try sweet potatoes for a healthier alternative. Cooking times may vary, so keep an eye on them.
- You can also make baby potatoes or fingerling potatoes for a different presentation.

2. Cooking Time:

- The cooking time may vary depending on the wattage and model of your air fryer. Keep an eye on the potatoes to avoid overcooking or undercooking.

3. Crispy Skin:

- To achieve an extra crispy skin, rub the potatoes with a bit of cornstarch or potato starch before air frying.

4. Preheating:

- Preheating the air fryer is recommended for even cooking, but you can skip it if you're in a hurry. Just add a few extra minutes to the cooking time.

5. Flipping:

- Flipping the potatoes halfway through cooking ensures that they cook evenly on all sides.

6. Oil Alternatives:

- You can use cooking spray or a spray bottle to apply oil evenly. This reduces the amount of oil needed.

7. Seasoning Ideas:

- Besides salt and pepper, try adding herbs like rosemary, thyme, or oregano for a flavorful twist.
- A pinch of paprika or smoked paprika can add a subtle smoky flavor.
- Garlic powder or onion powder can enhance the flavor of your potatoes.

8. Serve with Dips:

- In addition to traditional toppings, serve your air fryer baked potatoes with dipping sauces like garlic aioli, ranch dressing, or a homemade chipotle mayo.

9. Leftover Potatoes:

- If you have leftover baked potatoes, you can slice them and make potato wedges or hash browns in the air fryer. They'll be crispy and delicious.

10. Size Matters: - Try to choose potatoes of roughly the same size, so they cook uniformly.

11. Air Fryer Accessories: - You can use accessories like an air fryer rack to cook multiple layers of potatoes simultaneously.

12. Safety: - Be cautious when handling the hot air fryer basket or tray. Use oven mitts or a kitchen towel to prevent burns.

13. Keep Warm Function: - If you're making a larger batch, you can use the air fryer's "Keep Warm" function to keep the first batch warm while you cook the rest.

Air fryer baked potatoes are a versatile and simple side dish that you can customize to suit your taste. Experiment with different seasonings and toppings to create your favorite version of this classic comfort food. Enjoy!

Crispy Spicy Air Fryer Okra

Crispy and spicy air-fried okra is a delightful and healthy snack or side dish that's easy to make in an air fryer. Here's a recipe and some notes to help you make it:

Ingredients:

- 1 pound fresh okra, washed, dried, and trimmed
- 2 tablespoons olive oil
- 1/2 cup cornmeal or corn flour
- 1/4 cup all-purpose flour
- 1 teaspoon paprika
- 1/2 teaspoon cayenne pepper (adjust to your spice preference)
- 1/2 teaspoon garlic powder

- 1/2 teaspoon onion powder
- 1/2 teaspoon salt (adjust to taste)
- 1/4 teaspoon black pepper
- Cooking spray (to prevent sticking)

Instructions:

1. Preheat your air fryer to 375°F (190°C) for a few minutes to ensure it's hot when you start cooking.
2. In a mixing bowl, combine the cornmeal, all-purpose flour, paprika, cayenne pepper, garlic powder, onion powder, salt, and black pepper. Mix well to create your spicy coating.
3. Place the trimmed and dried okra in a separate bowl, and drizzle the olive oil over it. Toss the okra to ensure it's evenly coated with the oil.
4. Take the oiled okra pieces and add them to the bowl with the spicy coating mixture. Toss the okra until they are well coated with the mixture. You may want to do this in batches to ensure even coating.
5. Lightly spray the air fryer basket with cooking spray to prevent sticking.
6. Arrange the coated okra pieces in a single layer in the air fryer basket, making sure they are not overcrowded. You may need to cook in batches, depending on the size of your air fryer.
7. Air fry the okra at 375°F (190°C) for 10-12 minutes, shaking the basket or turning the okra halfway through the cooking time. The cooking time may vary depending on the size and thickness of the okra, so keep an eye on them. They should be golden brown and crispy.
8. Once the okra is crispy and cooked to your liking, remove them from the air fryer and let them cool for a minute or two before serving.
9. Serve your crispy and spicy air-fried okra immediately with your favorite dipping sauce, such as ranch dressing or a spicy aioli.

Notes:

- The key to achieving crispiness in the air fryer is to ensure that the okra is coated evenly with the spicy mixture and that the air can circulate around the pieces. This is why it's important not to overcrowd the air fryer basket.
- Feel free to adjust the level of spiciness by increasing or decreasing the amount of cayenne pepper in the coating mixture.
- You can experiment with different seasonings and spices to customize the flavor to your liking. Some people like to add a touch of smoked paprika or even a little grated Parmesan cheese for extra flavor.
- Make sure the okra is as dry as possible before coating it with oil and the spicy mixture. Excess moisture can affect the crispiness.
- Enjoy your air-fried okra as a snack, side dish, or even as a topping for salads. It's a healthier alternative to deep-frying, and the air fryer makes it quick and easy to prepare.

Certainly! Here are some additional tips and variations for your crispy and spicy air-fried okra:

Tips:

1. **Prep and Dry Thoroughly:** It's crucial to thoroughly dry the okra before coating it with oil and spices. Excess moisture can prevent the okra from getting crispy.
2. **Uniform Size:** Try to cut the okra into uniform-sized pieces to ensure even cooking. If you have very large okra pods, consider slicing them in half lengthwise.
3. **Bread Crumbs:** Instead of cornmeal or corn flour, you can use panko bread crumbs for a different texture. Panko will give your okra an even crunchier coating.
4. **Gluten-Free Option:** If you're following a gluten-free diet, use gluten-free flour and cornmeal for the coating.
5. **Experiment with Spices:** Don't hesitate to experiment with other spices and seasonings to suit your taste. For example, you can add a pinch of cumin, smoked paprika, or your favorite seasoning blend.

Variations:

1. **Garlic Parmesan Okra:** Toss the air-fried okra in a mixture of grated Parmesan cheese and minced garlic immediately after cooking for a flavorful twist.
2. **Lemon Zest and Herb Okra:** After air-frying, sprinkle some fresh lemon zest and chopped herbs like parsley or dill over the okra for a refreshing and herby flavor.
3. **Sesame Soy Okra:** For an Asian-inspired twist, add a sprinkle of sesame seeds and a drizzle of soy sauce after air-frying. You can also add a touch of honey or a sweet chili sauce for extra depth of flavor.
4. **Buffalo-Style Okra:** Toss the air-fried okra in your favorite buffalo sauce for a spicy and tangy kick. Serve with a side of blue cheese or ranch dressing for dipping.
5. **Taco Seasoned Okra:** Use taco seasoning in place of the paprika and cayenne in the coating mixture for a Southwestern flavor. Serve with a side of salsa or guacamole.
6. **Ranch Okra:** Make a ranch seasoning mix with powdered buttermilk, dried herbs, and spices, and use it as your coating. Dip the cooked okra in ranch dressing for a classic flavor.
7. **Sweet and Spicy Okra:** Add a touch of brown sugar and some red pepper flakes to the coating mixture for a sweet and spicy combination.

Remember to adjust these variations to your personal preferences for spice level and flavor. Air-frying offers a lot of versatility, and you can get creative with your favorite seasonings and dipping sauces. Enjoy your crispy and spicy air-fried okra, and don't be afraid to experiment with different flavors!

Air Fryer Radishes

Air frying radishes is a creative and delicious way to enjoy this root vegetable. Radishes take on a whole new flavor and texture when air-fried, becoming crispy on the outside while retaining a tender interior. Here's a simple air fryer radishes recipe along with some notes to help you make the most of this unique dish:

Ingredients:

- 1 bunch of radishes (about 1 pound), washed and trimmed
- 1-2 tablespoons olive oil
- Salt and pepper to taste
- Optional seasonings: garlic powder, paprika, or your favorite herbs and spices

Instructions:

1. **Prep the Radishes:**
   - Wash the radishes thoroughly and trim off the tops and tails. If the radishes are large, you can slice them into quarters or halves for even cooking. Smaller radishes can be left whole.
2. **Coat with Olive Oil:**
   - Place the radishes in a mixing bowl and drizzle with 1-2 tablespoons of olive oil. Toss them to ensure they are evenly coated with the oil.
3. **Seasoning:**
   - Add your preferred seasonings, such as salt, pepper, garlic powder, paprika, or any other herbs and spices you like. Mix well to distribute the seasonings evenly.
4. **Preheat the Air Fryer:**
   - Preheat your air fryer to 375°F (190°C). This helps the radishes cook evenly and get that nice crispy texture.
5. **Air Frying:**
   - Once the air fryer is preheated, place the seasoned radishes in the air fryer basket in a single layer. Avoid overcrowding to allow for proper air circulation. Cook in batches if necessary.
6. **Cooking Time:**
   - Cook the radishes for about 15-20 minutes, shaking the basket or flipping the radishes halfway through to ensure even cooking. The exact cooking time may vary depending on the size and thickness of your radishes and the specific air fryer model you're using.
7. **Check for Doneness:**
   - Radishes should be golden brown and crispy on the outside and tender on the inside. Taste one to check for your desired level of crispiness.
8. **Serve:**
   - Remove the air-fried radishes from the basket and serve immediately. They are best enjoyed hot and crispy.

Notes:

1. **Variations:** Feel free to experiment with different seasonings to suit your taste. Smoked paprika, cayenne pepper, or grated Parmesan cheese can add extra flavor.
2. **Tossing in Olive Oil:** Use just enough olive oil to lightly coat the radishes. Too much oil can make them soggy.
3. **Even Sizing:** Try to cut the radishes into similar-sized pieces to ensure they cook uniformly.
4. **Don't Overcrowd:** Overcrowding the air fryer basket can lead to uneven cooking. Cook in batches if needed.
5. **Preheating:** Preheating the air fryer is essential to achieve a crispy exterior.
6. **Serving Suggestions:** Air-fried radishes make a great side dish or a healthy snack. They pair well with a dipping sauce like garlic aioli or a yogurt-based dip.

Air-fried radishes are a delightful low-carb alternative to classic potato fries and are perfect for anyone looking to reduce their carb intake. Enjoy this crispy, flavorful treat as a side or a tasty snack.

Certainly! Here are some additional tips and ideas for making the most of your air fryer radishes:

Additional Tips:

1. **Don't Overload the Basket:** It's important to maintain a single layer of radishes in the air fryer basket. Overcrowding can result in uneven cooking, with some radishes remaining soft and undercooked.
2. **Monitor Cooking Time:** Keep an eye on the radishes as they cook, especially during the last few minutes. Cooking times can vary depending on the air fryer's make and model, so adjust as needed to achieve your desired level of crispiness.
3. **Serve Immediately:** Air-fried radishes are at their best when served fresh out of the air fryer. Their crispiness diminishes as they cool, so aim to enjoy them right away.
4. **Dipping Sauces:** Consider serving your air-fried radishes with a variety of dipping sauces. Options include homemade or store-bought ranch dressing, tzatziki, sriracha mayo, or a balsamic glaze for a sweet and tangy touch.
5. **Healthier Alternative:** If you're looking for a healthier option, you can use less olive oil or even try a light cooking spray. This will reduce the calorie content of the dish.

Recipe Variations:

1. **Parmesan Crusted:** Sprinkle grated Parmesan cheese over the radishes during the last few minutes of cooking. The cheese will melt and form a delicious, crispy crust.
2. **Spicy Radishes:** If you enjoy some heat, add a pinch of cayenne pepper or red pepper flakes to the seasoning mix.
3. **Herbed Radishes:** Experiment with fresh herbs like rosemary, thyme, or dill to enhance the flavor of your air-fried radishes.
4. **Cajun Seasoned:** Create a Cajun-inspired version by using a Cajun seasoning blend, or make your own by combining spices like paprika, cayenne, garlic powder, and onion powder.

5. **Sweet and Savory:** Drizzle a touch of honey or maple syrup over the radishes before cooking for a sweet and savory contrast.

Leftovers:

If you happen to have leftover air-fried radishes, you can reheat them in the air fryer for a few minutes to regain some of their crispiness. However, they may not be quite as crispy as when freshly cooked.

Air-fried radishes are a versatile and enjoyable side dish, and you can get creative with various seasonings and flavor profiles to suit your preferences. They make a healthy and satisfying alternative to traditional fried snacks.

Air Fryer Sweet Potato Fries

Air fryer sweet potato fries are a delicious and healthier alternative to traditional deep-fried fries. They come out crispy on the outside and tender on the inside. Here's a simple recipe and some notes to help you make perfect sweet potato fries in your air fryer:

Ingredients:

- 2 medium-sized sweet potatoes
- 1-2 tablespoons of olive oil or cooking spray
- 1/2 teaspoon of paprika (optional)
- 1/2 teaspoon of garlic powder (optional)
- Salt and pepper to taste

Instructions:

1. **Preheat the Air Fryer:** Preheat your air fryer to 375°F (190°C) for a few minutes. This helps ensure even cooking.
2. **Prepare the Sweet Potatoes:** Wash and peel the sweet potatoes. Cut them into evenly sized fries or wedges. Try to make them as uniform as possible to ensure even cooking.
3. **Coat with Oil and Seasoning:** Place the sweet potato fries in a large bowl. Drizzle olive oil over them, and add any optional seasonings like paprika and garlic powder. Season with salt and pepper to taste. Toss the fries to ensure they are evenly coated with the oil and seasonings.
4. **Arrange in the Air Fryer:** Place the sweet potato fries in a single layer in the air fryer basket. Avoid overcrowding to ensure proper air circulation. You may need to cook them in batches if your air fryer is small.
5. **Air Fry:** Cook the sweet potato fries at 375°F (190°C) for 15-20 minutes, shaking or flipping them halfway through the cooking time. Cooking time may vary depending on the

thickness of your fries and the air fryer model you're using. Keep a close eye on them to avoid overcooking.

6. **Check for Doneness:** Test the fries for doneness by piercing them with a fork or a toothpick. They should be tender on the inside and crispy on the outside. If they're not done to your liking, you can cook them for a few more minutes.
7. **Serve:** Once the sweet potato fries are cooked to your desired level of crispiness, remove them from the air fryer and serve immediately.

Notes:

1. **Sweet Potato Thickness:** The thickness of the sweet potato fries will affect the cooking time. Thinner fries will cook faster, while thicker ones will take longer.
2. **Oil:** You can use olive oil, avocado oil, or any cooking spray to coat the sweet potato fries. The oil helps them become crispy.
3. **Seasoning:** Feel free to get creative with your seasoning. You can use spices like cumin, smoked paprika, or chili powder to add extra flavor.
4. **Overcrowding:** Overcrowding the air fryer basket can lead to uneven cooking. Cook the fries in batches if needed.
5. **Serve Immediately:** Sweet potato fries are best served immediately while they're hot and crispy.

Enjoy your air fryer sweet potato fries as a tasty side dish or snack. They're a healthier alternative to regular fries and can be enjoyed with your favorite dipping sauces, such as ketchup, aioli, or sriracha mayo.

Certainly! Here are some additional tips and variations to enhance your air fryer sweet potato fries:

1. Soak in Water:

- For even crispier results, you can soak the sweet potato fries in cold water for about 30 minutes before patting them dry and coating with oil and seasonings. This can help remove excess starch and promote crispiness.

2. Preheating is Key:

- Preheating the air fryer is crucial for consistent and efficient cooking. Don't skip this step to ensure your fries cook evenly.

3. Basket Shaking:

- Shaking the air fryer basket or flipping the fries halfway through the cooking time is important. It helps ensure that all sides of the fries cook evenly and become crispy.

4. Parmesan Sweet Potato Fries:

- For a cheesy twist, sprinkle grated Parmesan or Pecorino Romano cheese over the fries during the last few minutes of cooking. The cheese will melt and add a savory kick to your sweet potato fries.

5. Cinnamon Sugar Sweet Potato Fries:

- If you prefer a sweet version, skip the savory seasonings and toss your sweet potato fries in a mix of cinnamon and sugar before air frying. Serve them with a side of marshmallow dip for a dessert-like treat.

6. Dipping Sauces:

- Experiment with different dipping sauces to complement your sweet potato fries. Popular choices include sriracha mayo, honey mustard, garlic aioli, or tzatziki.

7. Frozen Sweet Potato Fries:

- You can also make air fryer sweet potato fries using frozen store-bought fries. Just follow the package instructions for temperature and time, but they typically cook faster than homemade ones, so keep an eye on them.

8. Don't Overload:

- Ensure there is space between the fries in the air fryer basket. Overcrowding can lead to uneven cooking and less crispy results.

9. Serve with Fresh Herbs:

- After cooking, sprinkle some fresh herbs like chopped parsley, cilantro, or rosemary on the hot sweet potato fries for a burst of flavor and color.

10. Custom Seasonings:

- Get creative with seasonings. Try combinations like Cajun seasoning, Old Bay, curry powder, or smoked paprika for unique flavor profiles.

11. Reheat Leftovers:

- If you have leftover sweet potato fries, you can reheat them in the air fryer to restore their crispiness. Just heat them for a few minutes until they're warmed through.

Enjoy your air fryer sweet potato fries with these tips and variations. They're a versatile and tasty side dish that can be customized to your preferences, whether you like them savory, sweet, or with a unique twist.

Air Fryer Zucchini

Air frying zucchini is a quick and easy way to make a delicious and healthy snack or side dish. Here's a simple recipe and some notes to get you started:

Ingredients:

- 2 medium zucchinis
- 2 tablespoons olive oil
- 1/2 teaspoon salt
- 1/4 teaspoon black pepper
- 1/4 teaspoon garlic powder (optional)
- 1/4 teaspoon paprika (optional)
- Grated Parmesan cheese (optional, for serving)

Instructions:

1. **Preheat your air fryer:** Preheat your air fryer to 380°F (190°C). This preheating step helps ensure even cooking.
2. **Prepare the zucchini:** Wash the zucchinis and cut them into 1/4-inch thick rounds. You can also cut them into strips or sticks if you prefer a different shape.
3. **Season the zucchini:** In a large bowl, toss the zucchini slices with olive oil, salt, pepper, and any optional seasonings like garlic powder or paprika. Make sure the zucchini is evenly coated.
4. **Air frying:** Place the seasoned zucchini slices in a single layer in the air fryer basket. Avoid overcrowding to allow for proper air circulation. If needed, you may need to cook them in batches.
5. **Cooking time:** Air fry the zucchini at 380°F (190°C) for 10-12 minutes, or until they are golden brown and crispy, flipping them halfway through the cooking time. The cooking time may vary slightly depending on the thickness of the slices and your air fryer model.
6. **Serve:** Once the zucchini slices are golden and crispy, remove them from the air fryer. You can sprinkle them with some grated Parmesan cheese if you like. Serve immediately while they're still hot.

Notes:

1. **Slice thickness:** Try to cut the zucchini slices evenly so that they cook at the same rate. Thicker slices may need a little more cooking time.
2. **Oil:** You can use cooking spray instead of olive oil if you want to reduce the amount of oil used.
3. **Seasonings:** Get creative with your seasonings. You can experiment with different herbs and spices to suit your taste. Some people like to use a little lemon zest for a refreshing twist.

4. **Overcrowding:** Avoid overcrowding the air fryer basket as it can lead to uneven cooking. If you have a smaller air fryer, cook in batches.
5. **Dipping sauce:** Consider serving your air-fried zucchini with a dipping sauce like marinara, ranch, or tzatziki for extra flavor.
6. **Crispiness:** For the crispiest results, make sure the zucchini slices are well-coated with oil and spaced apart in the air fryer basket.

Air-fried zucchini is a healthy alternative to traditional deep-fried zucchini, and it's a great snack or side dish. Enjoy!

Certainly! Here are some additional tips and ideas for air frying zucchini:

Additional Tips:

1. **Temperature and Timing:** The suggested temperature and timing in the recipe are a good starting point. However, air fryers can vary, so it's a good idea to keep an eye on your zucchini during the cooking process. Adjust the time and temperature as needed to achieve your desired level of crispiness.
2. **Preheat the Air Fryer:** Preheating the air fryer is essential for consistent results. It ensures that the zucchini starts cooking immediately and prevents the food from sticking to the basket.
3. **Use Parchment Paper:** To make cleanup easier, you can line the air fryer basket with parchment paper. This prevents the zucchini from sticking to the basket and makes for an easier cleanup process.
4. **Spritz with Cooking Spray:** If you want to minimize the use of oil, consider spritzing the zucchini slices with cooking spray before air frying. This helps them become crispy without excess oil.
5. **Mix It Up:** Zucchini is a versatile vegetable. You can mix it with other vegetables like bell peppers, onions, or cherry tomatoes for a colorful and flavorful mix. Just adjust cooking times accordingly.
6. **Experiment with Dipping Sauces:** Zucchini pairs well with various dipping sauces. In addition to the options mentioned earlier, you can also try honey mustard, balsamic reduction, or a yogurt-based dip for a healthier alternative.

Variations:

1. **Zucchini Fries:** Instead of rounds, cut the zucchini into strips to make zucchini fries. Serve them with a side of marinara sauce or aioli.
2. **Stuffed Zucchini:** Halve the zucchini lengthwise, scoop out some of the flesh, and stuff them with a mixture of breadcrumbs, herbs, and cheese. Air fry the stuffed zucchini for a delicious appetizer or side dish.
3. **Parmesan Zucchini Chips:** Before air frying, coat the zucchini slices with grated Parmesan cheese for an extra layer of flavor and crispiness.
4. **Spicy Zucchini:** Add a pinch of cayenne pepper or red pepper flakes to the seasoning mix if you enjoy a little heat.

5. **Asian-Inspired:** Instead of the Mediterranean seasoning, try using a mix of soy sauce, garlic, and ginger for an Asian-inspired flavor. Serve with a soy-based dipping sauce.
6. **Ranch Seasoning:** Use a ranch seasoning mix for a tangy and flavorful twist.

Remember that air fryers are versatile appliances, and you can get creative with your recipes. Adjust the seasonings and ingredients to suit your preferences, and don't be afraid to try new combinations and flavors. Air-fried zucchini is a delicious and healthy treat that can be enjoyed in many ways!

Air Fryer Baby Potatoes

Air frying baby potatoes is a quick and easy way to achieve a crispy exterior and a soft, fluffy interior without using much oil. Here's a simple recipe and some notes to help you make delicious air fryer baby potatoes:

Ingredients:

- 1 pound (450g) baby potatoes
- 1-2 tablespoons olive oil or cooking spray
- 1 teaspoon salt (adjust to taste)
- 1/2 teaspoon black pepper (adjust to taste)
- 1/2 teaspoon garlic powder (optional)
- 1/2 teaspoon paprika (optional)
- Fresh herbs (rosemary, thyme, or parsley) for garnish (optional)

Instructions:

1. **Preheat the Air Fryer:** Preheat your air fryer to 400°F (200°C) for a few minutes.
2. **Prepare the Potatoes:** Wash and scrub the baby potatoes to remove any dirt. You can leave the skins on for extra texture and flavor. If the potatoes are larger, cut them into smaller, bite-sized pieces.
3. **Season the Potatoes:** In a large bowl, toss the baby potatoes with olive oil or use a cooking spray to lightly coat them. Add the salt, pepper, and any optional seasonings like garlic powder or paprika. Toss the potatoes to evenly coat them with the seasonings.
4. **Air Frying:** Place the seasoned baby potatoes in the air fryer basket in a single layer. It's essential not to overcrowd the basket to allow for even cooking. If needed, cook them in batches.
5. **Cooking Time:** Air fry the potatoes at 400°F (200°C) for about 15-20 minutes, shaking the basket or tossing the potatoes halfway through. Cooking time can vary depending on the size of your baby potatoes and the specific air fryer model. They should be golden brown and crispy on the outside and tender on the inside when done.

6. **Check for Doneness:** Test the potatoes with a fork or toothpick to make sure they are cooked through. If they are not quite done, continue to air fry for a few more minutes.
7. **Serve:** Once the baby potatoes are done, remove them from the air fryer and let them cool for a minute. Garnish with fresh herbs like rosemary, thyme, or parsley if desired. Serve hot.

Notes:

- **Potato Varieties:** You can use various baby potato varieties like fingerling, red, or Yukon Gold for this recipe. Each variety will offer a slightly different flavor and texture.
- **Oil:** While you can use olive oil, you can also use other oils like vegetable or canola oil. Using a cooking spray can help reduce the amount of oil needed.
- **Seasoning:** Feel free to customize the seasoning to your taste. You can add herbs, spices, or grated Parmesan cheese for additional flavor.
- **Shaking/Tossing:** It's essential to shake the air fryer basket or toss the potatoes halfway through cooking to ensure even browning.
- **Cooking Time:** Cooking times can vary depending on your air fryer's model and size, so it's a good idea to check the potatoes for doneness and adjust the cooking time if needed.

Air fryer baby potatoes make a great side dish for any meal. They're versatile and can be served with various dipping sauces, aioli, or as part of a breakfast hash. Enjoy your crispy and delicious air-fried baby potatoes!

Certainly! Here are some additional tips and variations for making air fryer baby potatoes:

Tips:

1. **Preheating:** Preheating your air fryer is essential to ensure even cooking and crispy results. It's like preheating an oven.
2. **Size Consistency:** Try to keep the baby potatoes as consistent in size as possible. This will help ensure they cook evenly.
3. **Coating Evenly:** Make sure to evenly coat the potatoes with oil and seasonings for a uniform flavor and texture.
4. **Cooking Temperature:** Adjust the cooking time and temperature based on your specific air fryer model. Keep an eye on the potatoes, so they don't overcook or burn.
5. **Don't Overcrowd:** Overcrowding the air fryer basket can lead to uneven cooking. If you're cooking a large batch, it's better to do it in multiple batches.
6. **Use a Trivet:** Placing a trivet or air fryer liner in the basket can prevent the smaller potatoes from falling through the holes.

Variations:

1. **Cheesy Potatoes:** Add shredded cheese like cheddar, parmesan, or feta during the last few minutes of cooking for a cheesy twist.

2. **Spicy Potatoes:** If you like heat, sprinkle some cayenne pepper or chili powder on the potatoes before air frying for a spicy kick.
3. **Herb Butter:** Instead of just olive oil, toss the potatoes in melted herb-infused butter for a rich and flavorful alternative.
4. **Crispy Skins:** For extra crispy skin, brush the potatoes with oil before air frying or even coat them with a thin layer of breadcrumbs.
5. **Balsamic Glaze:** After air frying, drizzle the potatoes with a balsamic glaze for a sweet and tangy flavor.
6. **Loaded Potatoes:** Top the air-fried baby potatoes with sour cream, bacon bits, chives, and shredded cheese for a loaded potato experience.
7. **Sweet Potatoes:** You can use the same method to make air fryer sweet potatoes for a sweeter and healthier side dish.
8. **Dipping Sauces:** Serve your air-fried baby potatoes with a variety of dipping sauces like aioli, ketchup, or a simple garlic yogurt dip.

Experiment with these variations to create a variety of delicious air-fried baby potato dishes. They are perfect for serving at parties, as a side for dinner, or even as a snack. Enjoy your culinary adventures with the air fryer!

Air Fryer Broccoli Cheese Bites

Air Fryer Broccoli Cheese Bites are a delicious and healthy snack or appetizer that you can make in your air fryer. These crispy, cheesy bites are perfect for parties, game day, or as a side dish. Here's a simple recipe along with some notes to make the process easier:

Ingredients:

- 2 cups fresh broccoli florets, steamed and finely chopped
- 1 cup shredded cheddar cheese
- 1/4 cup grated Parmesan cheese
- 1/4 cup breadcrumbs
- 1/4 cup mayonnaise
- 1 large egg
- 1/2 teaspoon garlic powder
- 1/2 teaspoon onion powder
- 1/4 teaspoon salt
- 1/4 teaspoon black pepper
- Cooking spray

Instructions:

1. **Prepare the Broccoli:**

- Steam the broccoli florets until they are tender. Drain and finely chop the broccoli. You can use a food processor for this step to make it easier.
2. **Mix the Ingredients:**
   - In a large bowl, combine the finely chopped broccoli, cheddar cheese, Parmesan cheese, breadcrumbs, mayonnaise, egg, garlic powder, onion powder, salt, and black pepper. Mix everything together until well combined.
3. **Form the Bites:**
   - Using your hands or a cookie scoop, form the mixture into small bite-sized balls or patties. Make sure they are compact and hold together well.
4. **Preheat the Air Fryer:**
   - Preheat your air fryer to 375°F (190°C).
5. **Air Fry the Bites:**
   - Place the broccoli cheese bites in a single layer in the air fryer basket, making sure they are not touching each other. You may need to cook them in batches depending on the size of your air fryer.
   - Lightly spray the bites with cooking spray. This will help them become crispy.
   - Cook for about 8-10 minutes, or until they are golden brown and crispy. Be sure to flip them over halfway through the cooking time for even browning.
6. **Serve:**
   - Once the broccoli cheese bites are done, remove them from the air fryer and let them cool slightly before serving. They are best enjoyed hot and crispy.

Notes:

- You can customize this recipe by adding other ingredients like chopped spinach, diced onions, or different types of cheese for extra flavor.
- If you don't have an air fryer, you can also bake these broccoli cheese bites in a preheated oven at 375°F (190°C) for about 15-20 minutes, flipping them over halfway through the baking time.
- Feel free to serve the broccoli cheese bites with your favorite dipping sauces like ranch dressing, marinara sauce, or honey mustard.
- These bites are best enjoyed fresh, but you can store any leftovers in an airtight container in the refrigerator. Reheat them in the air fryer or oven to maintain their crispiness.

Enjoy your homemade air fryer broccoli cheese bites as a tasty and nutritious snack or side dish!

Certainly! Here are some additional tips and variations for making your air fryer broccoli cheese bites:

Tips:

1. **Use Parchment Paper:** To prevent the broccoli cheese bites from sticking to the air fryer basket, you can place a piece of parchment paper at the bottom of the basket before cooking.
2. **Preheat Your Air Fryer:** Preheating your air fryer is essential for even cooking and achieving a crispy exterior. Allow it to preheat for a few minutes before adding the bites.
3. **Don't Overcrowd the Basket:** Ensure that the broccoli cheese bites are arranged in a single layer and not touching each other to allow for proper air circulation. If your air fryer is small, cook them in batches.
4. **Check for Doneness:** Cooking times may vary slightly depending on your specific air fryer model. It's a good idea to check the bites a few minutes before the recommended time to avoid overcooking. They should be golden brown and crispy.
5. **Experiment with Seasonings:** Feel free to customize the seasonings to your taste. You can add a pinch of cayenne pepper for some heat, or a dash of paprika or dried herbs for extra flavor.

Variations:

1. **Vegetarian/Vegan Options:** If you're vegetarian, these bites are already suitable for your diet. To make them vegan, simply substitute the cheese with vegan cheese, use a vegan egg substitute, and vegan mayonnaise.
2. **Gluten-Free:** If you're following a gluten-free diet, use gluten-free breadcrumbs or almond meal as a substitute for regular breadcrumbs.
3. **Protein Boost:** Add some cooked and crumbled bacon, diced ham, or even cooked ground sausage to the mixture for added protein and flavor.
4. **Spice it Up:** If you enjoy a bit of heat, consider adding some chopped jalapeños or red pepper flakes to the mixture for a spicy twist.
5. **Dipping Sauces:** Offer a variety of dipping sauces for added enjoyment. Try garlic aioli, sriracha mayo, or a balsamic reduction for a sweet and tangy touch.
6. **Mini Muffin Tin Method:** Instead of forming balls or patties, you can spoon the mixture into greased mini muffin tins. This creates bite-sized, uniform portions, and you can still air fry them or bake them in the oven.

These air fryer broccoli cheese bites are versatile and can be tailored to your preferences and dietary requirements. Get creative and enjoy experimenting with different ingredients and flavors to make them your own!

Healthy Air Fryer Eggplant

Air frying is a great way to make crispy and healthy eggplant without the need for excessive oil. Here's a simple recipe for healthy air-fried eggplant, along with some notes to help you make it just right:

Ingredients:

- 1 large eggplant
- 1-2 cups of breadcrumbs (you can use whole wheat or panko for added crunch)
- 2 eggs (or an egg substitute like aquafaba for a vegan option)
- 1/2 cup grated Parmesan cheese (or a vegan alternative)
- 1/2 teaspoon salt
- 1/2 teaspoon pepper
- 1/2 teaspoon garlic powder
- 1/2 teaspoon paprika (smoked paprika works well)
- Cooking spray (for the air fryer basket)

Instructions:

1. **Preheat Your Air Fryer**: Start by preheating your air fryer to 375°F (190°C) while you prepare the eggplant.
2. **Slice the Eggplant**: Cut the eggplant into 1/2-inch (1.27 cm) thick rounds. You can peel it or leave the skin on, depending on your preference. If you're using a particularly large eggplant, you may need to cut the rounds in half to fit them into the air fryer basket.
3. **Prepare the Breading Station**: In a shallow bowl, whisk the eggs (or your egg substitute) with a pinch of salt and pepper. In another bowl, combine the breadcrumbs, grated Parmesan cheese (or a vegan alternative), garlic powder, paprika, salt, and pepper. Mix well.
4. **Bread the Eggplant**: Dip each eggplant round into the egg mixture to coat it evenly, then press it into the breadcrumb mixture, ensuring it's well-coated on both sides. Place the breaded eggplant rounds on a plate or tray.
5. **Air Fry the Eggplant**: Lightly grease the air fryer basket with cooking spray to prevent sticking. Arrange the breaded eggplant rounds in a single layer in the air fryer basket, making sure they are not touching. You may need to cook them in batches depending on the size of your air fryer.
6. **Cook in the Air Fryer**: Air fry the eggplant at 375°F (190°C) for about 12-15 minutes, flipping them halfway through the cooking time. Keep an eye on them to ensure they don't burn. The eggplant should become golden brown and crispy.
7. **Serve**: Once the eggplant rounds are crispy and golden, remove them from the air fryer and let them cool for a minute. You can serve them with a dipping sauce like marinara, tzatziki, or a yogurt-based sauce. They're great as a snack, appetizer, or side dish.

Notes:

- Be sure to cut the eggplant into evenly sized rounds to ensure even cooking.
- Adjust the seasonings to your taste. You can add herbs like oregano or basil for extra flavor.
- Don't overcrowd the air fryer basket, as this can lead to uneven cooking. It's better to cook in batches if necessary.

- You can experiment with different coatings like almond flour or cornmeal for a different texture.
- The cooking time may vary depending on your specific air fryer model, so it's a good idea to keep an eye on the eggplant as it cooks.

Enjoy your healthy air-fried eggplant! It's a delicious and guilt-free way to enjoy this versatile vegetable.

Certainly! Here are some additional tips and variations for your healthy air-fried eggplant:

Tips:

1. **Sweat the Eggplant:** After slicing the eggplant, you can sprinkle some salt on both sides of the rounds and let them sit for about 30 minutes. This will help draw out excess moisture and can result in even crispier eggplant.
2. **Spray or Brush with Oil:** If you want to enhance the crispiness, lightly spray the breaded eggplant rounds with cooking oil or use a pastry brush to brush them with a small amount of oil before air frying. This will give them a more fried-like texture.
3. **Seasoning Variations:** Get creative with your seasonings. Try adding cayenne pepper for some heat, or use Italian seasoning for a Mediterranean twist.
4. **Vegan Options:** If you're following a vegan diet, use plant-based breadcrumbs, a vegan egg substitute, and dairy-free Parmesan cheese.
5. **Serve with Dipping Sauces:** Consider serving your air-fried eggplant with a variety of dipping sauces, such as hummus, baba ghanoush, or a lemon-garlic tahini sauce.

Variations:

1. **Eggplant Parmesan:** After air frying the eggplant, you can layer it with marinara sauce and mozzarella cheese, then return it to the air fryer for a few minutes to melt the cheese. This creates a healthier version of Eggplant Parmesan.
2. **Eggplant Fries:** Instead of rounds, cut the eggplant into thin strips to make eggplant fries. They'll cook faster and be great for dipping in your favorite sauce.
3. **Stuffed Eggplant:** Cut the eggplant in half lengthwise, scoop out some of the flesh to create a boat, and air fry it. You can stuff it with a mixture of vegetables, cheese, and herbs for a delightful side dish or appetizer.
4. **Eggplant Sandwich:** Use the air-fried eggplant rounds as a filling for a sandwich or burger. Stack them with fresh vegetables and your favorite condiments.
5. **Asian-Inspired Flavors:** Instead of the Italian seasoning, try a mix of soy sauce, ginger, and garlic for an Asian twist. Serve with a side of sweet chili dipping sauce.
6. **Baked Parmesan Eggplant:** If you don't have an air fryer, you can also bake the breaded eggplant rounds in a preheated oven at 375°F (190°C) on a wire rack set on a baking sheet for a similar crispy texture.

Feel free to adapt this recipe to your tastes and dietary preferences. Air-fried eggplant is a versatile and healthy dish that can be enjoyed in various ways.

Air Fryer Tortilla Chips

Air fryer tortilla chips are a delicious and healthier alternative to traditional deep-fried chips. They are crispy and flavorful, and you can customize them with your favorite seasonings. Here's a basic recipe along with some notes:

Ingredients:

- Corn tortillas (white or yellow, depending on your preference)
- Cooking spray or a small amount of vegetable oil (for a light coating)
- Salt or your preferred seasoning (e.g., chili powder, paprika, garlic powder)

Instructions:

1. **Preheat your air fryer:** Preheat your air fryer to around 350-375°F (175-190°C). The exact temperature may vary depending on your air fryer model.
2. **Prepare the tortillas:** While the air fryer is heating up, stack your corn tortillas and cut them into wedges or triangles. You can typically cut each tortilla into 6-8 pieces, similar to slicing a pizza. The size is up to you, but keep them fairly consistent for even cooking.
3. **Season the tortilla chips:** Lightly spray the tortilla chips with cooking spray or drizzle a small amount of vegetable oil over them. Toss them to ensure the oil is evenly distributed. You can also use a pastry brush to apply a thin layer of oil. Season the chips with salt or your preferred seasoning.
4. **Arrange in the air fryer:** Place the seasoned tortilla chips in a single layer in the air fryer basket. You may need to cook them in batches if you have a small air fryer. Make sure there's enough space for air to circulate around them.
5. **Cook the tortilla chips:** Air fry the chips for about 6-10 minutes, but check them frequently. The cooking time will depend on the thickness of the tortillas and your specific air fryer. The chips are done when they are golden brown and crispy. You might want to shake the basket or flip the chips halfway through to ensure even cooking.
6. **Cool and serve:** Once the tortilla chips are done, remove them from the air fryer and let them cool for a few minutes. They will continue to crisp up as they cool. Serve them with your favorite dips like salsa, guacamole, or queso.

Notes:

1. **Tortilla selection:** You can use either white or yellow corn tortillas, and you can also experiment with flavored tortillas for different taste variations.
2. **Seasoning:** Feel free to get creative with your seasoning. Besides salt, you can use chili powder, paprika, garlic powder, cumin, or even a sprinkle of grated cheese for extra flavor.

3. **Oil:** You don't need a lot of oil; just a light coating is enough to help the seasoning stick and crisp up the chips.
4. **Don't overcrowd:** Make sure not to overcrowd the air fryer basket. If you pile the chips on top of each other, they won't cook evenly. Cook them in batches if necessary.
5. **Watch them closely:** Air fryers vary in temperature and cooking times, so keep a close eye on the chips to prevent burning.
6. **Storage:** If you have any leftovers, store them in an airtight container to maintain their crispiness. Reheat them in the air fryer for a few minutes if needed.

Certainly, here are some additional tips and variations for making air fryer tortilla chips:

Variations:

1. **Flavored Tortillas:** Instead of plain corn tortillas, try using flavored tortillas like spinach, tomato, or whole grain for a different taste and added nutrients.
2. **Homemade Seasoning Blends:** Experiment with homemade seasoning blends to customize the flavor of your tortilla chips. For example, you can create a spicy seasoning with cayenne pepper and paprika, or a smoky flavor with chipotle powder and smoked paprika.
3. **Sweet Tortilla Chips:** For a sweet twist, brush the tortilla chips with a little melted butter and sprinkle them with a mixture of cinnamon and sugar before air frying. These are great for dipping in chocolate or fruit salsa.

Tips:

1. **Stacking Tortillas:** If you're making a large batch and need to stack the tortilla chips in the air fryer basket, consider placing a piece of parchment paper or a silicone mat between the layers to prevent sticking.
2. **Check for Doneness:** Keep a close eye on the chips as they cook. They can go from perfectly crispy to burnt quickly, so it's essential to check their progress, especially during the last few minutes of cooking.
3. **Uniform Sizing:** Try to cut the tortilla chips into uniform sizes to ensure even cooking. This will help you avoid some chips being undercooked while others are overcooked.
4. **Preheating the Air Fryer:** Preheating your air fryer helps ensure even cooking and consistent results. If your air fryer has a preheat function, use it. If not, simply turn it on for a few minutes at the desired cooking temperature before adding the chips.
5. **Serving Ideas:** Serve your air fryer tortilla chips with a variety of dips, such as classic salsa, guacamole, queso dip, hummus, or homemade pico de gallo.
6. **Storage:** If you happen to have leftovers, store the chips in an airtight container at room temperature. However, note that they may lose some of their crispiness over time. You can try re-crisping them in the air fryer for a few minutes before serving.

Air fryer tortilla chips are a versatile and healthy snack or side dish that you can enjoy in various ways. Whether you prefer a classic salty flavor or want to explore sweet and savory options, they are easy to make and customize to your taste.

Air Fryer Asparagus

Air frying asparagus is a quick and easy way to prepare this delicious and nutritious vegetable. It results in tender-crisp asparagus with a slightly charred flavor. Here's a simple recipe and some notes to help you make the perfect air fryer asparagus:

Ingredients:

- 1 bunch of fresh asparagus
- 1-2 tablespoons of olive oil
- Salt and pepper, to taste
- Optional: grated Parmesan cheese, lemon zest, or your favorite seasonings

Instructions:

1. **Preparation:** Start by washing the asparagus spears and trimming the tough ends. You can snap off the tough ends by bending the asparagus near the bottom; it will naturally break at the right spot. If you prefer, you can also use a knife to trim them.
2. **Seasoning:** Place the trimmed asparagus in a bowl and drizzle with olive oil. Season with salt and pepper, and any other seasonings you like. Toss the asparagus to coat it evenly with the oil and seasonings.
3. **Preheat the Air Fryer:** Preheat your air fryer to 400°F (200°C) for a few minutes. This ensures even cooking.
4. **Air Frying:** Place the seasoned asparagus spears in a single layer in the air fryer basket. You may need to do this in batches if you have a small air fryer. Cook for about 7-10 minutes, shaking or flipping the spears halfway through the cooking time. The exact cooking time may vary depending on the thickness of the asparagus and the specific model of your air fryer. Aim for a tender-crisp texture and slightly charred tips.
5. **Finishing Touches:** If you want to add some extra flavor, you can sprinkle some grated Parmesan cheese on the asparagus during the last minute of cooking or zest some lemon over them for a zesty kick.
6. **Serve:** Remove the asparagus from the air fryer, and serve immediately while they're still hot and crispy.

Notes:

- **Asparagus Thickness:** The cooking time can vary depending on the thickness of the asparagus spears. Thicker spears may require a bit more time, while thinner ones will cook faster. Adjust the cooking time accordingly.
- **Oil:** You can use different oils, such as avocado oil or melted butter, instead of olive oil for added flavor.

- **Seasonings:** Get creative with your seasonings. Try adding minced garlic, smoked paprika, red pepper flakes, or your favorite herbs for a different flavor profile.
- **Batches:** If you're cooking a large amount of asparagus, it's best to cook them in batches to ensure they cook evenly.
- **Serve Immediately:** Air-fried asparagus is best when served immediately. It tends to lose its crispiness as it cools.

Enjoy your air-fried asparagus as a side dish or a healthy snack. It's a versatile and tasty addition to any meal.

Certainly! Here are some additional tips and ideas for air fryer asparagus:

1. Flavor Variations:

- **Balsamic Glaze:** Drizzle balsamic glaze over the cooked asparagus for a sweet and tangy flavor.
- **Garlic Butter:** Melt some garlic butter and toss the cooked asparagus in it for a rich, savory twist.
- **Lemon Pepper:** Sprinkle lemon pepper seasoning for a zesty and aromatic flavor.
- **Sesame Ginger:** Add sesame oil and ginger to the asparagus for an Asian-inspired taste.

2. Cooking Time:

- If your asparagus is very thin, it may be done in as little as 5-7 minutes in the air fryer. Thicker asparagus may take closer to 10 minutes. Always check for tenderness as it cooks to avoid overcooking.

3. Asparagus Arrangement:

- For even cooking, try to arrange the asparagus in a single layer without overcrowding the air fryer basket. If needed, cook in batches.

4. Preheating:

- Preheating the air fryer is essential for consistent results. It helps ensure that the asparagus starts cooking immediately and cooks evenly.

5. Crispy Tips:

- If you want extra crispy tips on your asparagus, you can place them closer to the air fryer's heating element by layering them on top of each other in the basket.

6. Leftovers:

- If you have any leftover air-fried asparagus, you can use them in salads, omelets, or as a side for another meal. They won't be as crispy as when freshly cooked but still delicious.

7. Dietary Considerations:

- This method of cooking asparagus is naturally gluten-free and suitable for a variety of diets. To make it vegan, use a plant-based oil instead of butter and skip the Parmesan cheese.

8. Dipping Sauces:

- Consider serving your air-fried asparagus with dipping sauces like hollandaise, aioli, or a simple lemon garlic aioli for added flavor.

9. Experiment:

- Don't be afraid to experiment with different seasonings and flavors to suit your preferences. Asparagus is a versatile vegetable that pairs well with many herbs and spices.

Air fryer asparagus is a quick and healthy side dish that can complement a variety of main courses. It's perfect for weeknight dinners or when you need a simple but elegant side for a special occasion. Enjoy your cooking!

Air Fryer Pumpkin Fries

Air fryer pumpkin fries are a delicious and healthier alternative to traditional potato fries. They're crispy on the outside and tender on the inside, with the wonderful flavor of pumpkin. Here's a simple recipe along with some important notes:

Ingredients:

- 1 small sugar pumpkin (or any type of pumpkin)
- 1-2 tablespoons of olive oil
- 1 teaspoon of salt (adjust to taste)
- 1/2 teaspoon of pepper (adjust to taste)
- 1/2 teaspoon of paprika (optional, for added flavor)
- 1/2 teaspoon of garlic powder (optional)
- 1/4 teaspoon of cayenne pepper (optional, for a bit of heat)
- Cooking spray (for the air fryer basket)

Instructions:

1. **Prepare the Pumpkin:**
   - Start by peeling the pumpkin using a sharp knife or a vegetable peeler. Remove the seeds and fibrous pulp from the inside.

- Cut the peeled pumpkin into thin, even slices or sticks, similar to the size of traditional French fries.
2. **Season the Pumpkin:**
   - In a large bowl, combine the pumpkin slices, olive oil, salt, pepper, and any optional seasonings like paprika, garlic powder, or cayenne pepper. Toss to coat the pumpkin evenly with the seasonings.
3. **Preheat the Air Fryer:**
   - Preheat your air fryer to 375°F (190°C) for about 5 minutes.
4. **Arrange in the Air Fryer:**
   - Lightly grease the air fryer basket with cooking spray to prevent sticking.
   - Place the seasoned pumpkin slices in a single layer in the air fryer basket. Do not overcrowd; you may need to cook them in batches if your air fryer is small.
5. **Air Fry the Pumpkin:**
   - Air fry the pumpkin fries at 375°F (190°C) for 10-15 minutes, depending on your air fryer and the thickness of the fries. Check them at the 10-minute mark and continue cooking until they are golden brown and crispy. You may want to shake the basket or flip the fries halfway through for even cooking.
6. **Serve:**
   - Once the pumpkin fries are crispy and golden, remove them from the air fryer and serve immediately.

Notes:

1. **Pumpkin Selection:** Choose a small sugar pumpkin or any pumpkin variety with sweet and tender flesh for the best results. You can also use butternut squash or other similar vegetables.
2. **Uniform Sizing:** To ensure even cooking, try to cut the pumpkin slices or sticks as uniformly as possible.
3. **Oil and Seasonings:** Adjust the amount of oil and seasonings to your taste. You can experiment with different spices and herbs to create unique flavor profiles.
4. **Air Fryer Variations:** Cooking times can vary between different air fryer models, so keep an eye on your pumpkin fries to prevent overcooking.
5. **Serve with Dipping Sauce:** Consider serving the pumpkin fries with a dipping sauce like garlic aioli, ketchup, or a yogurt-based dip for extra flavor.

These air fryer pumpkin fries make for a tasty and nutritious snack or side dish that's perfect for the fall season. Enjoy!

Certainly, here are some additional tips and variations for making air fryer pumpkin fries:

Additional Tips:

1. **Soak in Water:** After cutting the pumpkin into fries, you can soak them in cold water for about 30 minutes. This helps remove some of the excess starch and can result in crispier fries.

2. **Pat Dry:** Make sure to pat the pumpkin fries dry with a paper towel after soaking. Excess moisture can hinder the crisping process in the air fryer.
3. **Single Layer:** Avoid overcrowding the air fryer basket. If the fries are too close together, they may not cook evenly. Cook them in batches if needed.
4. **Adjust Cooking Time:** Cooking time may vary depending on the thickness of your pumpkin fries and your air fryer's power. Keep a close eye on them, and adjust the cooking time as necessary.

Variations:

1. **Cinnamon Sugar Pumpkin Fries:** For a sweet twist, skip the savory seasonings and toss the pumpkin fries in a mixture of cinnamon and sugar before air frying. These make a delightful dessert or snack.
2. **Parmesan Pumpkin Fries:** Sprinkle grated Parmesan cheese over the pumpkin fries during the last few minutes of cooking for a cheesy and savory flavor.
3. **Herb-Infused Oil:** Instead of plain olive oil, infuse your oil with herbs like rosemary or thyme. This will add a fragrant and herbaceous element to the fries.
4. **Dipping Sauces:** Experiment with various dipping sauces like sriracha mayo, honey mustard, or ranch dressing for added flavor.
5. **Seasoning Blends:** Create your own seasoning blends using spices like cumin, chili powder, or curry powder for a unique flavor profile.
6. **Coconut-Curry Pumpkin Fries:** Toss the pumpkin fries in a mixture of coconut milk and curry powder before air frying for a flavorful and exotic twist.
7. **Glazed Pumpkin Fries:** After air frying, you can drizzle the pumpkin fries with a glaze made from maple syrup or honey for a sweet and sticky finish.

Remember that air fryer cooking is all about experimentation, so feel free to get creative and tailor the seasonings and flavors to your preferences. Whether you enjoy them as a side dish, snack, or dessert, air fryer pumpkin fries are a tasty and nutritious treat for any season.

Lemon Garlic Air Fryer Roasted Potatoes

Lemon Garlic Air Fryer Roasted Potatoes are a delicious and healthy side dish that you can make quickly and easily in your air fryer. Here's a recipe and some notes to help you make them:

Ingredients:

- 1 pound (450g) baby potatoes, washed and halved
- 2 tablespoons olive oil
- 4 cloves of garlic, minced
- 1 lemon, zest and juice

- 1 teaspoon dried oregano
- 1/2 teaspoon salt (adjust to taste)
- 1/4 teaspoon black pepper (adjust to taste)
- Fresh parsley, chopped (for garnish)

Instructions:

1. **Preheat your air fryer:** Set the air fryer to 400°F (200°C) and let it preheat for a few minutes.
2. **Prepare the potatoes:** In a large bowl, combine the halved baby potatoes, olive oil, minced garlic, lemon zest, dried oregano, salt, and pepper. Toss everything together to coat the potatoes evenly.
3. **Air fry the potatoes:** Place the seasoned potatoes in the air fryer basket in a single layer. You may need to cook them in batches if your air fryer is small. Cook for about 20-25 minutes, shaking the basket or tossing the potatoes halfway through to ensure even cooking. The cooking time may vary depending on the size of your potatoes and the air fryer model, so keep an eye on them. They are ready when they are golden brown and crispy on the outside, and tender on the inside.
4. **Add the lemon juice:** Once the potatoes are done, transfer them to a serving dish. Squeeze the lemon juice over the roasted potatoes while they are still hot.
5. **Garnish and serve:** Sprinkle fresh chopped parsley on top for some color and extra flavor. Serve your Lemon Garlic Air Fryer Roasted Potatoes hot as a side dish to your favorite main course.

Recipe Notes:

- You can use any type of baby potatoes for this recipe, such as red, yellow, or fingerling potatoes. If your potatoes are on the larger side, you can cut them into bite-sized pieces.
- Make sure the potatoes are evenly coated with the olive oil and seasonings to ensure even cooking and flavor distribution.
- Adjust the amount of garlic, lemon, and seasoning to your personal taste. If you love a strong lemon flavor, you can add more lemon zest and juice.
- Don't overcrowd the air fryer basket. Cooking the potatoes in a single layer allows them to crisp up nicely. If necessary, cook them in batches.
- Keep an eye on the cooking time, as it may vary depending on your air fryer model. Potatoes are done when they are golden brown and can be easily pierced with a fork.
- These potatoes are a great side dish for a variety of meals, from roasted chicken to grilled steak and fish.

Enjoy your Lemon Garlic Air Fryer Roasted Potatoes! They make a flavorful and satisfying addition to any meal.

Certainly! Here are some additional tips and variations for your Lemon Garlic Air Fryer Roasted Potatoes:

Additional Tips:

1. **Customize the Seasonings:** Feel free to get creative with the seasonings. You can add other herbs and spices like rosemary, thyme, paprika, or chili flakes to give the potatoes a different flavor profile.
2. **Preheat Your Air Fryer:** Preheating your air fryer for a few minutes helps the potatoes cook more evenly and crisply.
3. **Use a Non-Stick Basket or Liner:** To prevent sticking and make cleanup easier, consider using a non-stick air fryer basket or a parchment paper liner in the basket.
4. **Check for Doneness:** Keep an eye on the potatoes during the cooking process. If they're browning too quickly on the outside but aren't fully cooked on the inside, lower the temperature or reduce the cooking time.
5. **Serve with Dipping Sauce:** These potatoes go well with a dipping sauce like garlic aioli, tzatziki, or a simple Greek yogurt and lemon dip.

Variations:

1. **Cheesy Roasted Potatoes:** Sprinkle some grated Parmesan or cheddar cheese over the potatoes during the last few minutes of cooking for a cheesy twist.
2. **Spicy Roasted Potatoes:** Add a pinch of cayenne pepper or red pepper flakes for a spicy kick.
3. **Herb and Mustard Potatoes:** Mix in some whole grain mustard and fresh herbs like thyme and parsley for a tangy and herbaceous flavor.
4. **Mediterranean Flavors:** Use Mediterranean seasonings like dried oregano, dried basil, and a bit of feta cheese for a Mediterranean-inspired dish.
5. **Vegan Version:** To make this dish vegan, substitute the olive oil with a plant-based oil like avocado oil or use a vegan butter substitute.
6. **Sweet Potato Variation:** You can also make a variation of this recipe using sweet potatoes instead of regular potatoes for a sweeter, healthier option.

Experiment with these variations to suit your taste and dietary preferences. Air frying is a versatile cooking method, and you can adapt this recipe to create a wide range of delicious roasted potato dishes. Enjoy your culinary adventure!

Air Fryer Cauliflower

Air fryer cauliflower is a delicious and healthy side dish that's easy to make. Here's a basic recipe and some notes to help you get started:

Ingredients:

- 1 head of cauliflower, cut into florets
- 2 tablespoons olive oil

- 1 teaspoon garlic powder
- 1 teaspoon onion powder
- 1/2 teaspoon paprika
- Salt and pepper to taste
- Optional: grated Parmesan cheese, fresh herbs (such as parsley or thyme), lemon zest

Instructions:

1. **Prep the Cauliflower:** Wash and cut the cauliflower into florets of similar size. Dry them thoroughly using paper towels to ensure they get crispy in the air fryer.
2. **Season the Cauliflower:** In a large bowl, toss the cauliflower florets with olive oil, garlic powder, onion powder, paprika, salt, and pepper. You can adjust the seasoning to your taste.
3. **Preheat the Air Fryer:** Preheat your air fryer to 375°F (190°C) for a few minutes.
4. **Air Fry the Cauliflower:** Place the seasoned cauliflower florets in the air fryer basket in a single layer, making sure they don't overcrowd. You may need to cook them in batches depending on the size of your air fryer. This helps ensure they cook evenly and get crispy.
5. **Cooking Time:** Air fry the cauliflower at 375°F (190°C) for about 15-20 minutes. Shake the basket or flip the cauliflower florets halfway through to ensure even cooking. The exact time may vary depending on your air fryer and the size of the florets. Cook until they are tender and golden brown.
6. **Optional: Add Flavor:** If you'd like to add extra flavor, sprinkle grated Parmesan cheese over the cauliflower during the last few minutes of cooking, and let it melt and brown. You can also add fresh herbs or a touch of lemon zest for a zesty kick.
7. **Serve:** Once the cauliflower is cooked to your desired level of crispiness, transfer it to a serving plate. It's best enjoyed hot.

Notes:

1. **Don't Overcrowd the Air Fryer:** Make sure not to overcrowd the air fryer basket. This ensures that the cauliflower cooks evenly and gets crispy. If you have a small air fryer, cook in batches.
2. **Customize the Seasoning:** Feel free to customize the seasoning to your preference. You can add herbs, spices, or even a drizzle of balsamic vinegar for a different flavor profile.
3. **Check for Doneness:** Keep an eye on the cauliflower as it cooks since cooking times may vary with different air fryers. You want the cauliflower to be tender on the inside and golden brown on the outside.
4. **Serve with Dipping Sauce:** Air-fried cauliflower is delicious on its own, but you can also serve it with a dipping sauce like ranch, tzatziki, or hummus for extra flavor.
5. **Experiment with Different Variations:** You can try different variations of this recipe by using different seasonings and sauces to create a variety of flavors.

Air fryer cauliflower is a fantastic, healthier alternative to fried snacks, and it's a versatile dish that can be served as a side or even as a tasty appetizer. Enjoy!

Certainly! Here are some additional tips and variations for making air fryer cauliflower:

Tips:

1. **Preheat the Air Fryer:** Preheating the air fryer helps with even cooking and better results. It's a good practice to preheat for a few minutes before placing the cauliflower inside.
2. **Use Cooking Spray:** To help the cauliflower become even crispier, you can lightly spray the florets with cooking oil or use a cooking spray before placing them in the air fryer.
3. **Experiment with Seasonings:** Cauliflower is a versatile vegetable that pairs well with a wide range of seasonings. You can try adding cumin, chili powder, curry powder, or smoked paprika for different flavor profiles.
4. **Breadcrumbs or Panko:** For an extra crispy coating, consider dipping the cauliflower in breadcrumbs or panko before air frying. This will give it a crunchy texture.

Variations:

1. **Buffalo Cauliflower:** Toss the cooked cauliflower in buffalo sauce after air frying for a spicy and tangy twist. Serve with ranch or blue cheese dressing for dipping.
2. **Honey Sriracha Cauliflower:** Create a sweet and spicy glaze by combining honey and Sriracha sauce. Toss the cooked cauliflower in the glaze for a unique flavor.
3. **Cauliflower "Wings":** Dip the cauliflower florets in a batter made from flour, water, and seasonings. After air frying, toss them in your favorite wing sauce for a vegetarian alternative to chicken wings.
4. **Parmesan Roasted Cauliflower:** Instead of adding grated Parmesan during cooking, sprinkle it over the cooked cauliflower when serving for a cheesy, nutty flavor.
5. **Teriyaki Cauliflower:** Create a teriyaki glaze with soy sauce, ginger, garlic, and brown sugar. Toss the cooked cauliflower in the glaze and garnish with sesame seeds and green onions.
6. **Lemon Herb Cauliflower:** For a fresh and zesty flavor, drizzle the cooked cauliflower with lemon juice and sprinkle with fresh herbs like parsley and thyme.
7. **Sesame Ginger Cauliflower:** Create a marinade with sesame oil, soy sauce, ginger, and garlic. Toss the cauliflower in the marinade before air frying and sprinkle with sesame seeds.
8. **Mexican Cauliflower:** Season the cauliflower with taco or fajita seasoning before air frying. Serve it with salsa, guacamole, and sour cream.

Remember that the air fryer is a versatile appliance, and you can get creative with your cauliflower dishes. Feel free to combine different seasonings and sauces to create your own unique flavor combinations. Enjoy your air-fried cauliflower in various ways, whether as a side dish, snack, or even in salads and wraps.

Crispy Air Fryer Tater Tots

Crispy air fryer tater tots are a delicious and healthier alternative to traditional deep-fried tater tots. They come out perfectly golden brown and crunchy on the outside, with a fluffy interior. Here's a recipe and some notes to help you make the best air fryer tater tots:

Ingredients:

- Frozen tater tots
- Cooking spray or oil (optional)
- Salt and other seasonings (optional)

Instructions:

1. **Preheat your Air Fryer:** Preheat your air fryer to 400°F (200°C). Preheating ensures even cooking and better crisping.
2. **Arrange the Tater Tots:** Place the frozen tater tots in a single layer in the air fryer basket. You can lightly grease the basket or the tater tots with cooking spray or a small amount of oil to enhance the crispiness, but this step is optional.
3. **Cooking Time:** Cook the tater tots at 400°F for about 15-20 minutes. The exact time may vary depending on your specific air fryer model, so it's a good idea to check the tots periodically and shake the basket or flip them to ensure even cooking. You can add a few extra minutes if you prefer them crispier.
4. **Seasoning:** If desired, season the tater tots with salt or any other seasonings of your choice immediately after removing them from the air fryer. Common seasonings include paprika, garlic powder, onion powder, or grated Parmesan cheese.
5. **Serve:** Serve your crispy tater tots hot and enjoy them with your favorite dipping sauces, such as ketchup, ranch dressing, or aioli.

Notes:

1. **Preheating:** Preheating the air fryer is important because it helps the tater tots cook evenly and get that nice crispy texture. It also prevents them from sticking to the basket.
2. **Avoid Overcrowding:** Do not overcrowd the air fryer basket. It's crucial to leave enough space for air circulation to ensure that the tater tots cook evenly. If you have a lot of tater tots to cook, it's best to do it in batches.
3. **Shaking or Flipping:** To ensure uniform cooking and even browning, shake the basket or flip the tater tots halfway through the cooking time. This helps prevent any spots from getting too dark.
4. **Oil or Cooking Spray:** While oil or cooking spray is optional, it can help improve the texture and flavor of your tater tots. A light coating of oil will make them crispier, but you can omit it if you prefer a lower-fat version.

5. **Experiment with Seasonings:** Get creative with your seasonings! Tater tots are versatile and can be customized with various flavors to suit your taste.

Enjoy your homemade air fryer tater tots as a side dish or snack. They're quick and easy to make, and you can customize them to your liking.

Certainly! Here are some additional tips and ideas to make your air fryer tater tots even better:

1. Cheese-Stuffed Tater Tots: Make your tater tots extra special by stuffing them with cheese. Simply cut small cubes of your favorite cheese (cheddar, mozzarella, or pepper jack) and insert them into the center of each tater tot before air frying. The cheese will melt inside, creating a gooey, delicious surprise.

2. Seasoning Ideas:

- BBQ Tater Tots: Sprinkle tater tots with BBQ seasoning or rub before air frying for a smoky, tangy flavor.
- Cajun Tater Tots: Coat your tots in a mixture of Cajun seasoning for a spicy kick.
- Everything Bagel Tater Tots: Sprinkle tater tots with an "everything bagel" seasoning blend for a unique twist.
- Truffle Parmesan Tater Tots: After cooking, drizzle truffle oil and sprinkle grated Parmesan cheese on your tater tots for a gourmet touch.

3. Dipping Sauces: Elevate the tater tot experience with a variety of dipping sauces. Some popular options include sriracha mayo, buffalo sauce, honey mustard, or even a homemade cheese sauce for cheese lovers.

4. Mixing Varieties: Combine different varieties of frozen tater tots, such as regular, sweet potato, and seasoned tots, for a fun and flavorful mix.

5. Crisping Up Leftovers: If you have leftover tater tots, you can reheat them in the air fryer. They may not be as crispy as fresh ones, but a few minutes in the air fryer will help bring back some of the crunch.

6. Make Your Own Tater Tots: If you want to take it to the next level, consider making your own tater tots from scratch. Grate potatoes, season them, and form small cylinders or shapes before air frying.

7. Cleaning the Air Fryer: After you're done cooking tater tots, don't forget to clean your air fryer basket and tray. Use warm, soapy water and a non-abrasive sponge or brush to remove any residue.

8. Be Mindful of Allergies: If you or your guests have allergies or dietary restrictions, be sure to check the ingredients on the package of frozen tater tots. Some brands may contain allergens or additives.

Experiment with these tips and ideas to create your own unique spin on air fryer tater tots. Whether you prefer them classic or loaded with extras, tater tots are a versatile and satisfying snack or side dish that's sure to please.

Air Fryer Roasted Beets

Air fryer roasted beets are a delicious and easy way to prepare this nutritious root vegetable. Here's a simple recipe and some notes to help you make perfectly roasted beets in your air fryer:

Ingredients:

- Fresh beets (as many as you need)
- Olive oil or cooking spray
- Salt and pepper, to taste
- Optional: herbs and spices of your choice (rosemary, thyme, garlic powder, etc.)

Instructions:

1. **Prepare the Beets:**
   - Wash the beets thoroughly to remove any dirt or debris. You can leave the skin on or peel them if you prefer. Just make sure they are clean.
2. **Cut and Season:**
   - Trim off the tops and roots of the beets. Then, cut the beets into bite-sized pieces. You can also leave them whole if they are small enough.
   - Place the beet pieces in a bowl and drizzle with olive oil or use cooking spray to lightly coat them. Season with salt, pepper, and any optional herbs or spices. Toss to ensure the beets are evenly coated.
3. **Preheat the Air Fryer:**
   - Preheat your air fryer to 375°F (190°C).
4. **Air Fry the Beets:**
   - Once the air fryer is preheated, place the seasoned beet pieces in a single layer in the air fryer basket. It's important not to overcrowd the basket to ensure even cooking.
   - Cook the beets for about 15-20 minutes, shaking or flipping them halfway through the cooking time to ensure even browning. The cooking time may vary depending on the size of the beet pieces and the specific air fryer model.
5. **Check for Doneness:**
   - To check for doneness, pierce the beets with a fork or knife. They should be tender and easily pierced. If they're not done yet, continue to air fry in 5-minute increments until they reach your desired level of tenderness.
6. **Serve:**

- Once the beets are roasted to your liking, remove them from the air fryer, and let them cool slightly. Serve as a side dish or use them in salads, bowls, or other recipes.

Notes:

- Beets can release a vibrant red juice that can stain your hands and surfaces. Consider wearing gloves when handling beets and using a cutting board that's easy to clean.
- Be sure to cut the beets into uniform sizes to ensure even cooking.
- You can customize the seasoning to your taste. Beets pair well with a variety of herbs and spices, so feel free to experiment.
- Don't forget to shake or flip the beets during the cooking process to prevent sticking and ensure even crisping.
- The cooking time can vary depending on the air fryer's make and model. Be sure to check for doneness by testing the beets' tenderness rather than relying solely on the cooking time.

Air fryer roasted beets make for a healthy and flavorful side dish or ingredient in other recipes, and they have a delightful crispy exterior with a tender interior. Enjoy!

Certainly, here are some additional tips and ideas for air fryer roasted beets:

1. Seasoning Variations:

- Beets have a naturally sweet and earthy flavor, which pairs well with a variety of seasonings. You can add a touch of sweetness with a drizzle of honey or maple syrup, or a hint of acidity with balsamic vinegar.

2. Add Some Heat:

- For a bit of spice, you can sprinkle the beets with red pepper flakes or a pinch of cayenne pepper before air frying.

3. Parmesan-Crusted Beets:

- After air frying, you can sprinkle the beets with grated Parmesan cheese and return them to the air fryer for a couple of minutes until the cheese is melted and crispy. This creates a delicious Parmesan-crusted beet side dish.

4. Herbed Beets:

- Experiment with fresh herbs like rosemary, thyme, or dill to add a savory herbal element to your roasted beets.

5. Citrus Zest:

- Add a zesty twist by grating some citrus zest (lemon, orange, or lime) over the beets before serving. The citrus zest brightens up the flavors.

6. Dipping Sauces:

- Consider serving your air fryer roasted beets with dipping sauces. A classic choice is a garlic aioli, tzatziki, or a simple yogurt-based dip. These sauces can complement the sweetness of the beets nicely.

7. Serving Ideas:

- Air fryer roasted beets are a versatile ingredient. You can use them in salads, grain bowls, sandwiches, or as a side dish. They also work well in beet and goat cheese salads, or you can even puree them into a creamy beet soup.

8. Storage and Reheating:

- If you have leftover roasted beets, store them in an airtight container in the refrigerator. They will stay fresh for a few days. Reheat them in the air fryer for a few minutes to regain their crispiness, or you can warm them in the microwave.

9. Beets of Different Colors:

- Beets come in various colors, including red, golden, and Chioggia (candy-striped). You can mix and match different beet colors to create a colorful and visually appealing dish.

10. Complement with Greens:

- Pair air fryer roasted beets with fresh greens like arugula, spinach, or mixed lettuce for a tasty beet salad. Top it with some nuts and a vinaigrette for added texture and flavor.

Roasted beets are not only delicious but also nutritious, as they are packed with vitamins, minerals, and antioxidants. With these tips and ideas, you can enjoy this versatile vegetable in various ways and tailor the flavor to your preferences. Happy cooking!

Air Fryer Shrimp

Air frying shrimp is a quick and healthy way to enjoy crispy, succulent shrimp without the need for excessive oil. Here's a basic air fryer shrimp recipe along with some notes to help you make the most of your dish:

Ingredients:

- 1 pound of large shrimp, peeled and deveined

- 2 tablespoons of olive oil
- 1 teaspoon of paprika
- 1/2 teaspoon of garlic powder
- 1/2 teaspoon of onion powder
- 1/2 teaspoon of salt
- 1/4 teaspoon of black pepper
- 1/4 teaspoon of cayenne pepper (adjust to your spice preference)
- 1/2 cup of breadcrumbs or panko crumbs (for added crispiness)
- Cooking spray (optional)

Instructions:

1. Preheat your air fryer to 375°F (190°C).
2. In a mixing bowl, combine the olive oil, paprika, garlic powder, onion powder, salt, pepper, and cayenne pepper. Mix well to create a marinade.
3. Add the peeled and deveined shrimp to the marinade, ensuring they are evenly coated. Let them sit for about 10-15 minutes to absorb the flavors.
4. If you want extra crispy shrimp, coat them with breadcrumbs or panko crumbs. To do this, dip each shrimp into the breadcrumbs, pressing lightly to adhere the crumbs to the shrimp.
5. If desired, lightly spray the air fryer basket with cooking spray to prevent sticking.
6. Arrange the shrimp in a single layer in the air fryer basket, making sure they are not overcrowded. You may need to cook them in batches if you have a smaller air fryer.
7. Air fry the shrimp at 375°F (190°C) for 5-8 minutes, flipping them halfway through the cooking time. The exact cooking time will depend on the size of the shrimp and your air fryer model. Shrimp are done when they turn pink and the coating is golden brown.
8. Serve your air-fried shrimp hot with your favorite dipping sauce, such as cocktail sauce or tartar sauce.

Notes:

1. **Preheating**: Preheating your air fryer is important as it helps ensure even cooking and a crispy texture.
2. **Marinade**: Marinating the shrimp adds flavor, but you can also customize the seasonings to your liking. Try different herbs and spices to suit your taste.
3. **Breadcrumbs**: Using breadcrumbs or panko crumbs will give your shrimp an extra crunch. You can use regular or gluten-free breadcrumbs as per your dietary preferences.
4. **Don't overcrowd**: Make sure the shrimp are arranged in a single layer without overcrowding the basket. This allows the hot air to circulate around them, promoting even cooking.
5. **Cooking time**: The cooking time can vary depending on the size of your shrimp and the air fryer model. Keep an eye on them and adjust the time as needed.
6. **Dipping sauce**: Serve your air-fried shrimp with your preferred dipping sauce, whether it's a classic cocktail sauce, aioli, or something of your choice.

Enjoy your crispy and delicious air-fried shrimp as a snack, appetizer, or main course!

Certainly! Here are some additional tips and variations to consider when making air-fryer shrimp:

Additional Tips:

1. **Frozen Shrimp**: If you're using frozen shrimp, be sure to thaw them before marinating and cooking. Pat them dry with paper towels to remove excess moisture, which can affect the crispiness.
2. **Shrimp Size**: Larger shrimp work well for this recipe, but you can use smaller shrimp as well. Just adjust the cooking time accordingly. Larger shrimp may take 6-8 minutes, while smaller shrimp may only need 4-6 minutes.
3. **Shake Basket**: To ensure even cooking and avoid sticking, shake the air fryer basket halfway through the cooking time. This will help the shrimp cook evenly on all sides.
4. **Oil Options**: While olive oil is commonly used for its flavor, you can use other high-heat cooking oils like canola, vegetable, or avocado oil.
5. **Custom Seasonings**: Feel free to experiment with different seasonings and spices to create a flavor profile that suits your taste. Lemon zest, smoked paprika, Cajun seasoning, or Old Bay seasoning can add unique flavors.

Variations:

1. **Coconut Shrimp**: Instead of breadcrumbs, use shredded coconut for a tropical twist. Dip the shrimp in beaten egg before coating with coconut for better adhesion.
2. **Lemon Butter Shrimp**: Create a lemon butter sauce by melting butter and mixing it with lemon juice and zest. Drizzle this sauce over the cooked shrimp for a burst of citrus flavor.
3. **Honey Sriracha Shrimp**: For a sweet and spicy option, mix honey and sriracha sauce and glaze the shrimp with this combination before air frying. It's a delightful combination of flavors.
4. **Buffalo Shrimp**: Toss the cooked shrimp in your favorite buffalo sauce to make spicy buffalo shrimp. Serve with celery sticks and ranch or blue cheese dressing.
5. **Garlic Parmesan Shrimp**: After air frying, toss the shrimp in a mixture of melted butter, minced garlic, and grated Parmesan cheese for a creamy, savory coating.
6. **Mango Salsa**: Serve your air-fried shrimp with a homemade mango salsa for a refreshing and tropical twist. Mango, red onion, cilantro, lime juice, and a pinch of chili powder make a great salsa.
7. **Dipping Sauces**: Experiment with different dipping sauces like tzatziki, teriyaki, sweet chili, or a creamy garlic aioli to complement the shrimp.

Feel free to get creative and adapt this basic recipe to suit your personal preferences. Air frying allows you to enjoy shrimp with a variety of flavors and textures while keeping it healthier compared to traditional frying methods.

Easy Air Fryer Baby Back Ribs

Air fryers are a convenient way to cook baby back ribs, offering a quicker cooking time and less mess compared to traditional methods like grilling or baking. Here's an easy air fryer baby back ribs recipe along with some important notes:

Ingredients:

- 1 rack of baby back ribs
- 1/4 cup of your favorite BBQ sauce (homemade or store-bought)
- 1 tablespoon of olive oil
- 1 teaspoon of paprika
- 1 teaspoon of garlic powder
- 1 teaspoon of onion powder
- 1/2 teaspoon of salt
- 1/2 teaspoon of black pepper

Instructions:

1. **Prepare the Ribs:**
   - Remove the membrane from the back of the ribs. This helps the seasonings penetrate the meat better and makes for more tender ribs.
   - Rinse the ribs under cold water and pat them dry with paper towels.
2. **Season the Ribs:**
   - In a small bowl, mix together the olive oil, paprika, garlic powder, onion powder, salt, and black pepper to create a seasoning rub.
   - Rub the seasoning mixture all over the ribs, making sure to coat them evenly. You can also let them marinate in the seasoning for an hour or longer in the refrigerator for more flavor.
3. **Preheat the Air Fryer:**
   - Preheat your air fryer to 350°F (175°C). This will take about 5 minutes.
4. **Cook the Ribs:**
   - Cut the rack of ribs into sections that can fit comfortably in your air fryer basket. This usually means cutting them into 2-3 rib bone sections.
   - Place the ribs in the air fryer basket in a single layer, making sure not to overcrowd them. You may need to cook them in batches.
   - Cook the ribs at 350°F (175°C) for 25-30 minutes, flipping them halfway through the cooking time. You may need to adjust the time based on the size and thickness of the ribs.
5. **Apply BBQ Sauce:**
   - About 5 minutes before the ribs are done, open the air fryer and brush a layer of BBQ sauce onto both sides of the ribs. You can use a basting brush for this.

6. **Finish Cooking:**
    ○ Continue to cook the ribs for the remaining 5 minutes or until they reach your desired level of doneness and the sauce is caramelized.
7. **Serve:**
    ○ Once done, remove the ribs from the air fryer and let them rest for a few minutes before cutting them into individual ribs. Serve with additional BBQ sauce for dipping if desired.

Notes:

- Air fryers vary in size and power, so cooking times may need to be adjusted based on your specific model. Keep an eye on the ribs, so they don't overcook or burn.
- You can customize the seasoning and BBQ sauce to your liking. Experiment with different flavors to suit your preferences.
- Don't overcrowd the air fryer basket. It's important to leave enough space for proper air circulation to ensure even cooking.
- Use a meat thermometer to check for doneness. Baby back ribs are safe to eat at 145°F (63°C), but many people prefer them to be more tender, which may require a slightly higher internal temperature.
- Make sure to preheat your air fryer to ensure even and efficient cooking.

Enjoy your delicious air-fried baby back ribs!

Certainly! Here are some additional tips and notes to help you achieve the best results when making air fryer baby back ribs:

1. **Use the Right Equipment:**
    ○ Make sure you have an appropriate-sized air fryer that can accommodate the size of the baby back ribs without overcrowding. If your air fryer is on the smaller side, you may need to cut the ribs into smaller sections.
2. **Dry the Ribs Thoroughly:**
    ○ It's essential to pat the ribs dry with paper towels after rinsing. Moisture on the surface of the meat can prevent the seasoning from adhering properly and can affect the cooking process.
3. **Monitor Cooking Time:**
    ○ Keep a close eye on the cooking time, especially the first time you make ribs in your specific air fryer. Cooking times can vary, so it's important to check for doneness to prevent overcooking.
4. **Use a Meat Thermometer:**
    ○ Invest in a good meat thermometer to ensure your ribs are cooked to the desired internal temperature. The ribs are safe to eat at 145°F (63°C), but many people prefer them more tender, around 190-203°F (88-95°C).
5. **Baste and Layer the Sauce:**

- You can apply BBQ sauce in layers to create a nice glaze on the ribs. Apply a layer, let it cook for a few minutes, and then apply another layer until you achieve the desired level of caramelization.

6. **Experiment with Different Flavors:**
   - Feel free to experiment with different seasoning rubs, sauces, and marinades. You can create a variety of flavor profiles, from sweet and smoky to spicy and tangy, to suit your taste.

7. **Rest the Ribs:**
   - Let the ribs rest for a few minutes after cooking before cutting them. This allows the juices to redistribute and keeps the ribs moist and flavorful.

8. **Sides and Serving Suggestions:**
   - Baby back ribs are often served with classic barbecue sides like coleslaw, baked beans, cornbread, and potato salad. Consider your favorite sides to complete the meal.

9. **Cleaning Your Air Fryer:**
   - After cooking the ribs, make sure to clean your air fryer thoroughly. Many air fryer components are dishwasher safe, making cleanup easier.

10. **Safety First:**
    - Be cautious when working with hot air fryer baskets and racks. Use oven mitts or kitchen towels to handle them, and be careful when flipping the ribs.

With these tips and notes, you should be well-equipped to make delicious air fryer baby back ribs that are tender, flavorful, and a hit at your next meal. Enjoy your cooking!

Air Fryer Sponge Cake

Certainly! Here's a recipe for making a simple sponge cake in an air fryer along with some notes:

Air Fryer Sponge Cake Recipe:

Ingredients:

- 1 cup all-purpose flour
- 1/2 cup granulated sugar
- 3 large eggs
- 1/4 cup vegetable oil
- 1/4 cup milk
- 1 teaspoon vanilla extract
- 1 teaspoon baking powder
- 1/4 teaspoon salt

Instructions:

1. **Prepare the Air Fryer:** Preheat your air fryer to 320°F (160°C) for about 5 minutes. Use a parchment paper liner in the air fryer basket to prevent sticking.
2. **Sift Dry Ingredients:** In a bowl, sift together the all-purpose flour, baking powder, and salt. Sifting helps to aerate the flour and ensure a lighter texture.
3. **Whip Eggs and Sugar:** In another large bowl, whisk together the eggs and granulated sugar until the mixture is pale and slightly thick. This might take about 2-3 minutes of whisking.
4. **Add Oil and Milk:** Gradually add the vegetable oil and milk to the egg-sugar mixture, whisking continuously. This ensures even mixing.
5. **Incorporate Dry Ingredients:** Gently fold the sifted dry ingredients into the wet mixture using a spatula. Be careful not to overmix, as this can make the cake dense.
6. **Add Vanilla Extract:** Stir in the vanilla extract for flavor.
7. **Pour Batter:** Pour the cake batter into a greased and parchment-lined cake pan that fits inside your air fryer basket.
8. **Air Fry the Cake:** Place the cake pan in the preheated air fryer and set the temperature to 320°F (160°C). Air fry for about 25-30 minutes. The exact time may vary depending on your air fryer, so keep an eye on it. The cake is done when a toothpick inserted into the center comes out clean.
9. **Cool and Serve:** Once the cake is done, remove it from the air fryer and let it cool in the pan for a few minutes. Then, transfer it to a wire rack to cool completely. Once it's cool, you can frost or serve it as desired.

Notes:

1. **Preheating:** Preheating the air fryer is essential to get an even and consistent bake. Make sure to preheat it according to the specified temperature in the recipe.
2. **Cake Pan:** Ensure that the cake pan you use fits comfortably in your air fryer basket. You may need to adjust the size or shape of the pan to fit your specific air fryer.
3. **Temperature and Time:** Air fryer models can vary, so keep an eye on your cake to avoid overcooking. The suggested time and temperature are guidelines, and you may need to make slight adjustments.
4. **Parchment Paper:** Using parchment paper helps prevent the cake from sticking to the air fryer basket. Make sure it doesn't obstruct the air circulation in the air fryer.
5. **Frosting:** You can frost the sponge cake with your favorite frosting, or you can simply dust it with powdered sugar for a classic finish.

Enjoy your homemade air fryer sponge cake!

Certainly! Here are some additional tips and notes to help you make the perfect air fryer sponge cake:

1. **Greasing the Pan:** In addition to using parchment paper, you can lightly grease the cake pan with a thin layer of butter or cooking spray. This extra step helps ensure the cake doesn't stick to the sides of the pan.
2. **Mixing Techniques:** When incorporating dry ingredients into the wet mixture, use a gentle folding motion to maintain the cake's light and airy texture. Overmixing can lead to a denser cake.
3. **Size and Shape of the Pan:** The size and shape of the cake pan can affect baking time. A thinner, wider cake will cook faster than a thicker, smaller one. Keep this in mind when adjusting your baking time.
4. **Testing for Doneness:** Use a toothpick or a cake tester to check for doneness. Insert it into the center of the cake, and if it comes out clean or with just a few crumbs, your cake is done. If it comes out with wet batter, continue baking for a few more minutes and retest.
5. **Flavor Variations:** You can customize the flavor of your sponge cake by adding zest from citrus fruits, such as lemon or orange, or a teaspoon of your favorite extract (like almond or citrus) for added depth of flavor.
6. **Cooling:** It's essential to allow the cake to cool completely on a wire rack before serving or frosting. This helps the cake set and prevents it from becoming soggy.
7. **Frosting Options:** You can choose various frosting options, such as buttercream, cream cheese frosting, chocolate ganache, or a simple dusting of powdered sugar. Be creative and choose what suits your taste.
8. **Decorations:** Add fresh berries, fruit compote, chocolate chips, or edible flowers as decorative elements to enhance the cake's presentation.
9. **Storage:** Store any leftover cake in an airtight container at room temperature for a day or two, or in the refrigerator for longer shelf life.
10. **Experiment and Enjoy:** Sponge cake is a versatile dessert. Feel free to experiment with different flavors, fillings, and toppings to create a unique cake that suits your preferences.

Remember that practice makes perfect, so don't be discouraged if your first attempt isn't flawless. Baking in an air fryer can take some trial and error to get the timing just right for your specific model. Enjoy the process and the delicious results!

Air Fryer Grilled Cheese

Air fryer grilled cheese is a quick and easy way to make this classic comfort food with a crispy, golden exterior and gooey, melty interior. Here's a simple recipe and some notes to help you make the perfect air fryer grilled cheese:

Ingredients:

- 2 slices of bread (your choice of bread, but a sturdy one like sourdough works well)

- 2-4 slices of your favorite cheese (cheddar, American, Swiss, etc.)
- 1-2 tablespoons of softened butter or mayonnaise (for spreading)
- Optional additions: cooked bacon, tomato slices, caramelized onions, etc.

Instructions:

1. **Preheat the Air Fryer:** Preheat your air fryer to 350°F (175°C). This typically takes about 2-3 minutes.
2. **Assemble the Sandwich:**
   - Spread a thin layer of softened butter or mayonnaise on one side of each slice of bread.
   - Place the cheese slices between the slices of bread, with the buttered/mayo side facing out.
3. **Air Fry the Grilled Cheese:**
   - Place the sandwich in the air fryer basket. You can also use a piece of parchment paper to prevent sticking, but it's optional.
   - Air fry for about 5-7 minutes, flipping the sandwich halfway through, or until the bread is crispy and golden brown, and the cheese is melted.
   - The cooking time can vary based on your air fryer's model, so keep an eye on it to avoid overcooking.
4. **Serve:** Once done, carefully remove the grilled cheese from the air fryer, let it cool for a minute or two, then slice it diagonally and serve it with your favorite dipping sauce, such as tomato soup or ketchup.

Notes:

1. **Butter or Mayonnaise:** Both butter and mayonnaise work well for spreading on the bread before cooking. Butter gives it a classic flavor, while mayo can give the bread a crispy, tangy crust.
2. **Cheese Selection:** Use your favorite cheese or a combination of cheeses for the filling. Cheddar, American, Swiss, and mozzarella are popular choices, but feel free to experiment.
3. **Bread Choice:** Sturdy bread like sourdough, artisanal bread, or a good-quality white bread is ideal for air frying. Softer bread might become too crispy or dry.
4. **Preheating:** Preheating the air fryer is crucial for even cooking and a golden exterior.
5. **Optional Additions:** You can get creative with your grilled cheese by adding ingredients like cooked bacon, tomato slices, caramelized onions, or even a smear of mustard or pesto for extra flavor.
6. **Keep an Eye on It:** Cooking times may vary depending on your air fryer model, so be sure to monitor the sandwich's progress to avoid burning it.

Air fryer grilled cheese is a quick and satisfying meal that's perfect for lunch, dinner, or even as a late-night snack. Enjoy experimenting with different fillings and seasonings to create your perfect grilled cheese sandwich.

Certainly! Here are some additional tips and ideas for making air fryer grilled cheese:

Tips:

1. **Slice Thickness:** Use thin slices of cheese rather than thick chunks. Thin slices will melt more evenly and quickly, ensuring that your bread doesn't overcook while waiting for the cheese to melt.
2. **Prevent Sticking:** If you're worried about your grilled cheese sticking to the air fryer basket, you can place a piece of parchment paper or aluminum foil in the basket. Just make sure to cut it to the size of the basket and leave some space for air circulation.
3. **Temperature and Timing:** The recommended temperature and timing are starting points. Depending on your specific air fryer model, you may need to adjust the temperature and time slightly. Keep experimenting until you find the perfect settings for your appliance.
4. **Filling Ingredients:** Get creative with your fillings! Consider adding ingredients like sliced jalapeños for some heat, avocado for creaminess, or different herbs and spices for extra flavor.
5. **Two Sandwiches:** You can often make two sandwiches at once in most air fryers, as long as there's enough space for air circulation. Just make sure they're not overlapping.
6. **Flipping:** Flipping the sandwich halfway through the cooking process is essential for even browning on both sides. Use a spatula to do this gently.

Recipe Variations:

1. **Pesto Grilled Cheese:** Spread a thin layer of basil pesto on the inside of the bread before adding cheese for a delicious twist.
2. **Caprese Grilled Cheese:** Use mozzarella cheese, fresh basil leaves, and tomato slices for a Caprese-style grilled cheese sandwich.
3. **Bacon and Tomato:** Add crispy bacon strips and tomato slices to your grilled cheese for a savory and satisfying meal.
4. **Spicy Grilled Cheese:** Sprinkle some crushed red pepper flakes or add a slice of pepper jack cheese for a spicy kick.
5. **Sweet and Savory:** Try a sweet and savory combo by adding fig jam or apple slices to your grilled cheese.
6. **Herb-Infused Butter:** Mix finely chopped fresh herbs (e.g., rosemary, thyme, or parsley) into your butter or mayo for a fragrant twist.
7. **Mini Grilled Cheese:** Make mini grilled cheese sandwiches using slider-sized buns for a fun and party-friendly snack.
8. **Dipping Sauces:** Serve your grilled cheese with various dipping sauces like marinara sauce, ranch dressing, or even a balsamic reduction for added flavor.

Remember that the key to making the perfect air fryer grilled cheese is experimentation. Play around with different ingredients, seasonings, and cooking times to find your personal favorite. Enjoy your delicious air-fried grilled cheese sandwiches!

Air Fryer Onion Potatoes (Lipton Onion Soup)

Air Fryer Onion Potatoes with Lipton Onion Soup Mix is a delicious and simple side dish that's perfect for any meal. Here's a recipe and some notes to help you make this tasty dish:

Ingredients:

- 4-5 medium-sized potatoes, peeled and cut into wedges or cubes
- 1 packet of Lipton Onion Soup Mix
- 2-3 tablespoons of olive oil
- Salt and pepper to taste (optional)
- Cooking spray (for the air fryer basket)

Instructions:

1. **Preheat your air fryer:** Set your air fryer to preheat at 375°F (190°C) for a few minutes while you prepare the potatoes.
2. **Prepare the potatoes:** Peel and cut the potatoes into wedges or cubes. The size of the pieces will affect the cooking time, so try to keep them uniform for even cooking.
3. **Coat the potatoes:** In a large bowl, add the potato pieces. Drizzle olive oil over them, and then sprinkle the entire packet of Lipton Onion Soup Mix on top. You can add some salt and pepper to taste if you like. Toss the potatoes to coat them evenly with the oil and soup mix.
4. **Prep the air fryer:** Lightly spray the air fryer basket with cooking spray to prevent sticking.
5. **Air fry the potatoes:** Place the coated potato pieces in the air fryer basket in a single layer, without overcrowding. You may need to cook in batches if your air fryer is small. Cook the potatoes at 375°F (190°C) for about 20-25 minutes, shaking or flipping them halfway through the cooking time for even crispiness.
6. **Check for doneness:** After 20-25 minutes, check the potatoes for doneness. They should be golden brown and crispy on the outside and tender on the inside. If they need a bit more cooking, continue air frying for another 5-10 minutes, checking them periodically.
7. **Serve:** Once the potatoes are cooked to your liking, remove them from the air fryer and let them cool for a minute or two. Serve them hot as a side dish for your meal.

Recipe Notes:

- Be mindful of the potato size and the specific model of your air fryer, as cooking times may vary. Smaller potato pieces may cook faster, while larger ones may take longer.
- The Lipton Onion Soup Mix adds a lot of flavor to the potatoes, so be cautious with additional salt. Taste the potatoes after cooking and add more salt if needed.

- You can customize this recipe by adding other seasonings or herbs, like garlic powder, paprika, or rosemary, to enhance the flavor according to your preference.
- These air-fried onion potatoes are great as a side dish for various meals, from grilled meats to vegetarian options.
- Experiment with different potato varieties, such as russet, red, or Yukon gold, to find your favorite for this recipe.

Enjoy your crispy and flavorful air fryer onion potatoes with Lipton Onion Soup Mix!

Certainly, here are some additional tips and variations to enhance your Air Fryer Onion Potatoes with Lipton Onion Soup Mix:

Tips:

1. **Even Sizing:** Try to keep the potato pieces as uniform as possible. This ensures that they cook evenly and have a consistent texture when done.
2. **Preheat Your Air Fryer:** Preheating your air fryer helps achieve a more consistent cooking result. It's similar to preheating an oven.
3. **Shake or Flip:** It's important to shake or flip the potatoes halfway through the cooking time. This helps ensure that they cook evenly on all sides and become crispy all around.
4. **Don't Overcrowd:** Avoid overcrowding the air fryer basket. If you have a lot of potato pieces, cook them in batches to prevent them from sticking together and to ensure they cook properly.
5. **Check for Doneness:** Keep an eye on the potatoes towards the end of the cooking time. Cooking times can vary depending on the air fryer model, so be sure to adjust as needed to achieve your desired level of crispiness.

Variations:

1. **Cheese:** If you love cheesy potatoes, you can add some shredded cheese during the last few minutes of cooking. Cheddar, mozzarella, or Parmesan are great options.
2. **Herbs and Spices:** Experiment with additional seasonings to suit your taste. Consider adding dried herbs like thyme, oregano, or rosemary for extra flavor. Smoked paprika or cayenne pepper can add a nice kick.
3. **Bacon Bits:** For a smoky flavor and a bit of crunch, sprinkle some bacon bits on top of the potatoes before air frying. You can also add them after cooking as a garnish.
4. **Onions:** Since you're using Lipton Onion Soup Mix, you can enhance the onion flavor by adding some thinly sliced onions to the mix. They will caramelize beautifully in the air fryer.
5. **Sour Cream or Ranch:** Serve the potatoes with a side of sour cream or ranch dressing for dipping. The creamy dip complements the savory potatoes.
6. **Fresh Herbs:** After cooking, sprinkle some fresh chopped herbs like parsley or chives for a burst of freshness and color.
7. **Lemon Zest:** For a citrusy twist, try adding some lemon zest to the potatoes before air frying. The bright, fresh flavor pairs well with the savory onion seasoning.

Remember, this recipe is versatile, and you can adapt it to your taste preferences. The Lipton Onion Soup Mix provides a fantastic base of flavor, and you can build on it with your favorite ingredients and seasonings. Enjoy your customized Air Fryer Onion Potatoes!

Crispy Air Fryer Pork Belly

Crispy air-fried pork belly is a delicious dish that's easier to make and healthier than traditional deep-frying methods. Here's a simple recipe and some key notes to help you achieve that perfect crispy pork belly:

Ingredients:

- 1 lb (450g) pork belly, skin-on
- 1 tablespoon vegetable oil
- 1 teaspoon salt
- 1/2 teaspoon black pepper
- 1/2 teaspoon garlic powder
- 1/2 teaspoon paprika (optional, for extra flavor)
- Cooking spray (optional)

Instructions:

1. **Prep the Pork Belly:**
   - Start by ensuring the pork belly skin is dry. Use paper towels to pat it thoroughly, as moisture can prevent crispiness. Score the skin with a sharp knife, making diagonal or crosshatch cuts, about 1/2 inch apart. This helps the skin crisp up better.
2. **Season the Pork Belly:**
   - Mix the salt, pepper, garlic powder, and paprika in a small bowl. Rub this seasoning mixture evenly over the pork belly, including the sides and the meaty part. Allow it to marinate for at least 30 minutes (or overnight for even better flavor).
3. **Preheat the Air Fryer:**
   - Preheat your air fryer to 400°F (200°C) for about 5 minutes.
4. **Air Frying:**
   - Place the seasoned pork belly in the air fryer basket, skin side up. You can also use a trivet or rack if your air fryer has one; this will help air circulate around the pork better.
5. **Cooking Time:**
   - Cook the pork belly in the preheated air fryer for 25-35 minutes at 400°F (200°C). The cooking time may vary depending on your specific air fryer and the thickness of the pork belly. Check it after 25 minutes and continue cooking if needed.

6. **Check and Adjust:**
   - Keep a close eye on the pork belly. When the skin becomes crispy and the internal temperature reaches 160-165°F (71-74°C), it's ready. You can use a meat thermometer to ensure the internal temperature is safe.
7. **Rest and Slice:**
   - Once cooked, remove the pork belly from the air fryer and let it rest for a few minutes before slicing it into desired portions.
8. **Optional Final Crisp:**
   - If the skin isn't as crispy as you'd like, you can give it a quick blast under the broiler (grill) for a minute or two, but be very cautious not to burn it. You can also use a kitchen torch to crisp up the skin.
9. **Serve:**
   - Serve your crispy air fryer pork belly with your favorite side dishes, such as steamed vegetables, rice, or a refreshing salad.

Notes:

1. **Pork Belly Selection:** Choose pork belly with a good balance of meat and fat. Look for skin that's dry and not too wet.
2. **Scoring the Skin:** Scoring the skin is essential for better crisping and to prevent the pork belly from curling up.
3. **Preheating the Air Fryer:** Preheating the air fryer ensures even cooking and a crispy result.
4. **Temperature and Timing:** Cooking times may vary depending on your air fryer, so it's essential to monitor the process. The internal temperature is the most reliable indicator of doneness.
5. **Safety First:** Be cautious when using the broiler or kitchen torch to avoid burning the pork belly.

Enjoy your crispy air-fried pork belly! It's a delightful dish that combines the rich flavors of pork with the satisfying crunch of crispy skin.

Certainly! Here are some additional tips and information to help you perfect your crispy air fryer pork belly:

1. **Brining:** If you have the time, consider brining the pork belly for a few hours or even overnight before seasoning. A basic brine consists of water, salt, and sugar. This can enhance the flavor and tenderness of the meat.
2. **Patience Is Key:** Achieving crispy skin requires patience. After the initial air frying, let the pork belly rest for a few minutes to allow the juices to redistribute. This will help keep the meat moist and the skin crispy.
3. **Rack or Basket:** Using a rack or basket in your air fryer allows the hot air to circulate around the pork more effectively, promoting even cooking and crispiness.
4. **Basting:** Some recipes suggest basting the pork belly with oil during the cooking process to help the skin crisp up. However, this is optional and can add extra calories.

5. **Flavor Variations:** You can experiment with different seasoning blends or marinades. Consider adding herbs, spices, or even a glaze during the cooking process for additional flavor.
6. **Leftovers:** If you have leftover crispy pork belly, you can reheat it in the air fryer for a few minutes to regain some of its crispiness.
7. **Serving Suggestions:** Crispy pork belly is versatile and pairs well with a variety of sauces and side dishes. Popular choices include hoisin sauce, sweet chili sauce, or a simple soy dipping sauce. Served with steamed vegetables, rice, or noodles, it makes a complete meal.
8. **Customization:** Adjust the seasonings and cooking times to suit your taste. If you like it spicier, add some chili powder. If you prefer it less salty, reduce the salt in the seasoning mix.
9. **Safety Reminder:** Always follow safety guidelines when using your air fryer, and be cautious when handling hot equipment and food.
10. **Experiment:** Cooking times can vary depending on the thickness of the pork belly and your specific air fryer model, so don't be afraid to experiment to find the perfect timing for your preferences.

Remember that practice makes perfect. It may take a couple of tries to get the timing and settings just right for your specific air fryer and preferences. Enjoy your culinary journey to mastering crispy air-fried pork belly!

Best Air Fryer Salmon Recipe

Air fryer salmon is a quick and delicious way to prepare this healthy and flavorful fish. Here's a simple recipe along with some notes for the best results:

Ingredients:

- 2 salmon fillets (about 6-8 ounces each)
- 2 tablespoons olive oil
- 1 teaspoon lemon juice
- 1 teaspoon minced garlic
- 1 teaspoon dried herbs (such as dill, thyme, or rosemary)
- Salt and pepper, to taste
- Lemon wedges, for garnish
- Fresh herbs, for garnish (optional)

Notes:

1. **Preheat the Air Fryer:** Preheat your air fryer to 375°F (190°C) for a few minutes to ensure it's hot and ready to cook.

2. **Prepare the Salmon:** Pat the salmon fillets dry with paper towels. This helps the salmon to crisp up better in the air fryer. If your salmon has skin, you can leave it on or remove it, depending on your preference.
3. **Seasoning:** In a small bowl, mix together the olive oil, lemon juice, minced garlic, dried herbs, salt, and pepper. Brush this mixture onto the salmon fillets, making sure to coat them evenly. You can also marinate the salmon for 15-30 minutes if you have the time for added flavor.
4. **Cooking Time:** Place the seasoned salmon fillets into the air fryer basket, skin-side down (if you kept the skin). Make sure they are not overcrowded to ensure even cooking. Cook for about 10-12 minutes. The exact time may vary depending on your air fryer model and the thickness of the fillets. Salmon is done when it flakes easily with a fork, and the internal temperature reaches 145°F (63°C).
5. **Checking for Doneness:** Check the salmon after 8-10 minutes. You can use a fork to gently flake a small piece from the thickest part of the fillet. If it flakes easily and is opaque in the center, it's done. Be careful not to overcook, as salmon can become dry.
6. **Crispy Skin:** If you kept the skin on and want it crispy, you can flip the salmon and cook it for an additional 2-3 minutes. The skin should become crispy and golden brown.
7. **Serve:** Once the salmon is done, remove it from the air fryer. Squeeze some fresh lemon juice over the top, and garnish with fresh herbs if desired.
8. **Variations:** You can customize the seasonings to your liking. Try different herbs, spices, or marinades to create different flavor profiles.
9. **Side Dishes:** Air fryer salmon pairs well with a variety of side dishes such as steamed vegetables, rice, quinoa, or a fresh salad.

This air fryer salmon recipe is not only quick and easy but also a healthier cooking method compared to traditional frying. It results in a tender and flavorful salmon with a crispy exterior, and it's perfect for a quick weeknight dinner.

Certainly! Here are some additional tips and variations to enhance your air fryer salmon experience:

Tips:

1. **Frozen Salmon:** You can cook frozen salmon fillets in the air fryer. Just add a couple of extra minutes to the cooking time. However, thawing the salmon before cooking is recommended for the best texture and flavor.
2. **Prevent Sticking:** To prevent the salmon from sticking to the air fryer basket, you can line it with parchment paper or lightly brush the basket with a small amount of oil.
3. **Baking Paper:** Some people prefer to cook salmon on a piece of parchment paper inside the air fryer basket to avoid any potential sticking and make cleanup easier.
4. **Size Matters:** Adjust the cooking time based on the thickness of your salmon fillets. Thicker fillets may need a bit more time, while thinner ones will cook faster.

Variations:

1. **Glazed Salmon:** Brush the salmon with your favorite glaze, such as a honey mustard or teriyaki sauce, before cooking. The glaze will caramelize nicely in the air fryer.
2. **Spicy Salmon:** Add some heat by seasoning the salmon with chili powder, paprika, or cayenne pepper.
3. **Pesto Crust:** Spread a thin layer of pesto on the salmon fillets before air frying for a burst of fresh flavor.
4. **Coconut-Crusted Salmon:** Coat the salmon with a mixture of shredded coconut and breadcrumbs for a tropical twist.
5. **Soy and Ginger:** Marinate the salmon in a mixture of soy sauce, ginger, and garlic for an Asian-inspired flavor.
6. **Mediterranean Flavors:** Season with oregano, lemon, and a drizzle of olive oil for a Mediterranean-style salmon.
7. **Taco Seasoning:** For a different twist, rub the salmon with taco seasoning and serve it in tortillas for a salmon taco night.
8. **Herb Butter:** Top the cooked salmon with a pat of herb butter made with fresh herbs like parsley, chives, and thyme.
9. **Crispy Topping:** Add a crispy topping by mixing panko breadcrumbs, grated Parmesan cheese, and a bit of melted butter. Sprinkle it on top of the salmon before air frying.

Remember that the air fryer is a versatile kitchen appliance, so feel free to experiment with different seasonings and flavors to create a salmon dish that suits your taste. Enjoy your air fryer salmon with your favorite sides and garnishes for a satisfying and healthy meal.

Air Fryer Bacon Wrapped Scallops Recipe

Air fryer bacon-wrapped scallops are a delicious and easy-to-make appetizer or main course. The air fryer gives you a crispy bacon exterior while keeping the scallops tender and flavorful on the inside. Here's a simple recipe and some notes to help you make this tasty dish:

Ingredients:

- 12 large sea scallops
- 12 slices of bacon
- Salt and black pepper, to taste
- Toothpicks, for securing the bacon

For the Marinade (optional):

- 2 tablespoons olive oil
- 1 tablespoon lemon juice
- 2 cloves garlic, minced
- 1 teaspoon fresh thyme leaves (or 1/2 teaspoon dried thyme)

- 1/2 teaspoon paprika
- 1/4 teaspoon cayenne pepper (adjust to your spice preference)

Instructions:

1. If using the marinade, combine all the marinade ingredients in a bowl and mix well. Marinate the scallops for 15-30 minutes in the refrigerator. This step is optional, but it adds extra flavor to the scallops.
2. Preheat your air fryer to 400°F (200°C) for a few minutes.
3. While the air fryer is heating, wrap each scallop with a slice of bacon and secure it with a toothpick. Make sure the bacon completely covers the scallop.
4. Season the bacon-wrapped scallops with a little salt and black pepper.
5. Place the bacon-wrapped scallops in a single layer in the air fryer basket. Depending on the size of your air fryer, you may need to do this in batches.
6. Cook in the preheated air fryer at 400°F (200°C) for 10-12 minutes. The exact time may vary depending on the size of your scallops and the air fryer's power, so keep an eye on them. The bacon should be crispy, and the scallops should be cooked through but still tender. You can flip them halfway through the cooking time if desired.
7. Once they are done, remove the bacon-wrapped scallops from the air fryer, and let them rest for a minute or two before serving. The resting time will allow the bacon to crisp up a bit more and the scallops to set.
8. Serve your air fryer bacon-wrapped scallops hot as an appetizer or main course. You can garnish them with fresh herbs like chopped parsley or chives and serve with a dipping sauce, such as a garlic aioli or a sweet chili sauce, if desired.

Notes:

1. Be sure to use large sea scallops for this recipe, as smaller scallops may not wrap well with bacon.
2. The marinade is optional but adds extra flavor. You can adjust the seasonings to suit your taste.
3. The cooking time may vary based on the size and power of your air fryer, so keep an eye on them to prevent overcooking. The goal is crispy bacon and tender scallops.
4. Remember to soak the toothpicks in water for about 10 minutes before using them to prevent them from burning in the air fryer.
5. It's essential to space the bacon-wrapped scallops in the air fryer basket to allow for proper air circulation and even cooking.
6. Serve them immediately to enjoy them at their best. The combination of crispy bacon and succulent scallops is a crowd-pleaser.

Certainly, here are some additional tips and ideas for making air fryer bacon-wrapped scallops:

1. **Bacon Selection:** Choose good-quality bacon for this recipe. You can use regular or thick-cut bacon based on your preference. Smoked bacon adds extra flavor.

2. **Scallop Preparation:** Before wrapping the scallops with bacon, make sure to pat them dry with paper towels. Excess moisture can prevent the bacon from crisping up properly.
3. **Seasoning:** In addition to salt and black pepper, you can experiment with different seasonings. Try adding a pinch of smoked paprika, cayenne pepper, or your favorite seafood seasoning blend for extra flavor.
4. **Serving Options:** These bacon-wrapped scallops are delicious on their own, but you can also serve them over a bed of greens, with a side of rice, or as part of a seafood platter. They make a great addition to a surf and turf meal.
5. **Dipping Sauces:** While these scallops are tasty on their own, consider serving them with dipping sauces like garlic aioli, cocktail sauce, or a simple lemon butter sauce for added variety.
6. **Cooking Time:** The cooking time can vary between air fryer models, so it's essential to monitor them closely, especially the first time you make this recipe. You want the bacon to be crispy but not burnt.
7. **Crowd Pleaser:** This dish is a popular choice for parties and special occasions. You can prepare a larger batch of bacon-wrapped scallops in advance and keep them warm in the oven on low heat until ready to serve.
8. **Variations:** If you want to get creative, you can add a thin strip of jalapeño pepper or a small slice of cheese (like cheddar or Parmesan) inside the bacon wrap for extra flavor.
9. **Air Fryer Maintenance:** Make sure to clean your air fryer basket and tray promptly after making bacon-wrapped scallops. The bacon fat can cause smoking if it's left behind in the air fryer, and regular cleaning will help prevent this.
10. **Safety:** When using toothpicks to secure the bacon, be cautious when handling and eating to avoid any accidents. Inform your guests about the toothpicks, and consider using colored toothpicks to make them more visible.

Enjoy your air fryer bacon-wrapped scallops, and don't hesitate to get creative with the seasonings and dipping sauces to make this dish your own. It's a delightful appetizer or main course that's sure to impress your family and guests.

Succulent Garlic Butter Shrimp

Succulent Garlic Butter Shrimp is a delightful and easy-to-make dish that's perfect for seafood lovers. Here's a recipe and some notes to help you prepare this delicious dish:

Ingredients:

- 1 pound large shrimp, peeled and deveined
- 4 cloves garlic, minced
- 2 tablespoons unsalted butter
- 2 tablespoons olive oil
- 1/4 cup white wine (you can use chicken or vegetable broth as a substitute)

- Juice of 1 lemon
- Salt and black pepper to taste
- 2 tablespoons fresh parsley, chopped
- Optional: red pepper flakes for some heat

Instructions:

1. **Prepare the Shrimp:**
   - Make sure the shrimp are peeled and deveined. If you prefer, you can leave the tails on for presentation.
2. **Season the Shrimp:**
   - Season the shrimp with salt and black pepper. You can add a pinch of red pepper flakes if you like a little heat.
3. **Heat the Pan:**
   - In a large skillet or pan, heat the olive oil over medium-high heat.
4. **Cook the Shrimp:**
   - Add the shrimp to the hot skillet and cook for about 1-2 minutes per side or until they turn pink. Don't overcook the shrimp as they can become tough. Once cooked, transfer the shrimp to a plate and set them aside.
5. **Make the Garlic Butter Sauce:**
   - In the same pan, add the butter and minced garlic. Sauté the garlic for about a minute or until it becomes fragrant.
6. **Deglaze the Pan:**
   - Pour in the white wine (or broth) and lemon juice. Scrape up any browned bits from the bottom of the pan with a wooden spoon. Let the sauce simmer for a few minutes until it reduces slightly.
7. **Combine Shrimp and Sauce:**
   - Return the cooked shrimp to the pan and toss them in the garlic butter sauce. Cook for an additional minute to heat the shrimp through.
8. **Garnish and Serve:**
   - Sprinkle fresh parsley over the shrimp and sauce for a burst of freshness and color. Serve the succulent garlic butter shrimp hot over rice, pasta, or with crusty bread to soak up the delicious sauce.

Notes:

- Be sure not to overcook the shrimp. They cook quickly and become tough if left on the heat for too long.
- The white wine adds a nice depth of flavor to the sauce, but you can use chicken or vegetable broth as a substitute if you prefer a non-alcoholic version.
- Adjust the amount of garlic and red pepper flakes to your taste. If you love garlic, you can add more cloves for a stronger garlic flavor.
- Serve the garlic butter shrimp over pasta, rice, or with a side of crusty bread to soak up the sauce.

- Fresh parsley adds a fresh and vibrant touch to the dish, but you can also use other herbs like cilantro or chives.

This succulent garlic butter shrimp recipe is a crowd-pleaser and is perfect for a quick weeknight dinner or a special occasion. Enjoy!

Certainly! Here are some additional tips and variations for your succulent garlic butter shrimp recipe:

Tips:

1. **Quality of Shrimp:** Use fresh or frozen shrimp, but make sure they are properly thawed and patted dry with paper towels before cooking. This ensures they cook evenly and develop a nice sear.
2. **Size of Shrimp:** Large or jumbo shrimp work best for this recipe, as they are meatier and more succulent. You can use smaller shrimp, but adjust the cooking time accordingly.
3. **Butter and Oil:** The combination of butter and olive oil adds great flavor to the dish. Butter adds richness, while olive oil prevents the butter from burning.
4. **Lemon Zest:** If you want to intensify the lemon flavor, add some lemon zest to the dish along with the juice.
5. **Customize the Heat:** Adjust the amount of red pepper flakes to control the level of spiciness. You can omit them if you prefer a milder dish or increase the quantity for extra heat.
6. **Side Dishes:** Serve your garlic butter shrimp over a bed of pasta, rice, quinoa, or with steamed vegetables for a complete meal.

Variations:

1. **Creamy Garlic Butter Shrimp:** To make a creamy version, add heavy cream or half-and-half to the sauce and let it simmer until it thickens slightly. This creates a luscious and rich sauce.
2. **Garlic Butter Shrimp Scampi:** Enhance the garlic flavor by doubling the amount of garlic. Scampi is known for its garlic-forward taste.
3. **Cajun Garlic Butter Shrimp:** For a spicy twist, season the shrimp with Cajun seasoning or a mixture of paprika, cayenne pepper, and garlic powder.
4. **Linguine with Garlic Butter Shrimp:** Toss the garlic butter shrimp with cooked linguine, fresh herbs, and a sprinkle of grated Parmesan cheese for a classic pasta dish.
5. **Asian-Inspired Garlic Butter Shrimp:** Add a touch of Asian flair by incorporating soy sauce, ginger, and chopped scallions into the sauce. Serve over steamed jasmine rice.
6. **Garlic Butter Shrimp Skewers:** Thread the seasoned shrimp onto skewers and grill them for a smoky, charred flavor.

Feel free to get creative with this succulent garlic butter shrimp recipe and tailor it to your personal taste. Whether you keep it classic or experiment with different flavors, this dish is sure to be a hit at your table.

Golden Onion Rings with Tangy Dipping Sauce

Golden Onion Rings with Tangy Dipping Sauce Recipe

Note: This recipe makes approximately 4 servings of onion rings and dipping sauce.

Ingredients:

For the Onion Rings:

- 2 large yellow onions
- 2 cups all-purpose flour
- 2 teaspoons paprika
- 1 teaspoon garlic powder
- 1 teaspoon salt
- 1/2 teaspoon black pepper
- 1 1/2 cups buttermilk
- Vegetable oil, for frying

For the Tangy Dipping Sauce:

- 1/2 cup mayonnaise
- 2 tablespoons ketchup
- 1 tablespoon Dijon mustard
- 1 tablespoon pickle relish
- 1/2 teaspoon garlic powder
- 1/2 teaspoon onion powder
- 1/2 teaspoon paprika
- 1/4 teaspoon cayenne pepper (adjust to taste)
- Salt and black pepper to taste

Instructions:

For the Onion Rings:

1. Peel the onions and slice them into rings, about 1/2-inch thick. Separate the rings and discard the smaller pieces or save them for another use.
2. In a large bowl, combine the flour, paprika, garlic powder, salt, and black pepper. Mix well to create the dry coating for the onion rings.

3. Pour the buttermilk into another bowl.
4. Heat vegetable oil in a deep fryer or a large, deep pot to 350-375°F (175-190°C).
5. Dip each onion ring into the buttermilk, allowing any excess to drip off.
6. Next, coat the onion ring in the flour mixture, making sure it's evenly coated. Place the coated ring on a baking sheet.
7. Once all the onion rings are coated, carefully place them in the hot oil. Fry in batches, being careful not to overcrowd the pan. Fry for 2-3 minutes or until they are golden brown and crispy.
8. Using a slotted spoon, remove the onion rings from the oil and place them on a plate lined with paper towels to drain any excess oil.

For the Tangy Dipping Sauce:

1. In a small bowl, combine the mayonnaise, ketchup, Dijon mustard, pickle relish, garlic powder, onion powder, paprika, and cayenne pepper.
2. Mix well until all the ingredients are fully combined.
3. Season the sauce with salt and black pepper to taste. Adjust the cayenne pepper if you want more or less heat.
4. Serve the tangy dipping sauce alongside the golden onion rings for a delicious pairing.

Notes:

- You can add a bit of cayenne pepper or hot sauce to the flour mixture for the onion rings if you want them to have a bit of a spicy kick.
- Make sure the oil is hot enough before frying the onion rings. You can test it by dropping a small piece of onion or a bit of the flour mixture into the oil. If it sizzles and starts to fry, the oil is ready.
- It's important to fry the onion rings in batches to maintain the oil temperature and ensure even cooking.
- The dipping sauce can be prepared ahead of time and stored in the refrigerator until you're ready to serve the onion rings.
- You can customize the dipping sauce by adding ingredients like hot sauce, honey, or Worcestershire sauce to suit your taste.

Enjoy your homemade golden onion rings with this tangy dipping sauce - it's a delightful snack or appetizer for any occasion!

Certainly, here are some additional tips and variations to enhance your onion rings and dipping sauce:

Tips:

1. **Choose the Right Onions:** While yellow onions are a popular choice for onion rings, you can also use sweet onions like Vidalia or red onions for a different flavor profile.
2. **Let the Onion Rings Rest:** After coating the onion rings with flour, allow them to sit for a few minutes before frying. This helps the coating adhere better to the onions.

3. **Keep the Oil Clean:** As you fry multiple batches of onion rings, make sure to remove any loose bits of coating that may have fallen into the oil. This helps keep the oil clean and prevents burnt bits from sticking to the rings.
4. **Drain Excess Oil:** After frying, let the onion rings drain on a wire rack instead of paper towels. This will help keep them crispy by allowing excess oil to drip away.
5. **Double Coating:** For an extra crunchy texture, you can dip the coated onion rings in buttermilk and flour again before frying. This creates a thicker and crispier crust.

Variations:

1. **Beer-Battered Onion Rings:** Instead of using buttermilk, you can make a beer batter by substituting the buttermilk with beer. The carbonation in the beer creates a lighter, crispier coating.
2. **Gluten-Free Option:** Use gluten-free all-purpose flour and buttermilk to make gluten-free onion rings. Ensure your frying oil is uncontaminated by gluten if you have dietary restrictions.
3. **Spice it Up:** Add some extra spices to the flour mixture for a unique flavor. Try adding smoked paprika, cumin, or chili powder for a smoky and spicy twist.
4. **Herb-Infused Dipping Sauce:** Experiment with fresh herbs like chopped dill, parsley, or chives in the dipping sauce for a refreshing and herbaceous flavor.
5. **Sweet and Spicy Dipping Sauce:** Combine the mayonnaise and ketchup with honey and hot sauce to create a sweet and spicy dip for your onion rings.
6. **Ranch Dip:** If you prefer a creamier dip, serve your onion rings with a classic ranch dressing. You can make your own or use store-bought.
7. **Serve with a Side:** Enjoy your onion rings with a side of coleslaw, a green salad, or even alongside a juicy burger for a complete meal.
8. **Pickled Onion Rings:** For a unique twist, pickle your onion rings in a mixture of vinegar, sugar, and spices before frying. This adds a tangy and sweet flavor.

Feel free to get creative with your onion rings and dipping sauce. These variations and tips should help you create a memorable and delicious snack or appetizer.

Air Fryer Parmesan Roasted Potatoes

Air Fryer Parmesan Roasted Potatoes are a delicious and crispy side dish that's quick and easy to make. Here's a simple recipe along with some helpful notes:

Ingredients:

- 4 medium-sized russet or Yukon Gold potatoes
- 2 tablespoons olive oil
- 1/2 cup grated Parmesan cheese

- 1 teaspoon garlic powder
- 1 teaspoon paprika
- 1/2 teaspoon dried oregano
- 1/2 teaspoon dried thyme
- Salt and pepper to taste
- Cooking spray (for the air fryer basket)

Instructions:

1. **Preheat the Air Fryer:** Preheat your air fryer to 400°F (200°C).
2. **Prepare the Potatoes:** Wash and scrub the potatoes thoroughly. You can peel them if you prefer, but leaving the skin on adds a nice texture. Cut the potatoes into small, bite-sized pieces or wedges.
3. **Coat with Olive Oil:** In a large bowl, toss the potato pieces with olive oil until they are evenly coated. This will help the seasonings adhere and make the potatoes crispy.
4. **Season the Potatoes:** In a separate bowl, mix the grated Parmesan cheese, garlic powder, paprika, dried oregano, dried thyme, salt, and pepper.
5. **Coat with Seasonings:** Sprinkle the seasoning mixture over the oiled potatoes and toss to coat the potatoes evenly.
6. **Air Fry the Potatoes:** Lightly grease the air fryer basket with cooking spray to prevent sticking. Place the seasoned potatoes in the air fryer basket in a single layer. You may need to do this in batches, depending on the size of your air fryer. Do not overcrowd the basket as it will affect the crisping.
7. **Cook in the Air Fryer:** Air fry the potatoes at 400°F (200°C) for 15-20 minutes, shaking or stirring them halfway through to ensure even cooking. Cooking times may vary based on the size and type of your air fryer. The potatoes are done when they are crispy and golden brown.
8. **Serve:** Remove the potatoes from the air fryer and let them cool slightly before serving. You can garnish them with additional grated Parmesan cheese or fresh herbs if desired.

Recipe Notes:

- Make sure to preheat your air fryer to get the best results. This helps the potatoes start cooking immediately and become crispy.
- Be mindful of the size of the potato pieces. Smaller pieces will cook faster, so adjust the cooking time accordingly.
- Don't forget to shake or stir the potatoes halfway through the cooking time to ensure even browning.
- Feel free to customize the seasonings to your taste. You can add other herbs and spices, such as rosemary or cayenne pepper, for additional flavor.
- Serve your Air Fryer Parmesan Roasted Potatoes as a side dish with your favorite dipping sauce, like ketchup, sour cream, or a garlic aioli.

Enjoy your crispy and flavorful Air Fryer Parmesan Roasted Potatoes!

Certainly, here are some additional tips and ideas to make your Air Fryer Parmesan Roasted Potatoes even more delicious:

1. Experiment with Different Potatoes: While russet and Yukon Gold potatoes are commonly used, you can also try red or fingerling potatoes for a different flavor and texture. Each type of potato has its unique qualities.

2. Add Fresh Herbs: Fresh herbs like rosemary, thyme, or parsley can add a burst of freshness and flavor to your roasted potatoes. Simply chop them finely and sprinkle them over the potatoes just before serving.

3. Custom Seasoning Blends: Create your custom seasoning blend by experimenting with various spices and herbs. For a bit of heat, add a pinch of cayenne pepper. For a smoky flavor, try smoked paprika.

4. Grated Cheese Variations: While Parmesan cheese is the classic choice, you can also try other cheeses like cheddar, Pecorino Romano, or a mix of different cheeses for a unique flavor profile.

5. Panko Bread Crumbs: If you like extra crispy potatoes, you can toss the potato pieces in panko bread crumbs along with the seasonings and grated cheese. The bread crumbs will create an extra layer of crunch.

6. Cooking Time Adjustments: Cooking times can vary depending on your specific air fryer model, so keep a close eye on the potatoes. If they're not crispy enough after the recommended time, you can extend the cooking time by a few minutes.

7. Pre-soak or Blanch the Potatoes: To make the potatoes even crispier, you can pre-soak them in cold water for about 30 minutes or blanch them in boiling water for a few minutes before air frying. This can help remove excess starch and enhance the crispiness.

8. Oil Sprayer: Using an oil sprayer will help you evenly coat the potato pieces with oil and prevent them from becoming too greasy.

9. Serving Ideas: Air Fryer Parmesan Roasted Potatoes are versatile and can be served as a side dish with various meals. They pair well with grilled meats, roasted chicken, or as a snack with your favorite dipping sauces.

10. Leftovers: If you have any leftovers, you can reheat them in the air fryer for a few minutes to maintain their crispiness. Just be cautious not to overcook, as they can become too dry.

Remember, this recipe is highly customizable, so feel free to get creative and tailor it to your taste. Enjoy your homemade Air Fryer Parmesan Roasted Potatoes!

Air Fryer Hard Boiled Eggs

Making hard-boiled eggs in an air fryer is a quick and easy process, and they turn out perfectly cooked with a creamy yolk and easy-to-peel shells. Here's a simple recipe along with some important notes:

Ingredients:

- Fresh eggs (as many as you need)
- Cooking spray (optional)

Instructions:

1. **Prepare the Eggs:**
   - Start with fresh eggs at room temperature. You can use as many as you need, but make sure not to overcrowd the air fryer basket. It's best to cook them in a single layer.
2. **Preheat the Air Fryer:**
   - Preheat your air fryer to 250°F (121°C). If your air fryer doesn't have temperature settings, you can usually set it to the lowest temperature and let it preheat for a few minutes.
3. **Air Frying the Eggs:**
   - Place the eggs directly into the air fryer basket. You can use a little cooking spray to prevent sticking if you like, but it's not necessary.
   - Cook the eggs at 250°F (121°C) for about 15-17 minutes. The cooking time may vary depending on your air fryer, so it's a good idea to start with a shorter time and check for doneness.
4. **Ice Bath:**
   - While the eggs are cooking, prepare a bowl with ice water. This will be used to quickly cool the eggs after they're done cooking.
5. **Check for Doneness:**
   - After the cooking time, use tongs or a slotted spoon to transfer the eggs to the ice water bath. Let them sit in the ice water for about 5-10 minutes. This will help stop the cooking process and make them easier to peel.
6. **Peeling the Eggs:**
   - Gently tap each egg on a hard surface to crack the shell, then roll it between your hands to loosen the shell. You can start peeling from the wider end (where the air pocket is) or the narrower end.
7. **Serve or Store:**
   - Once peeled, you can serve the hard-boiled eggs immediately or store them in the refrigerator for later use. Hard-boiled eggs can be stored in the fridge for up to one week.

Notes:

- The air fryer cooking time may vary based on your specific air fryer model and the size of the eggs. You may need to experiment a bit to find the perfect cooking time that suits your preferences.
- Starting with room temperature eggs can help prevent them from cracking during the cooking process.
- Adding a bit of cooking spray can make it easier to peel the eggs, but it's optional.
- Make sure to place the eggs in an ice water bath immediately after air frying to stop the cooking process and prevent overcooking, which can lead to a greenish ring around the yolk.
- Always store your hard-boiled eggs in the refrigerator and use them within a week for the best quality.

Enjoy your perfectly cooked hard-boiled eggs made in the air fryer! They make a great snack, salad topping, or protein-packed breakfast.

Certainly! Here are some additional tips and variations for making air fryer hard-boiled eggs:

Tips:

1. **Egg Size:** The cooking time may need adjustment depending on the size of the eggs. Large eggs are the most common, but if you're using extra-large or jumbo eggs, you may need to extend the cooking time slightly.
2. **Room Temperature Eggs:** Starting with eggs at room temperature can help prevent them from cracking during cooking. If your eggs are refrigerated, you can let them sit in warm water for a few minutes to bring them to room temperature.
3. **Check for Freshness:** Fresher eggs are generally easier to peel. If you have the option, use the freshest eggs available.
4. **Customize Your Cooking Time:** If you prefer your hard-boiled eggs with a softer or firmer yolk, you can adjust the cooking time accordingly. Experiment to find your perfect level of doneness.

Variations:

1. **Seasoning:** Before air frying, you can season the eggs with a pinch of salt, pepper, or your favorite seasoning. This will infuse flavor into the egg whites while they cook.
2. **Deviled Eggs:** Hard-boiled eggs are the main ingredient for deviled eggs. After air frying, slice the eggs in half, remove the yolks, and mix them with mayonnaise, mustard, and other seasonings to create delicious deviled eggs.
3. **Smoked Paprika or Everything Bagel Seasoning:** Sprinkle some smoked paprika or everything bagel seasoning on the peeled hard-boiled eggs for extra flavor.
4. **Air Fryer Egg Salad:** Chop your air fryer hard-boiled eggs and mix them with mayonnaise, mustard, diced pickles, onions, and celery to make a tasty egg salad.
5. **Curried Eggs:** Add a twist to your hard-boiled eggs by mixing the yolks with mayonnaise, curry powder, and a pinch of cayenne for a flavorful, spicy kick.

6. **Avocado and Eggs:** Cut an avocado in half, remove the pit, and scoop out some of the flesh to create a well. Place a hard-boiled egg inside the avocado well for a nutritious and filling breakfast or snack.
7. **Bacon-Wrapped Eggs:** After air frying, wrap the hard-boiled eggs with bacon and air fry for a few more minutes until the bacon is crispy. This creates a tasty and savory treat.

Feel free to get creative and adapt these suggestions to your own taste preferences. Air fryer hard-boiled eggs are versatile and can be used in various dishes and snacks.

Scrumptious Air-Fried Donuts

Air-fried donuts are a delicious and healthier alternative to traditional deep-fried donuts. They are not only easier to make but also lower in calories and fat. Here's a scrumptious air-fried donuts recipe along with some notes to help you make them:

Ingredients:

For the dough:

- 2 1/4 cups all-purpose flour
- 1/4 cup granulated sugar
- 1 packet (2 1/4 tsp) active dry yeast
- 1/2 cup warm milk
- 1/4 cup warm water
- 2 tbsp unsalted butter, melted
- 1 large egg
- 1/2 tsp salt
- 1/2 tsp vanilla extract

For the glaze:

- 1 cup powdered sugar
- 2-3 tbsp milk
- 1/2 tsp vanilla extract

For the topping (optional):

- Sprinkles, chocolate chips, or your favorite toppings

Instructions:

1. **Prepare the Dough:**

- In a small bowl, combine warm milk and warm water. Sprinkle the yeast over the mixture, and let it sit for about 5-10 minutes until it becomes frothy.
- In a large mixing bowl, combine the flour, granulated sugar, salt, melted butter, egg, and vanilla extract.
- Pour the yeast mixture into the bowl with the other ingredients and mix until a dough forms.
- Knead the dough on a floured surface for a few minutes until it's smooth. Place it in a greased bowl, cover it with a kitchen towel, and let it rise for about 1 hour or until it has doubled in size.

2. **Shape the Donuts:**
   - Once the dough has risen, punch it down and roll it out to about 1/2-inch thickness.
   - Use a donut cutter or a round cutter to cut out donut shapes. You can also use a glass to cut out the donuts and a smaller round cutter for the donut holes.
   - Place the shaped donuts and donut holes on a baking sheet lined with parchment paper.

3. **Air Fry the Donuts:**
   - Preheat your air fryer to 350°F (175°C).
   - Lightly grease the air fryer basket with cooking spray or a brush of oil.
   - Place the donuts in the air fryer basket, making sure they don't touch each other. You might need to fry them in batches depending on the size of your air fryer.
   - Air fry the donuts for 5-7 minutes, flipping them halfway through. They should be golden brown and cooked through.

4. **Prepare the Glaze:**
   - In a small bowl, whisk together the powdered sugar, milk, and vanilla extract until you have a smooth glaze. Adjust the consistency by adding more milk or sugar as needed.

5. **Glaze the Donuts:**
   - Once the donuts are done, let them cool for a few minutes.
   - Dip each donut into the glaze, allowing any excess to drip off.
   - If desired, add your favorite toppings, like sprinkles or chocolate chips, while the glaze is still wet.

6. **Serve and Enjoy:**
   - Let the glaze set for a few minutes, and then your scrumptious air-fried donuts are ready to be enjoyed!

Notes:

- You can customize your donuts by adding flavored extracts or spices to the dough, such as cinnamon or nutmeg, to enhance the taste.
- The air fryer cooking time may vary depending on your specific model, so keep an eye on the donuts to prevent overcooking.
- If you prefer a cinnamon sugar coating, you can mix cinnamon and sugar together and toss the donuts in it while they're still warm.

- These donuts are best when freshly made but can be stored in an airtight container for a day or two.

Enjoy your homemade air-fried donuts!

Certainly! Here are some additional tips and information to help you perfect your air-fried donuts:

1. **Air Fryer Tips:**
   - Preheat your air fryer for a few minutes before cooking the donuts. This ensures even cooking.
   - You may need to lightly grease the air fryer basket or use parchment paper to prevent sticking, especially if your air fryer tends to stick.
2. **Dough Handling:**
   - When working with the dough, it's essential to roll it out to an even thickness. This helps ensure that the donuts cook uniformly.
3. **Donut Variations:**
   - Experiment with different glazes and toppings to create various donut flavors. Consider options like chocolate glaze, maple glaze, or a simple powdered sugar coating.
4. **Glazing Techniques:**
   - For a thicker glaze, dip the donuts twice in the glaze and let it set between each dip.
   - If you want to achieve a perfectly smooth glaze, you can heat it for a few seconds in the microwave, then dip the donuts.
5. **Donut Holes:**
   - Donut holes tend to cook faster than full-sized donuts. Keep an eye on them and adjust the cooking time accordingly.
6. **Serving Suggestions:**
   - These donuts are delicious when served warm. Enjoy them with a cup of coffee, tea, or a glass of cold milk.
7. **Storage:**
   - If you have leftovers, store them in an airtight container at room temperature for up to two days. You can also freeze them for longer storage. Just thaw and reheat in the air fryer for a few minutes when you're ready to enjoy them.
8. **Healthier Option:**
   - Air-frying significantly reduces the amount of oil used compared to deep-frying, making these donuts a healthier alternative. You can further reduce the sugar content or use whole wheat flour for a healthier twist.
9. **Safety:**
   - Always follow your air fryer's safety instructions and guidelines for proper usage.
10. **Donut Shapes:**
    - Don't limit yourself to just the classic ring-shaped donuts. You can get creative and make filled donuts by folding the dough in half with your choice of filling in the center.

Feel free to get creative with your air-fried donuts. They're a fun and delicious treat to make at home, and with a little experimentation, you can come up with your unique donut recipes to satisfy your taste buds. Enjoy your scrumptious air-fried donuts!

Crispy Fried Pickles

Crispy fried pickles are a popular and delicious snack or appetizer that combines the tangy flavor of pickles with a crispy, flavorful coating. Here's a basic recipe for crispy fried pickles along with some helpful notes:

Ingredients:

- 1 jar of dill pickles (sliced into thin rounds)
- 1 cup all-purpose flour
- 1 cup panko breadcrumbs
- 1/2 cup cornmeal
- 1 teaspoon paprika
- 1/2 teaspoon garlic powder
- 1/2 teaspoon onion powder
- 1/2 teaspoon cayenne pepper (adjust to taste)
- Salt and black pepper to taste
- 2 large eggs
- Vegetable oil for frying
- Ranch dressing or your favorite dipping sauce

Instructions:

1. **Drain and Dry the Pickles:** Open the jar of pickles and drain them in a colander. Lay the pickle slices out on a clean kitchen towel or paper towels to absorb excess moisture. You want the pickles to be as dry as possible to help the coating stick.
2. **Prepare the Coating:** In a shallow bowl, combine the all-purpose flour, panko breadcrumbs, cornmeal, paprika, garlic powder, onion powder, cayenne pepper, salt, and black pepper. Mix well to ensure all the ingredients are evenly distributed.
3. **Beat the Eggs:** In another shallow bowl, beat the eggs until well mixed.
4. **Dip and Coat:** Take each pickle slice and dip it into the beaten eggs, letting any excess drip off. Then, coat it with the breadcrumb mixture, pressing the coating onto the pickle slice to adhere it well. Place the coated pickles on a baking sheet or plate.
5. **Heat the Oil:** In a large, deep skillet or a deep fryer, heat about 2 inches of vegetable oil to 350-375°F (175-190°C). Use a thermometer to monitor the temperature. The oil should be hot but not smoking.
6. **Fry the Pickles:** Carefully add the coated pickle slices to the hot oil in batches, making sure not to overcrowd the pan. Fry for about 2-3 minutes, or until they are golden brown

and crispy. Use a slotted spoon to remove the fried pickles and place them on a plate lined with paper towels to drain any excess oil. Repeat this process with the remaining pickle slices.

7. **Serve:** Serve the crispy fried pickles while they are hot and crispy. You can dip them in ranch dressing or your favorite dipping sauce.

Notes:

- It's essential to ensure the pickles are well-drained and as dry as possible before coating them. Excess moisture can make the coating less crispy.
- Adjust the level of spiciness by adding more or less cayenne pepper to the coating mixture.
- You can use dill pickles or bread-and-butter pickles, depending on your preference for a tangy or slightly sweet flavor.
- For a healthier version, you can try baking the coated pickles in a preheated oven at 425°F (220°C) on a wire rack for about 15-20 minutes, turning them halfway through.
- Be cautious when working with hot oil and use a thermometer to maintain the correct frying temperature.

Enjoy your crispy fried pickles as a tasty and crunchy snack or appetizer!

Certainly! Here are some additional tips and variations to enhance your crispy fried pickles:

Tips:

1. **Pickles:** You can experiment with different types of pickles, such as spears or whole pickles. The slicing thickness can also vary to your preference. Thicker slices will have a different texture than thinner ones.
2. **Coating Variations:** Feel free to customize the coating mixture. You can add ingredients like grated Parmesan cheese, dried herbs, or even crushed potato chips for extra flavor and texture.
3. **Chill Before Frying:** After coating the pickles, you can place them in the refrigerator for 30 minutes to help the coating adhere better and stay crispy during frying.
4. **Double Coating:** For an extra crunchy texture, you can dip the coated pickles in the beaten egg and breadcrumb mixture twice before frying.
5. **Dipping Sauces:** Besides ranch dressing, you can serve your fried pickles with other dipping sauces like sriracha mayo, honey mustard, or blue cheese dressing for a variety of flavors.

Variations:

1. **Spicy Pickles:** Use spicy dill pickles or add hot sauce to the egg mixture for a spicier version of fried pickles.
2. **Sweet Pickles:** Try using bread-and-butter pickles for a sweeter, tangy flavor.
3. **Garlic Lovers:** Mix garlic powder into the coating mixture for a garlicky twist.

4. **Deep-Fried Pickle Spears:** Instead of slices, you can use pickle spears for a heartier snack. Adjust the frying time as needed.
5. **Pickle Chips with Cheese:** Place a small slice of cheese (like cheddar or pepper jack) between two pickle slices before coating and frying for a cheesy surprise.
6. **Dill Dip:** Make a dill-flavored dipping sauce by mixing chopped fresh dill, sour cream, and a little lemon juice.
7. **Sriracha Mayo:** Combine mayonnaise and sriracha sauce for a spicy, creamy dipping sauce.
8. **Pickle Po' Boy:** Place fried pickle slices in a po' boy sandwich with lettuce, tomato, and remoulade sauce.
9. **Keto Version:** Substitute almond flour or coconut flour for the all-purpose flour and crushed pork rinds for the breadcrumbs to make a keto-friendly version.
10. **Gluten-Free:** Use gluten-free flour and breadcrumbs to accommodate those with gluten sensitivities.

Crispy fried pickles are a versatile and delicious treat that can be adapted to suit your taste preferences. Get creative and enjoy experimenting with different flavors and textures!

Perfectly Crispy Air Fryer Carrots and Parsnips

Perfectly crispy air fryer carrots and parsnips make for a delicious and healthy side dish. Here's a simple recipe and some helpful notes to ensure your vegetables turn out perfectly crispy:

Ingredients:

- 2 large carrots
- 2 large parsnips
- 1-2 tablespoons of olive oil
- 1 teaspoon of salt
- 1/2 teaspoon of black pepper
- 1/2 teaspoon of paprika (optional, for added flavor)

Instructions:

1. **Preheat the Air Fryer:** Preheat your air fryer to 380°F (190°C) for a few minutes.
2. **Prepare the Vegetables:** Peel and trim the carrots and parsnips. Cut them into evenly sized sticks, about 1/2 inch thick and 3-4 inches long. This ensures even cooking.
3. **Season the Vegetables:** In a large bowl, toss the carrot and parsnip sticks with olive oil, salt, pepper, and paprika (if using). Make sure the vegetables are evenly coated with the oil and seasonings.

4. **Air Frying:** Place the seasoned vegetable sticks in a single layer in the air fryer basket. Be careful not to overcrowd, as this can lead to uneven cooking. You may need to do this in batches depending on the size of your air fryer.
5. **Cooking Time:** Cook the vegetables in the preheated air fryer for 15-20 minutes, shaking or flipping them halfway through the cooking time. Cooking times can vary depending on the air fryer model, so keep an eye on them. The vegetables should be tender on the inside and crispy on the outside.
6. **Serve:** Once the carrots and parsnips are golden brown and crispy, remove them from the air fryer and serve immediately. You can garnish with fresh herbs or a sprinkle of additional salt and pepper if desired.

Notes:

1. **Uniform Size:** Cutting the vegetables into evenly sized pieces ensures they cook at the same rate and come out uniformly crispy.
2. **Don't Overcrowd:** To achieve that perfect crispiness, make sure the vegetables are in a single layer in the air fryer basket. If they're too crowded, they may steam instead of crisping up.
3. **Oil:** Be mindful of the amount of oil you use. Too much oil can make the vegetables greasy, but you do need enough to help them crisp up. Use a light hand when tossing with oil and add more as needed.
4. **Seasonings:** Feel free to get creative with the seasonings. You can use garlic powder, thyme, rosemary, or any other spices that you enjoy.
5. **Checking for Doneness:** Cooking times may vary based on the air fryer's power and size, so it's essential to check for doneness as you go. If the vegetables need more time, cook them for an additional few minutes, keeping a close eye.

By following this recipe and these tips, you can enjoy perfectly crispy air fryer carrots and parsnips as a tasty and nutritious side dish for your meals.

Certainly, here are some additional tips and variations for making perfectly crispy air fryer carrots and parsnips:

1. Preheating: Preheating your air fryer is essential as it helps the vegetables cook more evenly. It's similar to preheating an oven. Make sure to do this for the best results.

2. Coat Evenly: When tossing the vegetables with oil and seasonings, it's important to coat them evenly. You can do this by using a large bowl and tossing them gently. This ensures that each piece gets the right amount of flavor.

3. Cooking Time Adjustments: Cooking times can vary depending on the thickness of your carrot and parsnip sticks. Thicker sticks may take a bit longer, while thinner ones may cook faster. Adjust the cooking time accordingly.

4. Crispy Texture: For an even crispier texture, consider lightly coating the vegetable sticks with a thin layer of cornstarch before air frying. This can help create a crispy crust.

5. Breading Options: If you want to take it a step further, you can create a breadcrumb or panko coating for your vegetables. Dip the seasoned sticks in a beaten egg, then coat them in breadcrumbs before air frying.

6. Dipping Sauces: Serve your crispy carrots and parsnips with a dipping sauce. Some great options include a simple garlic aioli, honey mustard, or tzatziki for a refreshing touch.

7. Experiment with Seasonings: Don't hesitate to experiment with different seasonings. Some tasty options include cumin, coriander, curry powder, or a sprinkle of Parmesan cheese for extra flavor.

8. Herb Garnish: After air frying, add fresh herbs like parsley, thyme, or chives for a burst of color and flavor.

9. Healthier Cooking: If you're looking for a healthier version, you can skip the oil and use a light cooking spray instead.

10. Mix and Match: Combine carrots and parsnips with other root vegetables like sweet potatoes, beets, or butternut squash for a colorful and flavorful medley.

11. Leftovers: If you have any leftovers, store them in an airtight container in the refrigerator. You can reheat them in the air fryer for a few minutes to regain their crispiness.

With these tips and variations, you can adapt the recipe to suit your preferences and create the perfect crispy air fryer carrots and parsnips that you and your family will love.

Air Fryer Omelette

Air fryers can be a convenient way to make omelettes, and they result in a fluffy, slightly crispy omelette with minimal oil. Here's a basic recipe and some notes to help you make an air fryer omelette:

Ingredients:

- 2-3 large eggs
- Salt and pepper, to taste
- Fillings of your choice (e.g., diced vegetables, cheese, cooked bacon, ham, etc.)
- Cooking spray or a small amount of oil (for greasing the air fryer basket)

Instructions:

1. **Preheat the Air Fryer:** Preheat your air fryer to 350°F (175°C) for about 5 minutes.
2. **Prepare the Eggs:** In a bowl, whisk the eggs and season with a pinch of salt and pepper. You can also add a splash of milk or cream if you like, but it's optional.

3. **Prepare the Fillings:** Chop or dice any vegetables or meats you plan to include in your omelette. Make sure they are pre-cooked or quick-cooking, as the air fryer cooks quickly.
4. **Grease the Basket:** Lightly grease the air fryer basket or tray with cooking spray or a small amount of oil to prevent sticking.
5. **Pour the Egg Mixture:** Pour the whisked eggs into the preheated and greased air fryer basket.
6. **Add Fillings:** Sprinkle your chosen fillings evenly over the eggs.
7. **Cook:** Place the filled basket back into the air fryer and cook at 350°F (175°C) for about 8-10 minutes. The cooking time may vary depending on your air fryer's wattage and the thickness of the omelette. Check after 6-8 minutes, and if it's not fully set, continue cooking.
8. **Fold and Serve:** Once the omelette is set and slightly golden brown on top, carefully fold it in half using a spatula.
9. **Serve:** Carefully slide the omelette onto a plate and serve immediately. You can garnish it with herbs or more cheese if you like.

Notes:

1. **Preheat the Air Fryer:** It's essential to preheat the air fryer, just like you would with an oven, for more consistent cooking results.
2. **Use the Right Size Basket:** Ensure the air fryer basket or tray is the right size for your omelette to avoid overflowing or underfilling.
3. **Quick-Cooking Fillings:** Use pre-cooked or quick-cooking fillings, as the omelette cooks relatively quickly in the air fryer.
4. **Adjust Cooking Time:** Cooking time may vary depending on your air fryer model, so keep an eye on it and adjust as needed. The omelette is done when it's set and slightly golden brown on top.
5. **Experiment:** Feel free to experiment with various fillings, herbs, and spices to customize your omelette to your taste.

An air fryer omelette is a quick and easy breakfast option. Once you get the hang of it, you can enjoy a delicious omelette with your favorite fillings in no time.

Certainly! Here are some additional tips and variations for making air fryer omelettes:

Tips:

1. **Avoid Overfilling:** Don't overfill the air fryer basket with too many eggs or fillings. This can cause the omelette to cook unevenly or spill over. You may need to make multiple omelettes if you have a lot of ingredients.
2. **Non-Stick Basket:** If you're concerned about sticking, use a non-stick air fryer basket or tray, and grease it lightly.
3. **Parchment Paper:** Placing a piece of parchment paper on the bottom of the basket can make it easier to remove the omelette after cooking and help prevent sticking.

4. **Temperature Adjustment:** Some air fryers may have slightly different temperature settings. If you find your omelette cooks too quickly or slowly, consider adjusting the temperature slightly.
5. **Cooking Time for Different Ingredients:** If you're adding ingredients like mushrooms or spinach, which release moisture when cooked, it's a good idea to sauté them briefly before adding to the omelette to avoid excess moisture in the omelette.

Variations:

1. **Cheese:** Add your favorite cheese for a creamy and gooey omelette. Cheddar, mozzarella, Swiss, and feta are great options.
2. **Vegetarian:** Make a vegetarian omelette with sautéed bell peppers, onions, tomatoes, and spinach. Top it with some grated Parmesan for extra flavor.
3. **Western Omelette:** Create a classic Western omelette with diced ham, bell peppers, and onions. You can even add a touch of salsa for a Tex-Mex twist.
4. **Mediterranean Omelette:** Combine diced tomatoes, feta cheese, olives, and fresh herbs like basil and oregano for a Mediterranean-inspired omelette.
5. **Spicy Omelette:** If you like it spicy, add some diced jalapeños, red pepper flakes, or a pinch of cayenne pepper for a kick.
6. **Sweet Omelette:** For a sweet twist, make a dessert omelette by adding a bit of sugar, cinnamon, and your choice of fruits like sliced bananas or berries. Top with a dollop of whipped cream or a drizzle of maple syrup.
7. **Low-Carb Omelette:** If you're watching your carbs, use egg whites or a combination of whole eggs and egg whites to reduce the calorie and carb content.
8. **Protein-Packed Omelette:** Boost the protein content by adding cooked chicken, turkey, or even tofu for a vegetarian option.

Remember that the beauty of omelettes is their versatility. You can create a wide range of flavor combinations to suit your preferences and dietary needs. Enjoy your air fryer omelette experiments!

Air Fryer Sausages

Air frying sausages is a convenient and healthier alternative to traditional frying methods. Here's a simple recipe for air fryer sausages along with some useful notes:

Ingredients:

- Sausages (your choice of sausage, such as pork, chicken, or vegetarian)
- Olive oil or cooking spray (optional)
- Salt and pepper (optional, for seasoning)

Instructions:

1. **Preheat the Air Fryer:** Preheat your air fryer to 375-400°F (190-200°C). The exact temperature may vary depending on your specific air fryer model, so consult your appliance's manual for guidance.
2. **Prepare the Sausages:** If the sausages are fresh, you can lightly pierce them with a fork to allow excess fat to escape while cooking. If they're frozen, it's best to thaw them first.
3. **Arrange the Sausages:** Place the sausages in a single layer in the air fryer basket. Don't overcrowd the basket; there should be some space between the sausages to allow for even cooking.
4. **Optional: Brush with Oil:** While sausages contain their own fats, you can lightly brush them with olive oil or use a cooking spray to promote browning and crispiness. This step is optional, but it can enhance the texture and flavor of the sausages.
5. **Cooking Time:** The cooking time will depend on the size and type of sausages, as well as the specific air fryer model. However, a general guideline is to cook fresh sausages for about 12-15 minutes, turning them halfway through. For frozen sausages, you may need to cook them for 20-25 minutes. Always refer to the appliance's manual for precise cooking times.
6. **Check for Doneness:** To ensure that the sausages are cooked through, use a meat thermometer to check the internal temperature. Pork sausages should reach 160-165°F (71-74°C), while chicken or turkey sausages should reach 165°F (74°C).
7. **Season:** If desired, season the sausages with a pinch of salt and pepper just before serving. Remember that some sausages may already be seasoned, so taste one before adding more seasoning.
8. **Serve:** Once the sausages are cooked to your satisfaction and have a crispy exterior, remove them from the air fryer and serve immediately.

Notes:

1. **Avoid Overcrowding:** It's essential not to overcrowd the air fryer basket, as this can lead to uneven cooking. Cook sausages in a single layer with some space between them for optimal results.
2. **Oil:** While adding a bit of oil or using a cooking spray can improve the texture of the sausages, it's optional. Some sausages release enough fat during cooking to achieve a crispy exterior.
3. **Cooking Time:** Cooking times can vary depending on the air fryer model and sausage type, so always refer to your appliance's manual and use a meat thermometer to ensure they're cooked to a safe temperature.
4. **Experiment:** Feel free to experiment with different sausage types, seasonings, and marinades to create unique flavors.

Air frying sausages is a quick and convenient way to enjoy a tasty meal. Adjust the cooking time and temperature based on your preferences and the specific sausages you're using.

Certainly! Here are some additional tips and ideas for air frying sausages:

1. Preheat Your Air Fryer: Preheating your air fryer is crucial for even cooking. Allow it to come up to temperature before adding the sausages.

2. Sausage Varieties: Experiment with different sausage varieties, such as bratwurst, Italian sausage, chorizo, or breakfast sausages. Each type may require slightly different cooking times and temperatures, so adjust accordingly.

3. Use a Sausage Rack: If you have a sausage rack or accessory for your air fryer, it can help keep the sausages from touching the basket's surface, allowing for better airflow and even cooking.

4. Sausage Wrapping: You can wrap sausages in bacon or pastry for a unique twist. Just keep in mind that wrapping them in additional ingredients may increase the cooking time.

5. Flavoring Options: Try adding additional flavor by brushing the sausages with BBQ sauce, mustard, or honey for the last few minutes of cooking.

6. Serve with Accompaniments: Sausages go well with a variety of side dishes. Serve them with sautéed onions and bell peppers, sauerkraut, coleslaw, or a fresh green salad for a complete meal.

7. Cleaning Your Air Fryer: Sausages can release a fair amount of grease during cooking, so be sure to clean your air fryer basket and tray thoroughly after each use to prevent any lingering odors or smoke.

8. Air Fryer Temperature Variability: Air fryers can vary in terms of temperature accuracy. It's a good practice to check the actual temperature inside your air fryer using an oven thermometer to ensure you're cooking at the desired temperature.

9. Basting: For extra flavor and moisture, you can baste the sausages with a flavorful liquid like broth, beer, or wine during the cooking process.

10. Monitor the Process: Keep an eye on the sausages as they cook to prevent burning or overcooking. You can flip or rotate them as needed to ensure even browning.

11. Serve with Sauces: Serve your air-fried sausages with various sauces, such as ketchup, mustard, mayo, or hot sauce, for dipping.

Remember that the key to successful air frying is to experiment and adjust your approach based on your preferences and your specific air fryer's performance. Enjoy your air-fried sausages!

Printed in Great Britain
by Amazon

34681237R00104